Foreign Direct Investment in Western China, 1994–2004

AF875331

Xianming Yang · Ning Huang · Guoqing Zhao

Foreign Direct Investment in Western China, 1994–2004

SSAP

Springer

Xianming Yang
Institute of Development Studies of Yunnan University
Kunming, China

Ning Huang
Institute of Development Studies of Yunnan University
Kunming, China

Guoqing Zhao
School of Statistics and Mathematics, Yunnan University of Finance and Economics
Kunming, China

With Contrib. by
Yue Ling
Beijing, China

Translated by
Song Zhiwei
Beijing, China

ISBN 978-981-97-7409-8 ISBN 978-981-97-7407-4 (eBook)
https://doi.org/10.1007/978-981-97-7407-4

Jointly published with Social Sciences Academic Press
The print edition is not for sale in China (Mainland). Customers from China (Mainland) please order the print book from: Social Sciences Academic Press.

Translation from the Chinese Simplified language edition: "中国西部外资问题研究" by Xianming Yang et al., © People's Publishing House 2008. Published by People's Publishing House. All Rights Reserved.

The translation was done with the help of an artificial intelligence machine translation tool. A subsequent human revision was done primarily in terms of content.

Supported by a Grant from the Yunnan University Double First-Class Initiative.

© Social Sciences Academic Press 2024

This work is subject to copyright. All rights are solely and exclusively licensed by the Publisher, whether the whole or part of the material is concerned, specifically the rights of translation, reprinting, reuse of illustrations, recitation, broadcasting, reproduction on microfilms or in any other physical way, and transmission or information storage and retrieval, electronic adaptation, computer software, or by similar or dissimilar methodology now known or hereafter developed.
The use of general descriptive names, registered names, trademarks, service marks, etc. in this publication does not imply, even in the absence of a specific statement, that such names are exempt from the relevant protective laws and regulations and therefore free for general use.
The publishers, the authors, and the editors are safe to assume that the advice and information in this book are believed to be true and accurate at the date of publication. Neither the publishers nor the authors or the editors give a warranty, express or implied, with respect to the material contained herein or for any errors or omissions that may have been made. The publishers remain neutral with regard to jurisdictional claims in published maps and institutional affiliations.

This Springer imprint is published by the registered company Springer Nature Singapore Pte Ltd.
The registered company address is: 152 Beach Road, #21-01/04 Gateway East, Singapore 189721, Singapore

If disposing of this product, please recycle the paper.

Preface

From the early 1990s to the early 2000s, the Chinese economy underwent fundamental changes. Through his speeches on the 1992 southern tour, Xiaoping Deng commenced a new round of reform and opening up in China, setting off accelerated economic growth. From 1994 to 2004, China's economy enjoyed a golden stage of rapid growth. Parallel to this major event is the foreign direct investment (FDI) in China, which grew apace, especially after China joined the World Trade Organization (WTO). Without doubt, FDI is pivotal in China's efforts to catch up with and surpass advanced economies as it has accelerated the industrial restructuring and technology transfer, profoundly reshaping the economic ties between China and the outside world. As the top destination for foreign investment, China has integrated into the international production system and global value chain. However, it is apparent that the FDI distribution was unbalanced during this period, as the eastern region absorbed far more FDI than its western counterpart, a situation that remained unchanged even after China launched the Western Development Strategy (WDS).

FDI is essentially a way of transferring such factors as capital, technology, market, and management. Therefore, its uneven distribution will produce a profound and long-term impact on regional development. FDI, which is highly concentrated in the east yet seriously insufficient in the west, will enlarge the gap in terms of regional development, industrial chains, market growth, and size between the two regions. Our study of foreign investment in the western region in this period is of significance in the following aspects.

First, we try to answer the question by examining the intrinsic relationship between the nature of FDI and the characteristics of the region. This requires us to study why it is difficult to introduce FDI in western China and to identify the factors. Why is it that the incentives offered by a large array of favorable policies and mechanisms, including the Western Development Strategy, often failed to attract foreign investors?

Second, from a historical perspective, we try to answer what impact the lack of FDI growth would produce on the development of the west in the long run? On this basis, we can better understand the failure of regional government in terms of development strategies and the complexity of the issue of regional coordinated development in a big country.

Third, the research on the development of the western region provides important historical perspectives and useful practices. Scholars at home and abroad have conducted many studies on the development of this region. As an exogenous variable, FDI did not induce the expected growth like that in the eastern region. This is an issue worth further exploring. The possible answer could be in most cases it is a combination of internal and external factors to make development possible. Changes in the western region's local conditions are the prerequisites for the positive effects of FDI and other exogenous variables.

This study begins with the question of why it is difficult to introduce FDI to western China, followed by discussions about technology, human capital, industrial foundation, location selection, institutional factors, and investment climate based on the gap theory. We then analyze how the lack of FDI growth affects the long-term growth of the western region. This book is the fruit of collective efforts, penned by Guoqing Zhao (Chapter One), Yonghua Yang (Chapter Two), Ying Chen, Jianmin Zhang (Chapter Three), Fan Yuan (Chapter Four), Ya Li (Chapter Five), Yaling Li (Chapter Six), Ning Huang (Chapter Seven), and Xiaolong Tao (Chapter Eight). Xianming Yang, apart from overseeing the research design, drafted and revised the entire book, Sujun Shao is responsible for proofreading and communication of the final draft. Recognizing there must be flaws and inadequacy on our end since it is a complicated and challenging task to study this important economic fact in this specific period, we welcome any feedback and comments.

Kunming, China

Xianming Yang
Ning Huang
Guoqing Zhao

Contents

1 Introduction 1
1.1 Past and Present of FDI in Western China 1
1.1.1 Shares of Western Region in China's FDI and GDP 1
1.1.2 The Development Stages of Foreign Investments in Western China 2
1.1.3 Distribution of FDI in Western China 3
1.1.4 Ways of FDI Inflow in Western China 3
1.2 Problems of FDI in Western China 5
1.2.1 FDI's Effect on Economic Growth in Western China 5
1.2.2 Lack of FDI's Effect on Economic Growth in Western China 6
1.2.3 Why It is Hard for FDI to Concentrate in Western China? 7
1.3 Literature Review and Theoretical Hypotheses 8
1.3.1 Review of Region-Based FDI Studies 8
1.3.2 Research Hypothesis: Gap Theory 9
1.3.3 The Economic Meanings of a Gap 12
References 15

2 Technology Gap and Technology Transfer Through FDI in Western China 17
2.1 Technology Gap Between Eastern and Western Regions and Its Representation 17
2.1.1 Technology Gap Stock and Increment of the Western Region From the Perspective of R&D Spending of Eastern, Central and Western Regions 18
2.1.2 Technology Gap Stock and Increment of the Western Region From the Perspective of R&D Output of the Eastern, Central and Western Regions 21

2.1.3 Technology Gap Stock and Increment of the Western Region From the Perspective of Comparison Between High-Tech Industries in the Eastern, Central and Western Regions ... 21
2.1.4 Technology Gap Stock and Increment of the Western Region From the Perspective of TFP of the Eastern, Central and Western Regions ... 24
2.2 Impact of the Technology Gap of the Western Region on its FDI ... 26
2.2.1 FDI in Western Region ... 26
2.2.2 Impact of the Technology Gap of Western China on FDI Inflow ... 26
2.2.3 Impact of the Technology Gap of Western China on the Quality of FDI ... 31
2.3 Impact of the Technology Gap of Western China on FDI Spillover ... 33
2.3.1 Model Description ... 35
2.3.2 Data Sources ... 37
2.3.3 Empirical Results and Analyses ... 38
2.4 Conclusion ... 40
References ... 41

3 Human Capital Gap and FDI Absorption of the Western Region ... 43
3.1 Empirical Analysis of the Impact of Human Capital in Western China on FDI Absorptive Capacity ... 43
3.1.1 Model of Human Capital and FDI ... 43
3.1.2 Variable Selection ... 44
3.2 Estimation and Explanation of the Model ... 45
3.2.1 Description of Data and Variables ... 45
3.2.2 Basic Description of Data ... 46
3.2.3 Estimation of Results ... 49
3.3 Conclusion ... 56
References ... 58

4 An Analysis of the Impact of Industrial Base on FDI in Western China ... 61
4.1 Impact of Industrial Gap of Western China on FDI ... 61
4.1.1 Industrial Gap Between the Western Region and the Eastern Region ... 62
4.1.2 Impact of the Industrial Gap of Western China on FDI ... 64
4.2 Impact of the Industrial Structure of Western China on FDI ... 65
4.2.1 Industrial Distribution of FDI in China ... 66
4.2.2 Impact of Dominant Industries of Western China on FDI ... 68

4.2.3 Impact of the Advantageous Industries of Western China on FDI ... 74
4.2.4 Western China's Position on the Industrial Chain and Its Influence on FDI Absorption ... 77
4.3 Impact of Supporting Industries in Western China on FDI ... 85
4.3.1 Industrial Supporting Capacity and Location Selection of FDI ... 85
4.3.2 A Comparison Between Industrial Supporting Capacity of the Manufacturing Industry in the Western Region and that in the Eastern Region ... 86
4.4 Conclusion ... 91

5 A Study on Location Issues of the Introduction of FDI in Western China ... 93
5.1 China's Attractiveness to FDI from Multinational Corporations ... 93
5.2 A Comparison of FDI Influencing Factors for FDI Location Selection Between the Western Region and the Eastern Region ... 94
5.3 Location Conditions of Western China ... 100
5.3.1 Evaluation of Location Factors in the Western Region ... 101
5.3.2 Constraints of Special Costs in the Western Region Over FDI ... 102
5.4 Conclusion ... 104
References ... 104

6 Institutional Factors and the Introduction of FDI in China's Western Region ... 107
6.1 Literature Review ... 107
6.2 Comparative Analysis of Institutional Factors Across Eastern, Central and Western Regions of China ... 108
6.2.1 Legal Factors ... 109
6.2.2 Economic Factors ... 112
6.2.3 Institutional Factors that Affect the Operating Costs of Businesses ... 119
6.2.4 Evolution of Informal Institutions ... 120
6.3 An Empirical Test of the Correlation Between Institutional Factors and FDI Across Different Regions ... 120
6.3.1 Hypothesis and Indicator Variables ... 120
6.3.2 Data, Measurement Methods and Measurement Models ... 121
6.3.3 Econometric Tests and Interpretation of Results ... 125
6.4 Empirical Research on the Relationships Between Regional Institutional Changes and FDI Inflows ... 132
6.4.1 The Impact of FDI Inflows on Institutional Changes ... 133
6.4.2 Test of the Causal Relationship Between FDI Inflows and Institutional Improvement ... 134

6.5 Conclusion ... 138
References ... 139

7 FDI Gap and Economic Growth in China's Western Region ... 141
7.1 FDI Gap in the Western Region ... 141
7.1.1 Disparity in Inbound FDI Per Unit of GDP Between Western and Eastern Regions and Between the Western Region and the National Average Level ... 142
7.1.2 FDI Gap of the Western Region ... 146
7.2 FDI and Economic Growth in the Western Region ... 147
7.2.1 The Impact of FDI on Capital Formation in the Western Region ... 148
7.2.2 The Impact of FDI on the Technological Landscape in the Western Region ... 151
7.2.3 The Impact of FDI on Foreign Trade of the Western Region ... 154
7.2.4 The Impact of FDI on Industries in the Western Region ... 157
7.3 Loss of Opportunities for Economic Development as a Result of the FDI Gap ... 160
7.3.1 The Economic Growth Function of the Western Region ... 160
7.3.2 FDI Gap and Loss of Opportunities for Economic Growth in the Western Region ... 163
7.3.3 Change in the Development Gap Between the Western Region and the National Average Level and Between the Western and the Eastern Regions After Filling the FDI Gap ... 173
7.4 Conclusion ... 174

8 Assessment of the Investment Climate of Western China ... 177
8.1 Key MNCs Considerations for Investment in China ... 177
8.1.1 MNCs and the Investment Climate of China ... 177
8.1.2 Key Considerations for Investment in China: Japanese, South Korean, and German Firms ... 178
8.2 Comparison of Investment Climate in Western Provinces ... 183
8.2.1 Comparison of Key Factors Affecting the Environment for Foreign Investments ... 183
8.2.2 Principal Component Analysis of the Environment for Foreign Investments ... 199
8.2.3 Types of Environment for Foreign Investments ... 205
8.3 Gaps Between the Central, Eastern and Western Regions in Investment Climate ... 207
8.3.1 Natural Environment ... 207
8.3.2 Legal and Administrative Systems ... 208
8.3.3 Economic Environment ... 209

8.3.4 Human Resources ... 214
8.3.5 Technological Environment ... 214
8.4 Strategies to Improve the Environment for Foreign Investments ... 218
8.5 Conclusion ... 219
References ... 220

Chapter 1
Introduction

The western part of China is comprised of Inner Mongolia, Guangxi, Sichuan, Chongqing, Guizhou, Yunnan, Shaanxi, Gansu, Qinghai, Ningxia, Xinjiang, and Xizang. Since China launched the strategy for large-scale development of its western region, great breakthroughs have been made in the region in transportation, communication and energy infrastructure, significantly improving the investment climate. Meanwhile, the governments of provinces, autonomous regions and municipalities in western China have taken effective measures to improve services and the investment climate on the whole. As a result, recovery growth has been seen in the region's level of FDI use, but there has been no substantive progress in FDI. Moreover, the structure of foreign investors in the region is far from ideal, and FDI distribution is extremely imbalanced.

1.1 Past and Present of FDI in Western China

1.1.1 Shares of Western Region in China's FDI and GDP

China pursues a non-egalitarian regional development policy and opened up its eastern part before the west by launching preferential policies for the east in finance, tax, credit, and access. Meanwhile, as the eastern region has a higher level of development and strong supporting capacities for various industries, it aggregates more FDI and has obvious advantages in using it. At present, FDI in eastern China accounts for 87% of the national total.

At the end of the 1980s, particularly since the 1990s, about 87% of the FDI flowing into China went to its eastern region, while merely about 4% went to the western region. Since the 9th Five-year Plan period, FDI flowing into western China has stayed above USD1.7 billion, but western China's share of China's total FDI dropped continuously from 5.60 to 2.88% in 2004, and western China's contribution

© Social Sciences Academic Press 2024

X. Yang et al., *Foreign Direct Investment in Western China, 1994-2004*,
https://doi.org/10.1007/978-981-97-7407-4_1

Table 1.1 FDI in western China and the region's share of FDI and GDP, 1997–2003

	1997	1998	1999	2000	2001	2002	2003	2004*
FDI (USD10,000)	254,445	235,050	183,977	184,486	192,219	200,527	172,260	174,370
FDI share (%)	5.60	5.09	4.57	4.57	4.15	3.82	3.20	2.88
GDP share (%)	17.76	17.75	17.51	17.17	17.25	17.02	16.93	16.88

Source Calculated based on relevant data of China Statistical Yearbooks (1998–2004)
**Source* Ministry of Commerce: China Foreign Investment Report 2005

to China's GDP declined from 17.76 to 16.88% over the same period. Obviously, although China implemented the strategy for large-scale development in the western region to stimulate GDP growth and FDI inflow of the region, the strategy was not able to reverse the declining trend in the western region's shares in China's GDP and total FDI, which was caused by the fact that western China's GDP and FDI growth rates were lower than the national average (see Table 1.1). It reflects two problems: the ability of western China to attract FDI is relatively low, and the FDI flowing into western China has reached a growth plateau, and FDI in western China has very little elasticity on the GDP growth.

1.1.2 The Development Stages of Foreign Investments in Western China

The development of foreign-invested enterprises in western China showed distinct characteristics in four different stages. The first stage (1980–1986) is the initial stage of FDI in western China. During this stage, the FDI scale was relatively small, the annual average FDI in actual use was merely about seven million US dollars with no upward trend. The second stage (1987–1993) featured growth of foreign-invested enterprises and the annual average FDI in actual use was about 190 million US dollars. The third stage (1993–1998) saw excellent development of FDI in western China and the annual average FDI in actual use was 2160 million US dollars. The fourth stage, from 1998 to the present, witnessed a clear fall in FDI in western China. The annual FDI in actual use was 1850 million US dollars, and there were no significant increase in the scale or the growth rate. Foreign investment grew slowly first and then sped up in western China, showing big fluctuations. As can be seen in Fig. 1.1, 1992 and 1997 are the turning points for FDI in western China, first up, then down. Historically, FDI in western China peaked at 2540 million US dollars, and then fluctuated around 1850 million US dollars, a level of FDI use suited to the FDI competitiveness of western China. This indicates great constraints and obstacles to the use of FDI in western China. To use FDI on a large scale, western China clearly needs to tackle various development obstacles.

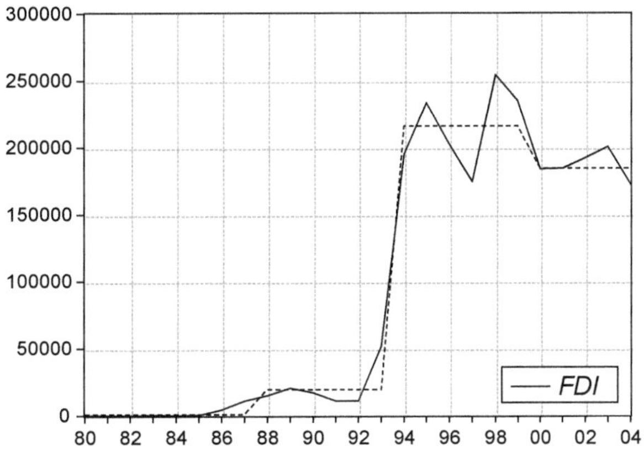

Fig. 1.1 The stages of FDI use in western China, 1984–2004

1.1.3 Distribution of FDI in Western China

Restricted by its geographical conditions, history and development level, western China has been the most backward region in terms of attracting FDI. On the one hand, it is plagued with poor transportation conditions manifested by a low railway coverage rate and low highway grades due to complicated landform and climatic conditions which caused difficulties and high costs for transportation development. On the other hand, communication infrastructure and means in western China had long been underdeveloped and IT infrastructure had also been poor, hampering FDI inflow and even causing capital outflow. Furthermore, the overall social environment in western China is also not conducive to foreign investment. Specifically, policies and regulations were not sufficient to properly protect the interests of investors; excessive review and approval procedures, complicated formalities, low work efficiency and poor services on the part of local authorities resulted in high transaction costs and investment risk, deterring potential investors.

The capabilities of different regions in western China for attracting FDI vary significantly due to economic scale and other factors. Since the 9th Five-year Plan period, Guangxi has been topping western China in attracting FDI, followed by Sichuan, Shaanxi, Chongqing and Yunnan, the last of which received nearly USD 920 million in FDI (see Table 1.2). Though Yunnan ranked fifth, relatively high in annual FDI, its accumulative FDI is below the average of western China, as the top four, Guangxi, Sichuan, Shaanxi and Chongqing claimed 82% of the total.

1.1.4 Ways of FDI Inflow in Western China

There are three ways of FDI inflow in China, namely Sino-foreign joint venture, Sino-foreign cooperative joint venture and wholly foreign-owned enterprise. Before the mid-1980s, FDI inflows in China were mainly in the form of Sino-foreign cooperative

Table 1.2 The size and share of FDI used in western China, 1996–2003, Unit: USD10,000, %

Region	FDI	Share	Region	FDI	Share	Region	FDI	Share	Region	FDI	Share
Guangxi	480,888	30.10	Chongqing	201,419	12.61	Gansu	43,251	2.71	Ningxia	15,580	0.98
Sichuan	338,981	21.22	Yunnan	91,878	5.75	Guizhou	30,412	1.90	Qinghai	13,559	0.85
Shaanxi	282,843	17.71	Inner Mongolia	77,875	4.87	Xinjiang	20,812	1.30			

Source Calculated on the basis of relevant data of China Statistical Yearbook (1998–2004)

Table 1.3 FDI in western China by business type, %

Business type	1996	1997	1998	1999	2002	2004*	1982–2004*
Sino-foreign joint venture	80.13	72.83	72.06	71.97	58.19	46.03	65.03
Sino-foreign cooperative joint venture	4.20	1.91	2.22	3.47	8.89	8.82	14.04
Wholly foreign-owned enterprise	15.67	25.27	25.71	24.56	32.92	42.94	28.53

**Source* Ministry of Commerce of the People's Republic of China, *China Foreign Investment Report 2005*, pp.150–151

joint venture. Later on, Sino-foreign joint venture gradually became the most form of investment. As foreign investors' strategy for technology transfer to China changed, wholly foreign-owned enterprises grew rapidly and became the dominant form of FDI. Nevertheless, although wholly foreign-owned enterprises in western China as a proportion of the national total showed an upward trend, the proportion of joint ventures in this region remained higher than 50% (see Table 1.3).

The distribution of foreign investors has a significant impact on regional technological development. Wholly foreign-owned enterprises have relatively low costs of transaction and management as they are able to make their own decisions and have a high degree of confidentiality. Under these circumstances, foreign investors are willing to transfer relatively advanced technologies, and even some core technologies. For the Chinese side, Sino-foreign joint venture brings greater technology spillover and offers more opportunities for having access to technologies and managerial experience of multinational corporations, while the foreign side is more concerned with market size, human capital and business risks. Western China features a low degree of openness, high uncertainty and high information costs, all of which determine that most FDI inflows there are in the form of Sino-foreign joint venture, and naturally only general technologies can be transferred.

1.2 Problems of FDI in Western China

FDI use in western China is unsatisfactory due to various factors. The scale of actual FDI is small and the portfolio of foreign investors in far from ideal. Thus, FDI in western China is not enough to bridge the gap between eastern and western China in economic development.

1.2.1 FDI's Effect on Economic Growth in Western China

Over the past 21 years, FDI has generally had a positive impact on the economic development of western China, however, its effect on economic growth is relatively weak due to the low quality and volume. First, the dependence of GDP on FDI in western China is low. Between 2001 and 2003, the FDI/GDP ratio of China was 4%, while that of western China was merely 0.5%, less than one tenth that of Shanghai and Guangdong. Second, as is seen from the contributions of foreign investors to industry, in 2003, the FDI-resulted industrial added value accounted for 27.62% of the national total on average, but none of the 12 western regions registered a figure higher than the national average in this regard and the contribution of FDI-resulted industrial value added to industry for western China was merely 8.24%. There is a low similarity between industries receiving FDI and the overall industrial structure in western China. Industries that highlights the region's resource advantage and comparative advantage are precisely industries that foreign investors are not willing to (e.g. phosphorus mining) or not allowed to (e.g. tobacco) enter. This not only hindered the inflow of foreign capital, but also bogged down the upgrading of industrial structure and the transformation of economic growth pattern in western China (Zhao 2004a, b). Third, interms of employment, in 2002, foreign investors in China employed 5.43% of China's urban workforce, but this share was merely 1.11% for western China. Obviously, this means that foreign enterprises provided less training for the local employees and contributed less to the formation of local human capital in western China. Lastly, 60% of China's current imports and exports are the result of FDI, while this share for western China is around 10%, roughly 1/6 of the national average. It shows that the exports of western China's FDI enterprises have little driving effect on economic growth. Simply, in western China, FDI concentration is relatively low, and FDI does not have a significant impact on industrial upgrading, transformation of economic growth pattern and increase in export competitiveness.

1.2.2 Lack of FDI's Effect on Economic Growth in Western China

In China, the economic development level, economic strength and FDI absorption capacity of different regions vary greatly. In general, between 1982 and 2004, the shares of eastern, central and western regions in China's GDP were 56.49%, 25.79% and 17.72%, respectively, and over the same period, the three parts' shares in FDI were 86.25%, 9.16% and 4.59%, respectively (Ministry of Commerce 2005). Assume a region's share in China's GDP is basically equal to its share in total FDI, then eastern China takes in 52.67% more of FDI that is assumed to, while central China and western China respectively take in 64.48% and 74.09% less, the greatest gap seen in western China.

Strictly, FDI's effect on economic growth can be more effectively demonstrated only within the theoretical framework of endogenous growth, and it is difficult to do this under current conditions. Here, we still managed to do this by setting up a double-log model for self-growth (moving average) using China's regional GDP and FDI between 1984 and 2004. First of all, with eastern China as the reference, FDI

Table 1.4 FDI's effect on growth by region

Variable	Ln (GDP_e)		Ln (GDP_m)		Ln (GDP_w)			
	Parameter estimation	t statistic	Parameter estimation	t statistic	Parameter estimation	t statistic	Parameter estimation	t statistic
Ln (FDI)	0.7158	56.44	0.0246	3.21	0.7924	56.25		
AR(1)	0.6007	2.57	1.0158	373.97	0.2769	11.72	1.0165	438.98
MA(1)	1.0874	7.04	1.4372	6.14	1.7055	3.37	0.7105	4.08
MA(2)	0.7003	3.45	0.4591	2.02	0.0406	0.08		
Adj. R^2	0.9861		0.9982		0.9564		0.9963	
CRDW	2.1322		1.5883		1.0603		1.6534	

has a long-term effect on GDP growth in the self-growing AR (1) error correction model. When all other factors remain the same, GDP grows by 0.75 percentage points whenever FDI increases by one percentage point. In the same model, the DW value for central China declines: GDP grows by 0.0245 percentage points when FDI increases by one percentage point. In comparison, the DW value of western China fell to 1, indicating no co-integration relationship between FDI and GDP. The GDP growth of western China is thus an ARMA process. Obviously, FDI has no growth effect in western China (see Table 1.4).

1.2.3 Why It is Hard for FDI to Concentrate in Western China?

In other less developed countries and regions, FDI has often filled the growth gap and become the engine and catalyst for economic growth. However, in western China, this has not been the case because FDI has has been small in scale and poor in quality.

FDI has been an important factor behind disparity in economic growth and income inequality between the eastern and western regions of China since the launch of the reform and opening up began (Sun 1998). Research work by Chinese scholars (Zhao 2001; Jiang et al. 2004) show that the widening gap in regional FDI absorption is a major factor behind the gaping regional gap in economic development. Between 1985 and 1999, about 90% of the differences between the GDP growth rates of eastern China and western China could be attributed to FDI (Wei 2002). FDI inflows increased in northern China, but not in western China. In the long term, foreign investors are not likely to come to western China in big strides (Wei 2003). Due to the competition between the eastern, central and western regions for FDI and the extremely adverse environment in western China, the region may find it hard to fully tap its ability to absorb FDI, and FDI tends to further decline (Zhao 2004a, b). Indeed, western China still faces the risk of being further marginalized in terms of FDI.

During the 10th Five-year Plan period, China failed to change the situation that its western region had low GDP growth and low foreign capital utilization rate in spite of its accession to the WTO, global economic restructuring, sub-regional cooperation, the strategy of large-scale development of the western region, and various other favorable factors. FDI in the western region failed to level up. Table 1.1 shows that western China's shares in the country's GDP and FDI kept declining as there is no substantial increase in FDI, and the large-scale development of the western region failed to reverse the situation. Why has FDI failed to concentrate in western China? Is possible for western China to attract more FDI? How to ensure that FDI inflow can help western China bridge the growth gap?

1.3 Literature Review and Theoretical Hypotheses

1.3.1 Review of Region-Based FDI Studies

To carry out region-based FDI studies, Chinese and foreign scholars would usually set up a measurement model for variables with statistical significance, explain the regional distribution of FDI with determining factors of regional FDI, thereby identifying the reason why FDI does not concentrate in western China. In this aspect, Wei (2002) made a comprehensive summary: (1) In the 1990s, Head and Ries (1996), Chen (1996), Qu and Green (1997), Broadman and Sun (1997), Chen (1997a), Wei et al. (1999), Coughlin and Segev (2000), Lu (1997), He and Liang (1999), and Feng and Zhang (1999) made intensive studies on the determinants of China's inter-provincial differences in FDI using the log-linear model and the multi-variable linear regression model. (2) In the twenty-first century, Cheng (2000), Buckley et al. (2002) and Qian et al. (2002) continued to follow the technological route of econometrics to study the determinants of regional distribution of FDI in China. In addition, Wei (2001, 2003), Wu (2002a; b) and Jiang et al. (2004) continued to pay attention to the issue from different perspectives of research.

In addition, some scholars studied FDI in central and western regions. Huang (2003) made a theoretical analysis of the impact of the gap in technological level between the FDI recipient and the foreign investor, discussed the types of FDI in central and western regions on the basis of local conditions, and put forward concrete measures to promote FDI. Wei (2003) analyzed the local characteristics and tendency of FDI in recent years, particularly after China's accession to the WTO.

Different from commonly used research methodology, Zhao (2004a, b) starts from the characteristics of integration of capital, technology and knowledge in FDI and regards each region as an FDI absorption capacity system. To address the deficiencies of Dunning's paradigm of OLI, Zhao Guoqing, on the basis of the concept of FDI absorption capacity, extends regional FDI absorption capacity (RAC) into the regional capacities of attracting, utilizing and spilling (AUS) FDI. By establishing this AUS analysis paradigm, Zhao evaluated the FDI absorptive capacities of Chinese regions in 2002, studied the distribution, level and category of FDI, and made a rank correlation test. From the perspective of FDI absorptive capacity, he put forward a new proposition about why FDI failed to concentrate in western China: The main reason for this is the FDI absorptive capacity gap and the lack of the structural effects of absorptive capacity in western China. Zhao (2004a, b) proves, using the dynamic economic approach, that the competition between the eastern, central and western regions of China for FDI determines that FDI would not concentrate in western China. Particularly, the extremely unfavorable environmental factors of the region restrict its FDI absorptive capacity. At present, the competition between Chinese regions for FDI corresponds to their respective absorptive capacity, and policy's facilitating effect on FDI in western China is not obvious. For every unit FDI increase in the western region, FDI in the central region will increase twice that much and that in the eastern region will increase by 18 times that. Thus, FDI in the western region tends to further decline. Meanwhile, there is competition rather than a symbiotic relationship between the GDP and FDI of western China, and such a mechanism can offset policy effects. According to Table 1.1, between 1997 and 2004, the FDI that western China absorbed showed a downward trend, and its share in China's total decreased year by year, initially validating the research finding.

1.3.2 Research Hypothesis: Gap Theory

1.3.2.1 FDI and Growth Gap

Currently, region-based research on FDI in China or research specifically on FDI in western China cover only dominant variables or factors. In this aspect, some determinants have been found for FDI distribution in China and reasonable explanations have been made for the western region's failure to attract more FDI. However, all these are far from enough to explain the continuous decline of western China's shares in the country's GDP and FDI. Why is it hard to accelerate the GDP growth of western China? Why FDI in western China has stayed around USD 2 billion or lower with no breakthrough? A reasonable solution can be worked out only when economic growth of western China in general is examined carefully. Assume the growth gap between eastern and western China can mainly be attributed to the uneven distribution of FDI. Eastern China's economic growth has benefited greatly from FDI as it helps fill the growth gap.

FDI may help narrow the growth gap between better developed and less developed regions in a holistic way. Development economists regard human resources, natural resources, capital formation and technology (including corporate management techniques) as the four major elements of economic development. Multinational corporations can provide capital, technology, ability to invent and corporate management skills, so FDI brings precisely all four elements and has the input–output function. Different from mere introduction of technology or capital, absorption of FDI brings in a highly efficient and advanced production function to modify the existing production function of backward regions and helps achieve leapfrog economic development (Zhao 2004a).

First, multinational corporations boast rich high-quality human resources, while backward regions have abundant low-cost labor due to the low per capita income, highly complementary. Multinational corporations can help train local workers and accelerate the formation and accumulation of human capital in backward regions, and the flow of trained labor causes technology and knowledge spillover, driving up the overall quality of the local workforce. Meanwhile, labor-intensive foreign investors create jobs enable workers to learn by doing and keep accumulating knowledge. This is extremely important for the technological level and technological absorptive capacity of backward regions as workers serve as the foundation of absorption at the micro level.

Second, in terms of capital formation, backward regions are mired in the "vicious cycle of poverty" because of their low income level, savings rate and capital formation rate. Although they may borrow from the outside to bring in capital, their absorptive capacity and capital operation efficiency tend to be low, making it hard to generate profits. Moreover, a debt crisis may occur as foreign debt increases given the heavy economic development burdens. As such, it is hard for backward regions to achieve a positive cycle of economic growth. In comparison, FDI, as capital without interest, in backward regions can make up for the lack of capital in these regions and accelerate capital accumulation. To this end, a better way to bring in FDI is to establish wholly foreign-owned enterprises and Sino-foreign cooperative joint ventures. The use of FDI via Sino-foreign joint ventures allows local capital to be more productively utilized. Meanwhile, the absorption of local capital by issuing shares is conducive to capital formation, increasing capital supply and narrowing the capital gap.

Third, in technological terms, the underdevelopment of backward regions is attributed to their low technological level and wide technological gap. The former means that economic growth relies mainly on the input of capital and labor, while technological advances make little contribution. The growth is mostly extensive with low production efficiency. It is of crucial importance that backward regions depend on FDI for technological advances and leverage the spillover effect of technologies brought by FDI to build their technological absorptive capacities and upgrade their overall technological structure. Only by making use of the technology spillover resulted from FDI to enhance the diffusion of advanced technologies, can backward regions progressively enter the stage of technological development featuring independent innovation and narrow the technological gap on the basis of a solid technological foundation and sound capacity for independent innovation. This largely determines whether a backward region can use FDI successfully.

Obviously, it is impossible for backward regions to break the vicious cycle of a gap by shoring up only one certain weak point (e.g. by purchasing technology or using foreign indirect capital). A breakthrough is only possible when FDI, a creative way of capital and technology can initiate changes and help overcome constraints in multiple areas relevant to the gap.

1.3.2.2 General Hypothesis of Regional Growth Gap

Japanese scholar Kiyoshi Kojima pointed out, "in the perspective of economics, FDI should be understood as the input of a whole package of resources, including capital, management skills, technical expertise and management resources to recipient countries." As such, FDI has obvious advantages in bridging regional growth gaps. Theoretically, FDI may modify the GDP production function of a country or a region, fill the gap and achieve a spillover effect for human capital and technology. However, the introduction of FDI has a threshold (Zhao 2004a, b). FDI's entry to less developed regions is restricted by gaps in technology, human resources, supporting funds and absorptive capacity. Therefore, for each region, there can be suitable and unsuitable FDI options.

Regarding the technology gap, although backward regions can promote technological advances by using FDI and narrow the technology gap with developing countries, they may not be able to make full use of the late-mover advantages due to difficulties in the commercialization and absorption of advanced technologies. According to theorists, there is a technology gap between multinational corporations and the overall level of backward regions. It is a kind of "dual technology gap", i.e., a technology transfer gap plus a technology accumulation gap. The former is mainly manifested as the gap between the technology of the investing multinational corporations and the existing technology in the backward regions involved (the technology recipient). This is a technology gap to be filled mainly by advanced technologies transferred by multinational corporations, who are the suppliers. The latter gap is mainly manifested as the practical difficulties in the absorbing FDI technologies. The main reason for this is that there is a gap between the recipient and the supplier in both technology and management, as well as the serious shortage of technical personnel in terms of quality and quantity, making it is difficult for the recipient to adapt to the technology transferred from the supplier. This is a technology gap that is mainly caused by the recipient. Such is the dualistic theory on technology gap. R&D (imitation) on the part of developing countries or regions narrows the technology gap and enables more advanced technologies to be transferred through FDI, while R&D (innovation) on the part of developed countries widens the technology gap, so that only less advanced technology is transferred through FDI.

Similarly, in accordance with the hypothesis of human capital threshold, a region can attract FDI only when its human capital stock has reached a specific threshold. For example, the Republic of Korea has a well-developed education system, so it has a relatively high capacity for attracting FDI which has accelerated its economic development. The theory on international industrial transfer indicates that multinational corporations transfer industries progressively to locations with narrow technology gap. Actually, FDI can facilitate the transformation of the economic growth pattern of a region and effectively reduce economic growth gaps, but regions will certainly get over the threshold of FDI effects. Therefore, we hereby propose a five-gap model:

$$Gap = f(gap_1, gap_2, gap_3, gap_4, gap_5) \tag{1.1}$$

wherein,

Gap refers to the total gap or growth gap;
gap_1 is the technology gap;
gap_2, the human resource gap;
gap_3, the industrial gap;
gap_4 the location gap; and
gap_5, the institutional gap.

Generally, the total gap function is a nonlinear function. Particularly, when the gap function is a linear homogeneous function,

$$Gap = gap_1^{a_1} gap_2^{a_2} gap_3^{a_3} gap_4^{a_4} gap_5^{a_5} \tag{1.2}$$

Formula (1.2) indicates that the total gap of undeveloped regions is not only a simple sum of to all the five gaps, it also involves how these gaps interact. It is not only about constraint of the maximum gap but also about various nonlinear mechanisms that may expand the gaps. This is why narrowing individual gaps in this portfolio may not be very helpful.

The following three ways may help backward regions fill or narrow the gap: (1) The endogenous model. The regions mainly rely on their own technological innovation and progress, their own accumulation of human resources, capital and institutional improvements to achieve independent growth and then gradually narrow the gap and overtake developed regions. (2) The extraneous model. The regions mainly rely on external forces, especially technology transfer and direct investment from multinational corporations. It is merely a makeshift and may cause the undeveloped regions to depend excessively on multinational corporations and become further marginalize. (3) In the case of an appropriate gap, effective imitation and innovation can be initiated through FDI inflow and the absorption of FDI resource spillover to narrow the gap and overtake developed regions. In this model, FDI can indeed bring resources to fill the gap for undeveloped regions. If FDI can accelerate regional human capital formation, transfer appropriate industries, narrow the industrial gap, promote institutional innovation, and improve transport communication infrastructures, then FDI integrates with local resources effectively and the region tends to enjoy the gap filling effect of FDI. Rapid economic growth is likely to follow and attract more FDI forming a positive circle. On the contrary, if FDI is low and integrates ineffectively with local resources, bringing no mutual benefit, then it will be hard for FDI to help fill the gap. In other words, regional gap has a restrictive effect on the absorption of FDI.

1.3.3 The Economic Meanings of a Gap

A gap, in economics, involves the supply and demand of resource factors. It involves many phenomena: the demand for FDI and how much of the demand is fulfilled,

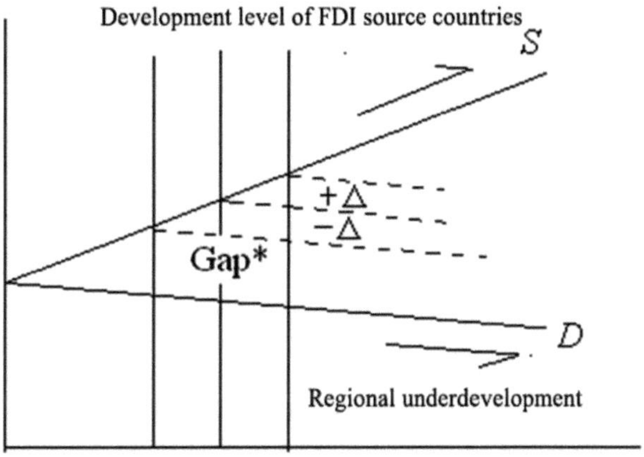

Fig. 1.2 Gap between an FDI recipient region and the FDI source country

as well as many forms of adjustments such as FDI's institutional demand and the institutional supply that a specific region can provide. FDI provides technology and demands human resources and supporting industries, while the recipient region demands high-quality factor input such as FDI and provides land and labor. It can be said that there is reciprocity between foreign investor and the recipient region. However, the investor certainly enjoys advantages in terms of internalization and monopoly, and is at a higher position than the recipient. In accordance with the FDI theory, the occurrence of FDI indicates a certain gap between the investor and the recipient region. However, the gap varies as the FDI source or the development level of the recipient region differs. For the same region, the gap is wide when FDI comes from a developed country, smaller when it comes from an emerging industrialized country, and even smaller or non-existent when it come from a developing country (see Fig. 1.2).

Before transferring technology to a region, foreign investors may consider the technology accumulation gap of the region and the suitability of the technology. When transferring technology through outbound direct investment, multinational corporations would carefully evaluate the market conditions, technological foundation, and absorptive capacity of the target region, for the transfer, though a subsidiary, would be maximally profitable for the multinational corporations only when the technology is suitable for the host country. Theoretically, according to Kiyoshi Kojima, the outward direct investment from Japan started from industries with a minimum technology gap between the investor and the recipient. The Flying Geese Paradigm proposed by Akamatsu also suggests a gradient for technology transfer between an investor and a recipient at an immediate lower development level. In other words, there is an optimal gap between the investor and the recipient regional.

A dynamic description of a region's gap is as follows:

$$\frac{dGap}{dt} = k(gap - gap^*)$$

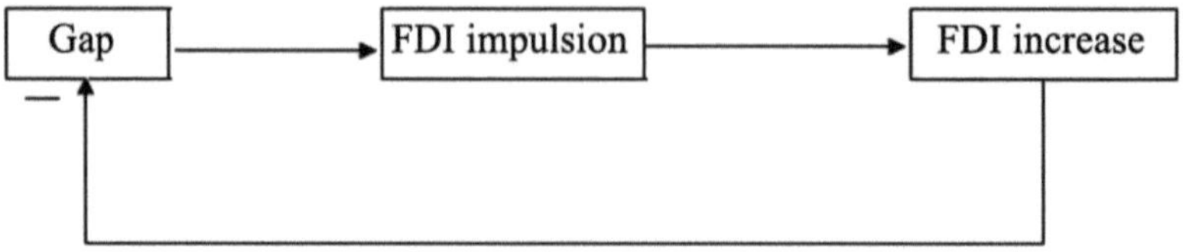

Fig. 1.3 Negative feedback mechanism that enables FDI to bridge the gap between regions with different development levels

The range of an appropriate gap, around *gap**, is (*gap** − △, *gap** + △). if the regional gap is greater than *gap** + △, then it is a non-convergent gap. This means that there is little suitable FDI, particularly from developed countries, and that there is severe gap constraint for the region. Only when the gap is within an appropriate range, can FDI initiate a positive mechanism to fill the gap (see Fig. 1.3).

The term "gap" refers to a collection of basic shortages in western China that made it difficult for the region to absorb FDI. A gap is relative and is a latent variable in the overall system of western China. A latent variable describes quantitatively the nature of a system. It hides behind some comparative indicators and cannot be directly observed. Its value can only be determined indirectly as estimates based on some explicit indicators. Therefore, the measurement of a gap is difficult and requires multiple methods:

1.3.3.1 Comprehensive Evaluation Method

A gap can be quantitatively measured. Originally, what is to be measured is the gaps in FDI-related elements between multinational corporations, the potential investors, and western China, a candidate FDI recipient region. Nevertheless, since the western, eastern and central regions of China naturally compete FDI, we can instead measure the gap between eastern China and western China according to the principle of transitivity. In other words, eastern China rather than multinational corporations can serve as the reference when we measure the gap of western China for FDI absorption. This enables us to design some indicators according to research needs and then categorize the various gaps of the western region.

1.3.3.2 Mathematical Economic Method

To study the association between the various gaps and FDI, it is necessary to set up some mathematical models such as the production function model and the total gap function model based on some hypotheses so as to determine the nature.

1.3.3.3 Econometric Method

This method is used to test the various hypotheses about the relationship between the gaps and FDI. Gap serial data is also employed to establish a total gap function. In parts of the study, dummy variables, causality test and the vector autoregression (VAR) model are also used.

References

Broadman, Harry G., and Xiaolun Sun. 1997. The distribution of foreign direct investment in China. *The World Economy* 20 (3): 339–361.

Buckley, Peter J., Jeremy Clegg, Chengqi Wang, and Adam R. Cross. 2002. FDI, regional differences and economic growth: Panel data evidence from China. *Transnational Corporations* 11 (1).

Chen, C.H. 1996. Regional determinants of foreign direct investment in China's mainland. *Journal of Economic Studies* 23 (2): 18–30.

Chen, Chunlai. 1997. *Provincial Characteristics and Foreign Direct Investment Location Decision within China.* Working Paper no. 97, p. 15. Chinese Economy Research Unit, University of Adelaide.

Cheng, Leoanrd K. 2000. What are the determinants of the location of foreign direct investment? The Chinese experience. *Journal of International Economics* 51: 379–400.

Coughlin, Cletus C., and Eran Segev. 2000. Foreign direct investment in China: A spatial econometric study. *The World Economy* 23: 1–23.

Feng, Yi, and Hui Zhang. 1999. *An Analysis of Inter-provincial FDI Distribution in China.* Economy and Management Publishing House.

He, Canfei, and Jinshe Liang. 1999. Regional differentiation and development of foreign direct investment in China. *Acta Geographica Sinica* 12.

Head, Keith, and John Ries. Inter-city competition for foreign investment: Static and dynamic effects of China's incentive areas. *Journal of Urban Economics* 40 (1): 38–60.

Huang, Xiaoling. 2002. Geographic advantage of Central/Western China and FDI promotion. *Journal of International Trade* 1.

Jiang, Xiaojuan, Yingxin Wang, Laike Yang, Shijia Chu, Rui Li, Li Deng, Pin Wu, Lin Chen, Gang Song, and Li Li. 2004. A study on gradient transfer of foreign investment in China. *China Industrial Economics* 4.

Ministry of Commerce of the People's Republic of China, *China Foreign Investment Report 2005*, pp.150–151

Lu, Minghong. 1997. Regional distribution of foreign direct investment and assessment of China's investment environment. *Economic Research* 12.

Qu, Tao, and Milford B. Green. 1997. *Chinese Foreign Direct Investment: A Subnational Perspective on Location.* Routledge Press.

Sun, H. 1998. *Foreign Investment and Economic Development in China, 1979–1996*. London: Ashgate Publishing Limited.

Sun, Q., Wilson Tong, and Qiao Yu. 2002. Determinants of foreign direct investment across China. *Journal of International Money and Finance* 21: 79–113.

Wei, Yingqi, Xiaming Liu, David Parker, and Kirit Vaidya. 1999. The regional distribution of foreign direct investment in China. *Regional Studies* 33: 857–867.

Wei, Houkai. 2002. The impact of foreign direct investment on regional economic growth in China. *Economic Research* 4.

Wei, Houkai. 2003. The location changes and the prospect of FDI in Western China after WTO. *Management World* 7.

Wei, Houkai, and Canfei He. 2001. Motivation and geographical factors of foreign direct investment in China. *Economic Research* 2.

Wu, Jian. 2002a. Regional distribution and growth effect of foreign direct investment. *Economic Research* 4.

Wu, Jian. 2002b. The regional distribution of foreign direct investment and its effect on economic growth. *Economic Research* 4.

Zhao, Jinping. 2001. *Foreign Investments and China's Economic Growth.* People's Publishing House.

Zhao, Guoqing. 2004a. Why doesn't FDI come to Western China? *Management World* 11.

Zhao, Guoqing. 2004b. *A Study on FDI Competitiveness of Western China.* China Social Sciences Press.

Chapter 2
Technology Gap and Technology Transfer Through FDI in Western China

As a kind of special and important production factor, technology plays an important and decisive role in promoting economic development of the entire country or region and even world economy. Just as what has been underlined by the theory on endogenous growth, namely technological advance plays a key role in long-term and sustained economic growth, experience shows that most inter-country gaps of income level and growth rates can be explained by technology. The technologies of a country or region can come from independent innovation, or introduction and absorption of innovative technologies of other countries or regions, namely international technology transfer and diffusion. As what Sachs (2000) points outs: “at the core of the global divide is the vast inequality in innovation and diffusion of technology”. Compared with less developed regions, developed regions are in an advantageous position in terms of technological innovation. However, the cost of transfer and imitation of existing technologies is much lower than that of invention and creation of new technologies. Therefore, under-developed regions can narrow their technology gap with technologically advanced countries or regions and even overtake them by transferring and imitating innovative technologies of developed regions.

2.1 Technology Gap Between Eastern and Western Regions and Its Representation

The technological level and absorptive capacity of a country or region are important factors determining the introduction of FDI and the technology transfer effects. An excessively wide technology gap will affect the volume of the introduction of FDI, and the positive effect of FDI is relatively low. In the case of a moderate technology gap, it may attract a good deal of FDI, and FDI exporters tend to transfer those sub-cutting-edge technologies to the host country. Along with the application and

© Social Sciences Academic Press 2024

X. Yang et al., *Foreign Direct Investment in Western China, 1994-2004*,
https://doi.org/10.1007/978-981-97-7407-4_2

leakage of such sub-cutting-edge technologies, local enterprises will gradually get familiar with and imitate these technologies, thereby narrowing the technology gap and intensifying the competitions. To ensure their advantages in the market of the host country in terms of technology and product quality, technology transfer parties must keep transferring some more advanced technologies, certainly, on the premise that the technology transfer parties must have strong impetus and capabilities for innovation. Eventually, the technology gap between the two sides of FDI is related to the ratio between the imitation speed of the technologically-lagged party and the innovation speed of the technologically advanced party.

2.1.1 Technology Gap Stock and Increment of the Western Region From the Perspective of R&D Spending of Eastern, Central and Western Regions

As is seen from spending on science and technology, namely the absolute quantity of R&D spending, the total R&D spending of China's eastern, central and western regions keeps increasing. However, the growth rate of the R&D spending in eastern region has greatly exceeded that in western region (see Fig. 2.1), thereby expanding the gap between the western region and the eastern region in R&D spending, the ratio between the R&D spending of the eastern region and that of the western region increased from 3.3 times in 1998 to 5.6 times in 2004 (see Table 2.1). This shows that there is a relatively large gap between the western region and the eastern region in terms of R&D spending, and the gap keeps expanding.

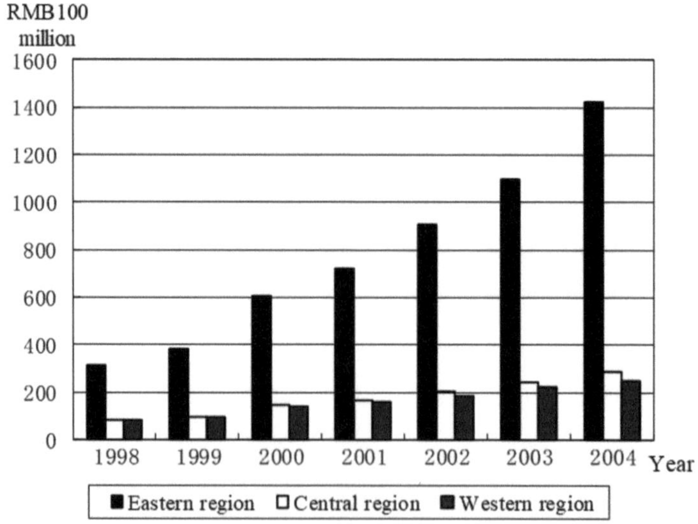

Fig. 2.1 R&D spending by region

Table 2.1 R&D spending of eastern, central and western regions and the proportions to regional GDP

Region	Year						
	1998	1999	2000	2001	2002	2003	2004
R&D spending in eastern region (USD100 million)	314.9	386.5	609.6	719.6	907.94	1094.7	1423.79
R&D spending in eastern region as a percentage of GDP	0.68	0.78	1.09	1.17	1.33	1.38	1.49
R&D spending in central region (USD100 million)	86.3	98.1	145.2	165.4	204.94	244.81	289.71
R&D spending in central region as a percentage of GDP	0.40	0.43	0.58	0.61	0.69	0.74	0.72
R&D spending in western region (USD100 million)	84.9	98.8	140.8	158.6	183.99	223.05	252.85
R&D spending in western region as a percentage of GDP	0.58	0.64	0.85	0.87	0.92	0.97	0.92
National R&D spending (USD100 million)	486.1	583.4	895.6	1043.6	1296.87	1562.56	1966.35
National R&D spending as a percentage of GDP	0.59	0.67	0.92	0.98	1.10	1.15	1.20

Source China Statistical Yearbook on Science and Technology (1998–2005), National Bureau of Statistics http://www.stats.gov.cn/, http://www.chinainfo.gov.cn/, http://www.sts.org.cn/; China Statistical Yearbook (1999–2005)

Research and development (R&D) activities are the core of the entire scientific and technological activities, R&D spending as a percentage of GDP is a very important indicator measuring the scientific and technological development level and capacity of a country or region. As is seen from R&D spending as a percentage of GDP, the R&D spending as a percentage of GDP in the eastern, central and western regions shows a rising trend. Generally, the proportion ranges from 2 to 3% in some developed countries, from 1 to 2% in moderately developed countries, and is less than 1% in developing countries. In 1998, the R&D spending as a percentage of GDP in the eastern, central and western regions was 0.68%, 0.40% and 0.58%, respectively, all of the above were at a relatively low level. At that time, the proportional gaps between the regions and developed countries were relatively large, but that gap between eastern, central and western regions was not very large. However, as is seen from Table 2.1 and Fig. 2.1, the R&D spending as a percentage of GDP in both the eastern region and the western region has been significantly increased, but the gap between them are expanding. The ratio between the eastern region and the western region was 1.49% and 0.92 in 2004, respectively, and the gap has significantly expanded.

As is seen from the numbers of research personnel in the eastern, central and western regions, the absolute totals of research personnel varied greatly (see Fig. 2.2), and the numbers of research personnel per 10,000 persons in the eastern, central and western regions also varied greatly (see Fig. 2.3). As is seen from the absolute total of research personnel, it kept rising in the eastern region, but rose and then declined and maintained at a relatively stable level in the western region, thereby widening the gap between research personnel in the eastern region and that in the western region. As is seen from the number of R&D personnel per 10,000 persons, it kept growing in the eastern region on the whole (except for the slight decline in 2000 and 2001), while in the western region, it rose and then declined and maintained at a relatively stable level. Therefore, the gap kept widening.

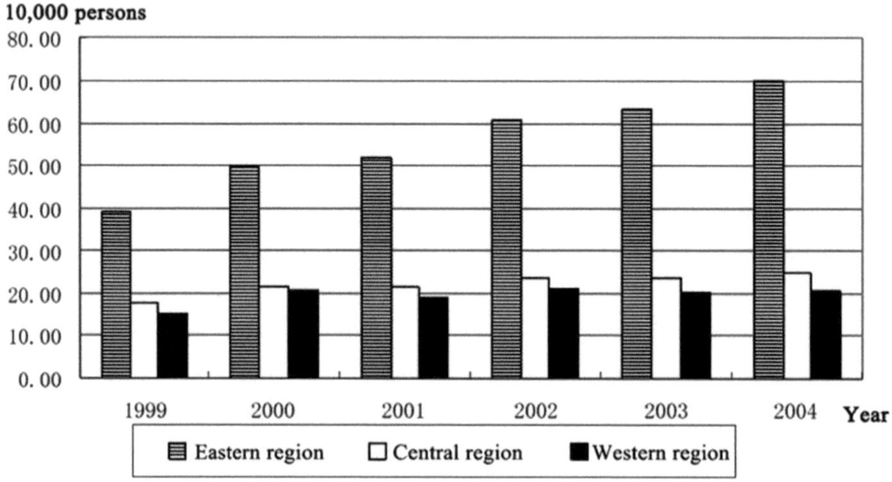

Fig. 2.2 R&D personnel by region

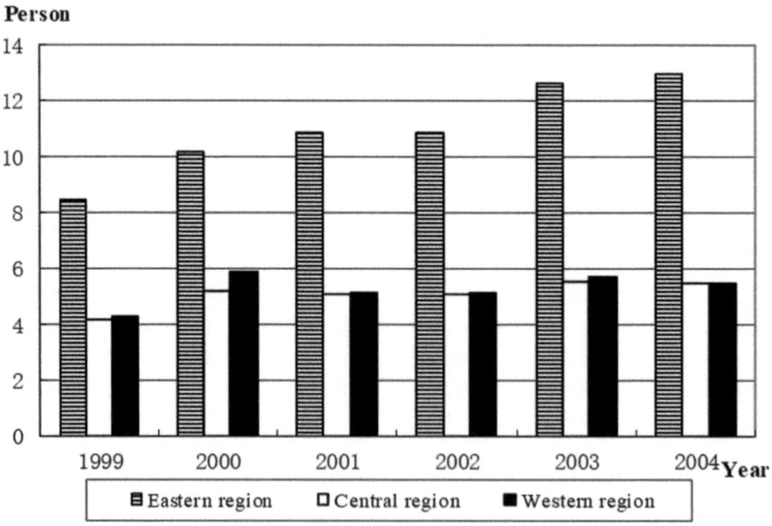

Fig. 2.3 Number of R&D personnel per 10,000 persons by region

From this we can see that in the western region the absolute quantity of R&D spending, R&D spending as a percentage of GDP, absolute total of research personnel and the number of R&D personnel per 10,000 persons kept rising. However, as the original base number of the western region was smaller than that of the eastern region, and the growth speed of the western region was not faster than that of the eastern region, and there was still a relatively large gap between the western region and the eastern region, and the gap was widening.

2.1.2 Technology Gap Stock and Increment of the Western Region From the Perspective of R&D Output of the Eastern, Central and Western Regions

Globally, patent is an important indicator measuring the output of science and technology. As is shown in Table 2.2, the number of patent applications and grants of China's eastern, central and western regions has significantly increased over the past decade, indicating that the R&D output of the above regions generally kept improving, but great inter-regional differences existed. In the western region, the number of patent applications and grants increased from 9741 and 5774 in 1995 to 25,912 and 15,834 in 2004, respectively, increasing by about 2.7 times, respectively. In the eastern region, the number of patent applications and grants increased from 40,257 and 23, 877 in 1995 to 194,909 and 104,158 in 2004, respectively, increasing by about 4.8 times and 4.4 times, respectively. This shows that the growth of patent applications and grants in the western region was much lower than that in the eastern region. As the base of patent applications and grants in the western region was smaller than that in the eastern region, there was a wide gap between patent applications and grants in the western region and that in the eastern region, and the gap continued to widen.

2.1.3 Technology Gap Stock and Increment of the Western Region From the Perspective of Comparison Between High-Tech Industries in the Eastern, Central and Western Regions

New and high-tech industries have increasingly become a key factor promoting national economic development and determining the international competitiveness of a country, and has become a important indicator measuring the technological development level of a country/or region. As is seen from this indicator, the situations of eastern, central and western regions varied. A substantial growth has been achieved in the added value of enterprises above designated size of new and high-tech industries in the eastern region, which reached RMB132,602 million in 1998 and has been on

Table 2.2 Number of patent applications and grants in the eastern, central and western regions, 1995–2004

Year		1995	1996	1997	1998	1999	2000	2001	2002	2003	2004
Eastern region	Application	40,257	48,729	53,789	57,997	68,152	89,851	107,548	139,299	171,874	194,909
	Grants	23,877	23,928	28,259	38,076	56,273	59,231	63,738	75,099	104,868	104,158
Central region	Application	13,927	15,893	16,341	17,485	19,164	21,942	24,300	28,044	34,042	38,124
	Grants	7556	6952	7309	9601	14,903	14,943	13,824	14,133	17,514	18,798
Western region	Application	9741	11,439	11,661	12,109	13,148	16,381	17,497	20,527	25,376	25,912
	Grants	5774	5443	5426	7317	10,968	11,299	11,360	11,496	14,297	15,834

Source China Statistical Yearbook on Science and Technology (1998–2005), National Bureau of Statistics, http://www.stats.gov.cn/, http://www.chinainfo.gov.cn/, http://www.sts.org.cn/; China Statistical Yearbook (1999–2005)

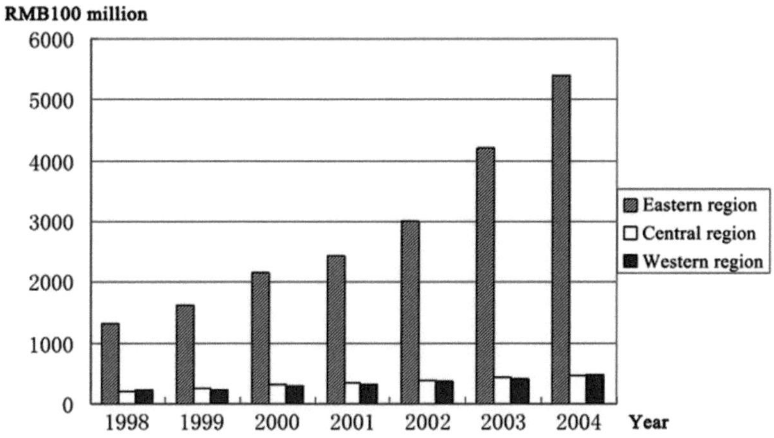

Fig. 2.4 Added values of high-tech enterprises above designated scale by region

the rise since then. Particularly, the added value of enterprises above designated size of new and high-tech industries in the eastern region achieved a significant growth in 2003 and 2004, up by 39.8% and 28.6% on a year-on-year basis, respectively. The added value of enterprises above designated size of new and high-tech industries in the central region has achieved certain limited growth, reached RMB21,805 million in 1998, but failed to exceed RMB50,000 million even in 2004. The added value of enterprises above designated size of new and high-tech industries in the western region showed a growing tendency (except for the slight decline in 1999), but grew moderately in the following years. The added value of enterprises above designated size of new and high-tech industries in the western region was RMB24,124 million in 1998 and RMB48,180 million in 2004, lagging far behind that in the eastern region, and the gap was widening (see Fig. 2.4).

The gap between the western region and the eastern region in the aspect of new and high-tech industries is also embodied in the indicator of the proportion of added value of enterprises above designated size of new and high-tech industries to the national total (see Fig. 2.5). The indicator of the proportion of added value of enterprises above designated size of new and high-tech industries in the eastern region to the national total was 74.29% in 1998. Subsequently, it had been on the rise and rose to 85.16% in 2004. The indicator in the western region declined on the whole from 13.5% in 1998 to 7.6% in 2004, except for a sudden increase to 35.2% in 2002. Therefore, the gap between the western region and the eastern region further expanded.

Fig. 2.5 Share of added value of high-tech enterprises above designated scale in the national total

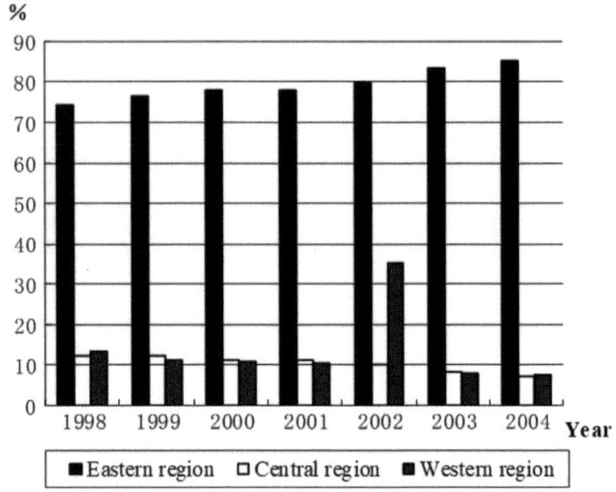

2.1.4 Technology Gap Stock and Increment of the Western Region From the Perspective of TFP of the Eastern, Central and Western Regions

The computational formula of TFP often depends on the selection of production function. In other words, the computational formula of TFP varies with production function. In the analyses and computations below, this paper adopts the Cobb-Douglas production function, i.e.,

$$\Upsilon = AK^{\alpha}L^{1-\alpha} \tag{2.1}$$

wherein, Y is output, L and K indicates labor input and capital input, respectively, A refers to the coefficient of technological advance, and α and $(1 - \alpha)$ are share of capital and that of labor factors, respectively. As many Chinese scholars assume that the share of capital factor is 0.35 when computing TFP, the share of labor factors is 0.65, and many scholars have proved that the data are relatively close to the actual situation of China. Therefore, this paper uses the data to calculate the TFP of the eastern, central and western regions. This paper adopts the 1995 data in China's inter-provincial material capital stock estimation of Zhang et al. (2004) in representative years, uses Goldsmith's perpetual inventory system to calculate the capital stocks of different provinces, autonomous regions and municipalities directly under the central government, and uses the formula below:

$$K_{it} = K_{it-1}(1 - \delta_{it}) + I_{it} \tag{2.2}$$

wherein i refers to ith province, t refers to tth year, I refers to investment, and δ refers to the rate of economic depreciation. According to the researches conducted by Huang et al. (2002) and Zhang et al. (2004), 4% is used and capital stocks (1996–2004) of the eastern, central and western regions are estimated on the basis of (2.2), and TFP (1996–2004) of the eastern, central and western regions is calculated on the basis of (2.1) (Table 2.3).

As is seen from TFP, there is a relatively wider gap between the eastern, central and western regions. The TFP of the eastern region was 1.66 times that of the western region in 1996, while it rose to 1.88 times that of the western region in 2004. This shows that there has been a technology gap between the western region and the eastern region represented by TFP, and the gap has been widening (see Fig. 2.6).

To sum up, the western region lagged far behind the eastern region in the aspects of the absolute amount of R&D spending, R&D spending as a percentage of GDP, the absolute total of research personnel, the number of R&D personnel per 10,000 persons, the absolute amount of and increase in patent applications and grants, the added value of enterprises above designated size of new and high-tech industries, the proportion of added value of enterprises above designated size of new and high-tech industries to the national total, and TFP, and the gap was widening. Therefore, compared with the eastern region, the western region has a great technology gap, which continued to widen.

Table 2.3 TFP of eastern, central and western regions, 1996–2004

Indicator	1996	1997	1998	1999	2000	2001	2002	2003	2004
Eastern region	1.42	1.36	1.34	1.32	1.37	1.41	1.46	1.57	1.73
Central region	1.08	1.01	0.95	0.90	0.92	0.94	0.96	1.03	1.15
Western region	0.86	0.81	0.77	0.74	0.75	0.77	0.79	0.83	0.92

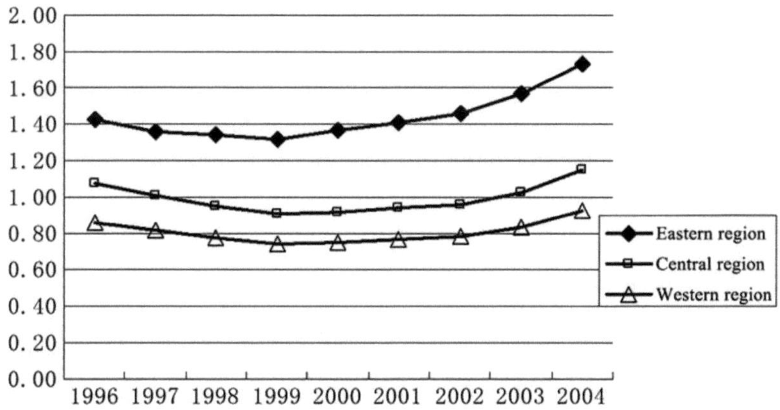

Fig. 2.6 TFP by region (1996–2004)

2.2 Impact of the Technology Gap of the Western Region on its FDI

2.2.1 FDI in Western Region

Since the 1990s, China has accelerated its utilization of foreign capital, which became an important factor for China's rapid economic development. However, as mentioned before, there is a very wide gap between the eastern, central and western regions in terms of the amount of foreign investments. As is shown in Table 2.4, FDI has always been concentrated in the eastern region, and was seldom attracted to the western region, and the gap was expanding. As is seen from the changes of FDI of different provinces, the FDI shares of Guangdong in which FDI accounts for a large proportion declined significantly, the FDI shares of Shanghai, Jiangsu, Zhejiang and Shandong increased to a certain extent, the FDI shares of Sichuan, Chongqing, Shaanxi and Guangxi dropped, while FDI shares of Xinjiang, Ningxia, Gansu, Qinghai and Guizhou were very small. It indicates that FDI distribution was extremely unbalanced and the FDI distribution has been varying greatly between the eastern region and the western region.

2.2.2 Impact of the Technology Gap of Western China on FDI Inflow

Generally speaking, the technological advantages of multinational corporations are necessary for their outward direct investment and a technology gap is necessary for FDI inflow. However, the gap shall not be excessively wide, otherwise FDI would not be fully used, a combination of knowledge, technology and capital, cannot maximize the profits of multinational corporations, and thereby reducing the FDI inflow. At present, FDI concentrates in the manufacturing industry with higher technical content, further explaining that more FDI inflows can be attracted only at a certain technological level.

2.2.2.1 Analytical Framework

According to relevant theories and literature, the main influence factors of FDI's regional distribution in China are shown below:

A. Technological level and technology gap
B. Market size
C. Economic development level
D. Infrastructure
E. Labor cost

Table 2.4 Distribution of FDI among Chinese regions

	1996		1999		2001		2003	
	Amount (USD10,000)	Share %	Amount (USD10,000)	Share %	Amount (USD10,000)	Share %	Amount (USD10,000)	Share %
Beijing	155,290	3.71	197,525	4.95	176,818	3.81	219,126	4.14
Tianjin	215,273	5.14	176,399	4.42	213,348	4.60	153,473	2.90
Hebei	83,022	1.98	104,202	2.61	66,989	1.44	96,405	1.82
Shanxi	13,808	0.33	39,129	0.98	23,393	0.50	21,361	0.40
Inner Mongolia	7186	0.17	6456	0.16	10,703	0.23	8854	0.17
Liaoning	173,782	4.15	106,173	2.66	251,612	5.43	282,410	5.33
Jilin	45,155	1.08	30,120	0.75	33,766	0.73	19,059	0.36
Heilongjiang	56,691	1.35	31,828	0.80	34,114	0.74	32,180	0.61
Shanghai	394,094	9.41	283,665	7.10	429,159	9.26	546,849	10.33
Jiangsu	521,009	12.44	607,756	15.22	691,482	14.91	1,056,365	19.95
Zhejiang	152,050	3.63	123,262	3.09	221,162	4.77	498,055	9.41
Anhui	50,661	1.21	26,131	0.65	33,672	0.73	36,720	0.69
Fujian	408,455	9.75	402,403	10.08	391,804	8.45	259,903	4.91
Jiangxi	30,126	0.72	32,080	0.80	39,575	0.85	161,202	3.04
Shandong	263,355	6.29	225,878	5.66	352,093	7.59	601,617	11.36
Henan	52,356	1.25	52,135	1.31	45,729	0.99	53,903	1.02
Hubei	68,079	1.63	91,488	2.29	118,860	2.56	156,886	2.96
Hunan	74,530	1.78	65,374	1.64	81,011	1.75	101,835	1.92
Guangdong	1,175,407	28.07	1,165,750	29.19	1,193,203	25.73	782,294	14.78
Guangxi	66,313	1.58	63,512	1.59	38,416	0.83	41,856	0.79
Hainan	78,908	1.88	48,449	1.21	46,691	1.01	42,125	0.80

(continued)

Table 2.4 (continued)

	1996		1999		2001		2003	
	Amount (USD10,000)	Share %	Amount (USD10,000)	Share %	Amount (USD10,000)	Share %	Amount (USD10,000)	Share %
Chongqing	–	–	23,893	0.60	25,649	0.55	26,083	0.49
Sichuan	44,090	1.05	34,101	0.85	58,188	1.25	41,231	0.78
Guizhou	3138	0.07	4090	0.10	2829	0.06	4521	0.09
Yunnan	6537	0.16	15,385	0.39	6457	0.14	8384	0.16
Xizang	–	–	–	–	–	–	–	–
Shaanxi	32609	0.78	24,197	0.61	35,174	0.76	33,190	0.63
Gansu	9002	0.21	4104	0.10	7439	0.16	2342	0.04
Qinghai	100	0.00	459	0.01	3649	0.08	2522	0.05
Ningxia	555	0.01	5134	0.13	1680	0.04	1743	0.03
Xinjiang	6390	0.15	2404	0.06	2035	0.04	1534	0.03

Note The eastern region includes Beijing, Tianjin, Hebei, Liaoning, Shanghai, Jiangsu, Zhejiang, Fujian, Shandong, Guangdong, and Hainan; the central region includes Shanxi, Jilin, Heilongjiang, Anhui, Jiangxi, Henan, Hubei, and Hunan; the western region includes Inner Mongolia, Guangxi, Chongqing, Guizhou, Yunnan, Shaanxi, Gansu, Qinghai, Ningxia, Xinjiang, and Xizang; indicates data unavailable.

F. Level of openness
G. Preferential policy.

2.2.2.2 Determination of Variables, Data Source and Modeling

Next, based on the data of China's provinces, municipalities and autonomous regions in 2000 and 2004, we obtain results by means of model regression, and then analyze the results. Explained variable is the incremental 1nFDI of FDI inflow amount. The explaining variables include: (1) T: The output value of enterprises above designated size of high-tech industries, representing the technological level. (2) PGDP: per capita GDP, representing the economic development level. (3) W: average wage level of employees, representing labor cost. (4) TC: total retail sales of consumer goods, representing the market size. (5) TRA: foreign trade dependence, representing the degree of opening-up. (6) BF: the ratio between the output value of the tertiary industry and the GDP, presenting the infrastructure level. (7) FP: dummy variable, representing preferential policies, Beijing, Tianjin, Shanghai, Jiangsu, Zhejiang, Fujian and Guangdong are assigned with 1, while other provinces are assigned with 0.

Source: China Statistical Yearbook on Science and Technology, the National Bureau of Statisticshttp://www.stats.gov.cn/, http://www.sts.org.cn/, http://www.chinainfo.gov.cn/, and relevant statistical data in the China Statistical Yearbook.

The following models are used for econometric regression:

$$\begin{aligned} 1\text{n}\,(\text{FDI}) &= \alpha + \beta 1\ 1\text{n}\,(\text{T}) + \beta 2\ 1\text{n}(\text{PGDP}) + \beta 3\ 1\text{n}(\text{W}) \\ &\quad + \beta 4 1\text{n}(\text{TC}) + \beta 5 1\text{n}(\text{TRA}) + \beta 6\ 1\text{n}(\text{BF}) + \beta 7\text{FP} + \varepsilon \end{aligned}$$

wherein, α and $\beta I(i = 1 - 7)$ are regression coefficients, ε is residual. If the logarithmic form is taken for a variable, the regression coefficient is the value of elasticity of dependent variables with respect to other explaining variables.

2.2.2.3 Regression Results and Analyses

The OLS regression results based on the above model and relevant data are shown in Table 2.5.

Model 1 regresses all variables. The table of regression results indicates that policy variables and infrastructure variables are insignificant. In Model 2, policy variables are removed and infrastructure variables are insignificant. In Model 3, regression results are eventually obtained after repeated regressions. All variables are relatively significant.

From the regression results of the above three models we can see that the technological level and FDI inflows are significantly positively correlated; the economic development level and FDI inflows are positively correlated; market demand and FDI inflows are positively correlated, the higher the market demand, the more FDI; the

Table 2.5 An analysis of determinants of China's FDI inflow

	2000			2004		
	Model 1	Model 2	Model 3	Model 1	Model 2	Model 3
Constant term C	13.79 (– 2.08)**	15.36 (2.59)***	17.25 (3.25)***	7.74 (1.67)*	8.73 (2.18)**	8.72 (2.22)**
LNT	0.42 (2.54)***	0.39 (2.54)***	0.41 (2.80)***	0.46 (3.20)***	0.43 (3.42)***	0.44 (3.53)***
LNPGDP	0.58 (1.26)*	0.56 (1.27)*	0.61 (1.36)*	0.47 (1.34)*	0.47 (1.39)*	0.47 (1.39)*
LNTC	0.35 (1.31)*	0.378 (1.43)*	0.30 (1.25)*	0.25 (1.24)*	0.27 (1.41)*	0.27 (1.42)*
LNW	– 1.24 (– 1.65)*	– 1.44 (– 2.24)**	– 1.31 (– 2.13)**	– 1.12 (– 1.72)**	– 1.26 (– 2.25)**	– 1.18 (– 2.68)***
LNTRA	0.50 (2.13)**	0.45 (2.11)**	0.48 (2.33)**	0.46 (2.24)**	0.42 (2.30)**	0.42 (2.36)**
LNBF	0.72 (0.59)	0.88 (0.74)		0.06 (0.07)	0.17 (0.20)	
FP	0.33 (0.56)			0.22 (0.44)		
Adj. R^2	0.88	0.88	0.89	0.93	0.93	0.93
DW	1.43	1.49	1.45	1.97	1.98	2.00
SE	0.53	0.52	0.52	0.41	0.40	0.40

Note Presented in the table are regression coefficients, with t values provided in parentheses. * indicates a significance level of 10%, ** a significance level of 5%, and *** a significance level of 1%

infrastructure level and FDI inflows are positively correlated; labor cost (i.e., salary) and FDI inflows are negatively correlated; the level of openness and FDI inflows are positively correlated; preferential policies and FDI inflows are positively correlated. Meanwhile, we can see that effects of infrastructures and preferential policies are not so significant for FDI inflows. The preferential policies of different provinces vary greatly, and simple assignments of 1 and 0 cannot fully reflect the differences in preferential polices. Infrastructure covers highways, railways, ports, IT and business facilitation. It cannot fully reflect the level of infrastructures of a region by merely using the output value of the tertiary industry.

From the regression results of 2000 and 2004 we can see that the technological level plays an important role in the introduction of FDI. The coefficients in Model 3 are 0.41 and 0.44, respectively. That is, whenever the output value of new and high-tech industries increases by one unit, FDI inflow increases by 0.41 units and 0.44 units, respectively. Through comparison between two time frames we can find that technology is becoming increasingly important.

Industry is the carrier of technology. In the western region, the industrial level is relatively low due to the low technological level. Particularly, the proportion of new and high-tech industries in western region to the national total was relatively small.

Table 2.6 The proportions of the added value of enterprises above designated size of high-tech industries to the national total and that of the eastern region, %

Indicator	1998	1999	2000	2001	2002	2003	2004
The proportion of the eastern region to the national total	74.29	76.40	77.82	78.15	79.72	83.40	85.16
The proportion of the eastern region to the eastern region	100.00	100.00	100.00	100.00	100.00	100.00	100.00
The proportion of the central region to the national total	12.23	12.30	11.36	11.36	10.26	8.51	7.25
The proportion of the central region to the eastern region	16.46	16.10	14.60	14.54	12.87	10.20	8.51
The proportion of the western region to the national total	13.50	11.26	10.80	10.49	35.20	8.08	7.60
The proportion of the western region to the eastern region	18.17	14.74	13.88	13.42	44.15	9.69	8.92

The proportion of the added value of high-tech industries in the western region to the national total was 13.5% in 1998, it dropped year by year and decreased to 7.6% in 2004. The proportion of the added value of high-tech industries in the eastern region to the national total was 74.29% in 1998, and increased to 85.16% in 2004, while the proportion of the added value of high-tech industries in the western region to that in the eastern region declined from 18.17% in 1998 to 8.92% in 2004 (see Table 2.6).

Compared with the eastern region, the western region was obviously deficient in high-tech industries and its overall technological level lags far behind. For example, in the western region, there were few R&D spending and scientific and technological advances, the high-tech industries were still in the initial stage, high-quality human capital was in critical shortage, and the technological absorptive capacity was relatively weak, all these factors severely hindered FDI inflow in the western region as foreign investors consider that it is hard for them to give play to its monopolistic advantages and seek for drawing on each other's strengths. The fact that FDI is mainly concentrated in the eastern region also proved that only regions with a certain technological base can attract more FDI, and such characteristic has been maintained for many years.

2.2.3 *Impact of the Technology Gap of Western China on the Quality of FDI*

What factor determines the technological level of FDI? The technology gap between local enterprises and multinational corporations is an important determinant of the quality of FDI. What technological level can FDI bring depends on the following two factors: (1) The technological level of the parent company, which generally transfers lower-level technologies so as to maintain its monopoly over advanced technologies. Multinational corporations engage in internationalized production, sale and other business activities by making international direct investments in and establishing branches or subsidiaries in other countries and regions by relying on their monopolistic advantages of abundant capital and advanced technologies. The ultimate purpose of international foreign investments made by multinational corporations is to gain higher profits. (2) The current technological level of the host country, multinational corporations generally transfer technologies higher than that of local enterprises so as to gain a competitive edge. Chen (2003) believes that China's current overall industrial level is equivalent to industrial level of developed countries in the 1970s, featuring little technological accumulation, low capacity for research and development and lack of strong competitiveness, for this, multinational corporations can obtain a competitive edge without the need to adopt very advanced technologies in the Chinese market. Therefore, the technologies transferred by multinational corporations are higher than that of the host country but lower than the most advanced technology of the parent company. It shows that the narrower the technology gap the higher the technological level of FDI inflows.

In accordance with the International Standard Industrial Classification formulated by the UN, OECD selected 22 manufacturing industries in 1986. On the basis of 1979–1981 data of its 13 typical member states, OECD used a weighted method (weight: the value of output of each country as share of the total output) to calculate the R&D spending intensity of these industries, and classify the industries on the basis of the R&D spending intensity (see Table 2.7). According to the industrial classification method of OECD, the technological levels of FDI can be divided into high technological level, medium technological level, medium-low technological level, and low technological level.

Foreign investments in the eastern region are mainly concentrated in manufacturing, real estate, resident service and other services. Between 1997 and 2004, the proportions of the actual FDI absorption in the three industries in the eastern region to the actual use of foreign capital in the eastern region were 66.49%, 10.93% and 4.48%, respectively, amounting to a sum of 82.35% (see Table 2.8).

Likewise, the foreign investments in the western region are mainly concentrated in manufacturing, real estate, resident service and other services. Between 1997 and 2004, the actual FDI amount absorbed in the above four industries in the western region accounts for 50.35%, 14.76%, 8.79%, and 8.49%, respectively, of the actual use of foreign capital in the central region, with a proportional sum of 82.39%. Different from the fact that FDI in the eastern region is highly concentrated in the manufacturing industry, although in the western region FDI was also highly concentrated in the manufacturing industry, its degree of concentration was merely 50.35%, much lower than 66.49% of the eastern region measured by the actual absorption of foreign capital. It is worth noting that, the proportion of FDI absorption of agriculture, forestry, animal husbandry, and fishing to the total utilization of foreign capital of the western region reached 3.01%, higher than 1.56%, that of the eastern region. This shows that the FDI technological level in the western region is far below that in the eastern region (Table 2.9).

Table 2.7 OECD's classification of industrial R&D spending intensity

	1960s–1970s	1980s–1990s
High technology	1. Aerospace 2. Computer, office equipment 3. Pharmaceuticals 4. Electronics—communication 5. Scientific instruments and equipment 6. Electronic machinery	1. Aerospace 2. Computer, office equipment 3. Electronics—communication 4. Pharmaceuticals
Middle technology	7. Automobile 8. Chemical industry 9. Non-electrical machinery 10. Rubber and plastic equipment 11. Other manufacturing industries	5. Scientific instruments and equipment 6. Electronic machinery 7. Automobile 8. Chemical industry 9. Non-electromechanical equipment
Lower middle technology	–	10. Shipbuilding 11. Rubber and plastic equipment 12. Other transportation equipment 13. Stone, earth and glass 14. Non-ferrous metals 15. Other manufacturing industries 16. Metal products
Low technology	12. Other transportation equipment 13. Stone, earth and glass 14. Petroleum refining 15. Shipbuilding 16. Non-ferrous metals 17. Ferrous metals 18. Metal products 19. Paper-making and printing 20. Food and beverage 21. Timber and furniture 22. Textiles and clothing	17. Petroleum refining 18. Ferrous metals 19. Paper-making and printing 20. Textiles and clothing 21. Timber and furniture 22. Food and beverage

2.3 Impact of the Technology Gap of Western China on FDI Spillover

The relationship between technology gap and effect of technology transfer through FDI is uncertain. Theoretically, there are two types of effects that are related to technology gap and completely opposite to each other: one type is positive effects from late-mover advantages. The wider the technology gap, the greater the technology transfer and spillover. The other type is negative effects. Influenced by absorptive capacity, the wider the technology gap, the lower the absorptive capacity, and the smaller the effects of technology transfer and spillover. Now, we make an empirical analysis of the influence of the technology gap on effect of technology transfer through FDI in the western region from the perspectives of the absorptive capacity and R&D level in western China. We know that FDI may produce technology transfer effects on the host country through imitation, competition, association and human capital flow, thereby influencing the economic growth rate of the host country. Therefore, we may conduct a test by using the models below:

Table 2.8 Distribution of foreign investment in industries in the eastern region between 1997 and 2004, Unit: USD 100 million

Industry	Contract item	Contract item	Contract amount	Contract amount	Amount actually used	Amount actually used
	Number	Percentage (%)		Percentage (%)		Percentage (%)
Eastern region (total)	196281	100	5512.34	100	3388.5	100
Agriculture, forestry, animal husbandry, and fishing	5720	2.91	106.2	1.93	52.9	1.56
Mining	807	0.41	35.28	0.64	41.54	1.23
Manufacturing	142204	72.45	3866.81	70.15	2253.07	66.49
Production and supply of electricity, gas and water	1047	0.53	116.33	2.11	132.24	3.9
Construction	1899	0.97	93.01	1.69	62.11	1.83
Transportation, warehousing and postal services	2636	1.34	156.53	2.84	88.28	2.61
Information transmission, computer services and software	1521	0.77	18.98	0.34	8.43	0.25
Wholesale and retail trade	10024	5.11	129.15	2.34	77.2	2.28
Hotel and catering services	899	0.46	16.86	0.31	6.16	0.18
Finance	89	0.05	14.97	0.27	7.78	0.23
Real estate	6297	3.21	479.99	8.71	370.47	10.93
Leasing and business services	5553	2.83	175.2	3.18	110.67	3.27
Scientific research, technical services and geological survey	1821	0.93	32.7	0.59	9.23	0.27

(continued)

Table 2.8 (continued)

Industry	Contract item	Contract item	Contract amount	Contract amount	Amount actually used	Amount actually used
	Number	Percentage (%)		Percentage (%)		Percentage (%)
Water conservancy, environmental and public facilities management	94	0.05	4.76	0.09	1.33	0.04
Resident service and other services	14979	7.63	239.5	4.34	151.97	4.48
Education	217	0.11	6.83	0.12	3.01	0.09
Health, social security and social welfare	274	0.14	11.19	0.2	8.49	0.25
Culture, sports and entertainment	198	0.1	7.91	0.14	3.6	0.11

Source Foreign trade statistics of the Ministry of Commerce
The bold part indicates that this is the total for the eastern region, which includes Beijing, Tianjin, Hebei, Liaoning, Shanghai, Jiangsu, Zhejiang, Fujian, Shandong, Guangdong, and Hainan; Central region: Shanxi, Jilin, Heilongjiang, Anhui, Jiangxi, Henan, Hubei, Hunan.

$$\ln GDP_{it} = C + \alpha \ln FDI_{it} + \beta \ln K_{it} + \gamma \ln L_{it} + \delta H_{it}$$

$$\ln GDP_{it} = C + \alpha H_{it} + \ln FDI_{it} + \beta \ln K_{it} + \gamma \ln L_{it} + \delta H_{it}$$

$$\ln GDP_{it} = C + \alpha RG_{it} \times \ln FDI_{it} + \beta \ln K_{it} + \gamma \ln L_{it} + \delta H_{it}$$

2.3.1 Model Description

In the model, GDP_{it} denotes the GDP of region i in the period t, FDI_{it} denotes the FDI inflow amount of region i in the period t, K_{it} denotes the total capital of region i in the period t, L_{it} denotes employees of region i in the period t, H_{it} denotes the human capital level of region i in the period t, RG_{it} denotes R&D spending (R&D) as share of GDP of region i in the period t. Specifically, we use the logarithmic model for regression. The reason why we choose the logarithmic model is that if we take the log of the both sides of the equation, the coefficient before the explaining variable is a concept of flexibility, for the convenience of comparison of empirical results.

Table 2.9 Distribution of foreign investment in industries in the western region between 1997 and 2004, Unit: USD 100 million

Industry	Contract item	Contract item	Contract amount	Contract amount	Amount actually used	Amount actually used
	Number	Percentage (%)		Percentage (%)		Percentage (%)
Western region (total)	10552	100	297.49	100	134.31	100
Agriculture, forestry, animal husbandry, and fishing	752	7.13	17.27	5.81	4.04	3.01
Mining	292	2.77	9.13	3.07	3.02	2.25
Manufacturing	5976	56.63	142.58	47.93	67.62	50.35
Production and supply of electricity, gas and water	207	1.96	26.48	8.9	11.4	8.49
Construction	292	2.77	17.09	5.74	5.11	3.8
Transportation, warehousing and postal services	117	1.11	5.74	1.93	2.89	2.15
Information transmission, computer services and software	49	0.46	0.42	0.14	0.14	0.1
Wholesale and retail trade	369	3.5	3.31	1.11	2.77	2.06
Hotel and catering services	105	1	1.87	0.63	0.8	0.6
Finance	4	0.04	0.27	0.09	0.04	0.03
Real estate	779	7.38	34.06	11.45	19.83	14.76
Leasing and business services	226	2.14	5.96	2	2.34	1.74
Scientific research, technical services and geological survey	105	1	2.52	0.85	0.78	0.58

(continued)

Table 2.9 (continued)

Industry	Contract item	Contract item	Contract amount	Contract amount	Amount actually used	Amount actually used
	Number	Percentage (%)		Percentage (%)		Percentage (%)
Water conservancy, environmental and public facilities management	24	0.23	1	0.34	0.25	0.19
Resident service and other services	1175	11.14	27.38	9.2	11.8	8.79
Education	33	0.31	0.39	0.13	0.33	0.25
Health, social security and social welfare	25	0.24	0.91	0.31	0.97	0.72
Culture, sports and entertainment	22	0.21	1.11	0.37	0.18	0.13

Data source Foreign capital statistics of the Ministry of Commerce
The bold part emphasizes that this is the total of the western region: Inner Mongolia, Guangxi, Sichuan, Chongqing, Guizhou, Yunnan, Shaanxi, Gansu, Qinghai, Ningxia, Xinjiang, Tibet.

The model is mainly used to test: interaction between technology gap an effect of technology transfer through FDI in the western region. Through technology transfer effects, FDI may facilitate narrowing of the technology gap, which is mainly manifested in the influence of FDI on economic growth, namely the influence on GDP. Meanwhile, the technology transfer effect of FDI, particularly the technology spillover effect of FDI, depends on the technological absorptive capacity and technology gap. The technological absorptive capacity is measured with human capital level, while the gap of the technological level is measured with R&D spending (R&D) as share of GDP.

2.3.2 Data Sources

All data adopted in the process of metrological analysis are from *1997 to 2005 China Statistical Yearbooks*, the official website of the National Bureau of Statistics, http://www.chinainfo.gov.cn/, and http://www.sts.org.cn/. This paper regresses the data of eastern, central and western regions calculated on the basis of relevant data of China's 31 provinces, municipalities and autonomous regions between 1996 and 2004. For human capital, H_{it}, the index of average educational year, which is commonly adopted, is used. It is the ratio between the total education years of the population aged six and above and the total population aged six and above. By referring to the commonly-used method, we set the years of elementary schooling, junior secondary schooling, senior secondary schooling and college education as 6, 3, 3 and 4, respectively.

In order to analyze the relationship of technological absorptive capacity, technology gap and effect of technology transfer through FDI of China's different economic regions (eastern, central and western regions), we make empirical researches by using panel data consisting of cross-section data and time series data.

2.3.3 Empirical Results and Analyses

We have regressed the data of eastern, central and western regions respectively in accordance with model (1), and the results are shown in Table 2.10.

From the regression results of Model 1 we can see that the coefficients of lnFDIit, lnKit, lnLit and Hit are positive, indicating that FDI, total capital, workforce and human capital level are main influence factors of economic growth. By comparing the regression coefficients of all explaining variables we can found that the regression coefficients of total capital and quantity of employment are higher than that of FDI. Therefore, in essence, the total capital and quantity of employment are still the

Table 2.10 Table of regression results based on model (1)

	Eastern region	Central region	Western region
	$\ln GDP_{it}$	$\ln GDP_{it}$	$\ln GDP_{it}$
Constant term C	− 11.25 (− 2.23)**	− 37.19 (1.48)***	− 15.11 (− 1.43)***
$\ln FDI_{it}$	0.42	0.24	0.13
	(2.48)**	(1.82)**	(1.88)**
$\ln K_{it}$	0.43	1.34	0.39
	(4.17)*	(1.78)***	(4.31)*
$\ln L_{it}$	2.09	4.85	2.62
	(3.26)*	(1.84)**	(2.04)**
H_{it}	0.21	0.18	0.15
	(4.64)*	(1.65)***	(2.72)**
Adj. R^2	0.96	0.97	0.95
DW	2.85	1.83	2.50
SE	0.02	0.04	0.001

Note The values in the parentheses are *t* test values, ***, ** and * indicate the significance levels of 10%, 5% and 1%, respectively primary influence factors of economic growth and play a non-negligible role in increasing the FDI spillover effects.

Through analyses of the three sets of regression results of eastern, central and western regions, we can work out the differences of technology spillover effects of foreign capital in the three regions. Wherein, the technology spillover effect of FDI in the eastern region is the most significant one. Among the three groups of regression results, the coefficients of FDI are 0.42, 0. 24 and 0.13, respectively, indicating that whenever the FDI inflow amount increases by 1 unit, the economic growth rates will rise 0.42 units, 0.24 units and 0.13 units, respectively. We have measured the promoting effects of international technology spillover with FDI as a transmission channel on the economic growth rates of the eastern, central and western regions. Obviously, FDI plays the biggest role in the economic growth in the eastern region, followed by the central region and the western region.

Although developing countries and regions can introduce and study foreign advanced technologies by attracting FDI, their technology learning effect or the technology transfer effect of FDI tends to be influenced by their technological absorptive capacity and the original technological development level (technology gap). Model 2 and Model 3 investigate the influences of technological absorptive capacity, which is measured with human capital, and technological development level measured with R&D spending as share of GDP, on the technology transfer effects of FDI.

In accordance with Model 2, we have regressed data in eastern, central and western regions, and the results are shown in Table 2.11.

Table 2.11 Table of regression results based on model (2)

	Eastern region	Central region	Western region
	$\ln GDP_{it}$	$\ln GDP_{it}$	$\ln GDP_{it}$
Constant term C	− 10.42 $(-2.19)^{**}$	− 36.65 $(-1.92)^{**}$	− 14.98 $(-1.53)^{***}$
$H_{it} \times \ln FDI_{it}$	0.06	0.03	0.02
	$(2.48)^{**}$	$(1.63)^{***}$	$(1.89)^{**}$
$\ln K_{it}$	0.44	0.34	0.39
	$(4.32)^{**}$	$(1.77)^{***}$	$(4.32)^{*}$
$\ln L_{it}$	2.04	4.86	2.63
	$(3.30)^{*}$	$(1.47)^{***}$	$(2.05)^{**}$
H_{it}	0.15	0.09	0.12
	$(3.10)^{*}$	$(1.58)^{***}$	$(1.77)^{**}$
Adj. R^2	0.96	0.97	0.96
DW	2.86	1.86	2.50
SE	0.001	0.007	0.001

Note The values in the parentheses are *t* test values, ***, ** and * indicate the significance levels of 10%, 5% and 1%, respectively

Table 2.12 Table of regression results based on model (3)

	Eastern region $lnGDP_{it}$	Central region $lnGDP_{it}$	Western region $lnGDP_{it}$
Constant term C	4.17 $(2.25)^{**}$	− 31.59 $(-1.90)^{**}$	− 8.11 (− 0.62)
$RG_{it} \times lnFDI_{it}$	0.06	0.03	0.02
	$(6.21)^{*}$	$(2.75)^{**}$	$(-1.50)^{***}$
lnK_{it}	0.60	0.50	0.43
	$(15.47)^{*}$	$(4.44)^{*}$	$(4.56)^{*}$
lnL_{it}	0.44	4.32	1.86
	$(2.08)^{**}$	$(2.42)^{**}$	$(1.30)^{***}$
H_{it}	0.04	0.03	0.16
	(− 0.99)	$(-1.26)^{***}$	(0.96)
Adj. R^2	0.94	0.98	0.94
DW	2.61	2.83	2. 66
SE	0.003	0.003	0.001

Note The values in the parentheses are *t* test values, ***, ** and * indicate the significance levels of 10%, 5% and 1%, respectively

In accordance with Model 3, we have regressed data in eastern, central and western regions, and the results are shown in Table 2.12.

From the regression results of model (2) and model (3) we can see that the regression coefficients of $H_{it} \times lnFDI_{it}$ and $RG_{it} \times lnFDI_{it}$ are less than that of $lnFDI_{it}$ in Model 1. The regression coefficient in Model 2 has dropped from 0.42, 0. 24, 0.13 to 0.06, 0.03, 0.02 in Model 2, respectively, and fell from 0.42, 0. 24, 0.13 to 0.06, 0.03, 0.02 in Model 3, respectively. It further demonstrates that technological absorptive capacity and technological development level of the host country have a very important influence on the technology transfer effect of FDI. Whether the technological absorptive capacity and technological development level of the host country are considered, the western region has the minimum effect of technology transfer through FDI, as the technological absorptive capacity and the technological development level of the western region are lower than those of the eastern region and the central region.

2.4 Conclusion

Through over 20 years of policy changes and development practices, China has gradually formed a technology import model with FDI as the mainstay and simultaneous use of other approaches. The development over the past two decades represents a development course in which developing countries gave play to their late-mover technical advantages, filled the technology gap and overtook developed countries. Over the past two decades, China has imported a large number of foreign advanced technologies and promoted the high-speed, sustained and steady economic development. Particularly, over the past decades since the implementation of the strategy of exchanging market for technology, it has played a great role in increasing China's industrial development, production capacity and production technology level. The above researches indicate that the technology gap of a country or region plays an important role in the introduction of FDI and FDI technology spillover. The comparative researches on the western region and the eastern region indicate that, as there is a wide technology gap between the western region and the eastern region, the western region lags far behind the eastern region in introduction and use of FDI. Therefore, the western region shall attract more FDI to narrow its technology gap with through the technology spillover effect of FDI, starting from the aspects of accelerating the development of high-tech industries, increasing the R&D ability, attracting FDI at high technological level and facilitating the connections between foreign subsidiaries and local enterprises.

References

Chen, Mingsen. 2003. Location and industry orientation of international capital flow. *Asia-Pacific Economic Review* 5.

Huang, Yongfeng, Ruo'en Ren, and Xiaosheng Liu. 2002. Estimation of the capital stock of China's manufacturing industry by using the perpetual inventory method. *Economics (Quarterly)* 1.

Sachs, Jeffrey. 2000. Globalization and patterns of economic development. *Review of World Economics (Weltwirtschaftliches Archiv)* 136 (4): 579–600.

Zhang, Jun, Guiying Wu, and Jipeng Zhang. 2004. China's inter-provincial material capital stock estimation: 1952–2000. *Economic Research* (10).

Chapter 3
Human Capital Gap and FDI Absorption of the Western Region

Since the introduction of FDI in China, multinational corporations' investments in China have been concentrated in the eastern coastal areas, and the western region has been a marginal region attracting FDI. Undoubtedly, multiple factors affect the location selection of FDI, then what role does the level of human resources in a region play in it? The researches of relevant experts and scholars at home and abroad have found that human capital plays a very important role in FDI absorption, and some of them indicate that there are no necessary and obvious connections between them. Does the human capital level of western China lag behind that of eastern China? Is the state of human capital an important reason for preventing FDI flowing in China? This chapter will conduct a study on this.

3.1 Empirical Analysis of the Impact of Human Capital in Western China on FDI Absorptive Capacity

Currently, most existing empirical researches on the relationship between human capital and FDI consider that there is a stable relationship between China's human capital and FDI, and the accumulation of human capital play an important role in China's absorption of FDI. This paper focuses on whether there is a stable relationship between China's human capital and FDI, as well as the relationship between the differences in FDI and human capital in the eastern region and the western region.

3.1.1 Model of Human Capital and FDI

Previous empirical researches on the relationship between human capital and FDI acquired regression formulas from the neoclassical theory of economic growth or the

© Social Sciences Academic Press 2024

X. Yang et al., *Foreign Direct Investment in Western China, 1994-2004*,
https://doi.org/10.1007/978-981-97-7407-4_3

endogenous economic growth theory to analyze the relationship of human capital, FDI and economic growth. According to the needs of this research, we learn from the empirical approaches of Lai et al. (2005) and Noorbakhash and Paloni (2001) and use the regression formula below:

$$FDI_{it} = \alpha HK_{it} + \beta^t CV_{it} + \lambda + \varepsilon_{it} \tag{3.1}$$

wherein, FDI is an explained variable and the proportion of the net FDI flow to GDP, HK is human capital, CV is control variable vector (i.e., the determinant of FDI except for human capital), λ is a co-fixed effect term, ε is an error term, i.e., the white noise. FDI here uses flow rather than stock, as if regional and time factors are considered, the explanatory power of stock on FDI inflow is not strong, and stock generally expresses book value and has not been adjusted by inflation and exchange rate movements. As what Root and Ahmed (1979) believe, FDI flow data are seldom attacked by deviation from book value. The selection of control variables are determined on the basis of the prior experience in FDI. However, the problem arising from time series is that FDI flow changes every year, and most fluctuations of FDI make the effects of human capital and other factors on FDI flow indistinct. This paper, by making an analysis of the panel data of 17 years, strives to reduce the influence of random fluctuation of data and fluctuations of data by using time series. Therefore in the above formula, subscript i refers to region, and subscript t refers to time. We consider the specific issue of choice of explaining variable in the model on the basis of the existing models.

3.1.2 Variable Selection

The educational level of the population (or labor force) is usually the most important indicator measuring the development level of human capital. In essence, the enhancement of the educational level of a country/region may help increase the human resource quality of the country/region, and the increase in supply and quality of human capital is conducive to increasing the geographical advantages of a country (region) for attracting FDI. Lucas (1998) considers that human capital can be accumulated by two ways: education and "learn from work". Education can be measured by some statistical data, but there is almost no statistical data about the effect of "learn from work". As this section mainly studies whether the human capitals in different regions are different in attracting FDI, we continue to use the traditional average schooling when choosing the data indicators of human capital level. This indicator remains effective for the accumulation of human capital. In addition, we measure the human capital level by using two other variables, namely proportion of junior secondary educated population and that of senior secondary educated population, proportion of educated population above the university level.

As China further deepens its opening-up, it has realized rapid economic growth, which is conducive to attracting multinational corporations. In practice, FDI inflows tend to occur in China's regions with most brisk and highest economic growth, which high economic growth tends to be accompanied by large-scale FDI, so it is reasonable that in many empirical researches GDP growth rate has been used as an alternative to degree of marketization.

In addition, time trend should be included in regression to replace some variables that cannot be observed, such as the change of the environment for attracting investments, or the supply factors of the countries where multinational corporations are located in, such factor endowment and economic conditions, etc. Those factors have a time trend and can make the departmental composition and location distribution of FDI change over time.

Regression estimation includes the lagging occurrence of explaining variable, which can be normalized by all means. First of all, previously, FDI flows reflect the investment conditions of the region with FDI inflows, and this can be also used as a reference for guiding potential investors to choose specific investment locations. Second, just as Johanson and Paul (1975) have pointed out, inventors tend to like to invest in the countries they are familiar with as it is dangerous to invest in countries/regions that they are unfamiliar with.

Therefore, explaining variables mainly consist of average educational level, economic growth rate, accession rate, time trend and time-delayed terms of explained variable. In addition, it is necessary to explain that the variable of openness has not been included in the model due to the incomplete data of openness of 29 provinces, municipalities and autonomous regions in the 17 years.

3.2 Estimation and Explanation of the Model

3.2.1 Description of Data and Variables

From the modeling and variable selection we can conclude that data needed for estimation include: annual GDP, human capital level, FDI flow, and number of employed persons. Relevant basic data are from the Statistical Data of New China over the Past 50 Years (1999) and China Statistical Yearbook (main year). Based on availability of variable data, the data we select include 28 provinces, municipalities and autonomous regions (the data for Xizang, Qinghai, Chongqing are included in that of Sichuan) between 1987 and 2004, wherein the average schooling data (1987–1998) calculated by Chen et al. (2004) are used. When examining the issue of human capital structure, that is, when the proportion of population receiving secondary and university education is used as a regression variable, the data availability is limited. We have adopted data of 28 provinces for regression analyses (1998–2004). The meanings of the signs are shown below:

FDI foreign direct investment as share of GDP, here, exchange rates of different years are used here to convert FDI amount;

Edu average schooling (in consideration of the availability and comparability of data, this paper continues to use average schooling to denote human capital, and the computational formula of average schooling is shown below:

$$h = 6d_1 + 9d_2 + 12d_3 + 16d_4,$$

wherein, $d_i\ (1, 2, 3, 4)$ denotes the proportions of persons at the educational levels of elementary, junior secondary, senior secondary and junior college and above to the populations at an age of six or above);

GDPGR	GDP growth rate;
Time	Time tendency;
Secondary	The proportion of persons with educational levels of junior secondary and senior secondary to the populations at an age of six or above;
College	The proportion of persons with an education level of college to the populations at an age of six or above;
West, *East*	denotes the individual dummy variables of the western region and the eastern region, respectively;
*D*1993–1997; *D*1998–2004	denotes the dummy variables of time between 1993 and 1997 and between 1998 and 2004, respectively.

3.2.2 Basic Description of Data

In this section, we expound on the relationship between human capital and FDI inflow and pay particular attention to whether there are differences between the eastern region and the western region. First of all, we need to graphically describe the relationship between human capital level represented by average schooling and FDI flow, as are shown in Figs. 3.1, 3.2 and 3.3.

According to the scatter diagrams (Figs. , 3.2 and 3.3) of FDI flow and human capital level (average schooling) in 28 regions in 19 years, we can make the following basic judgments:

The overall level of FDI inflows to most provinces in the eastern region is higher than that in western region, but the dispersion degree of FDI in eastern region is higher than that in western region, and the FDI intensity in the western region is greater than that in the eastern region;

The dispersion degree of the relationship between human capital level and FDI in the eastern region is higher than that in the central and western regions;

It seems that the relationship between human capital level and FDI is not positively correlated as shown in relevant empirical researches;

There is a certain time trend among regional FDI levels, but the time trend varies with region and is mainly concentrated between 1993 and 1997.

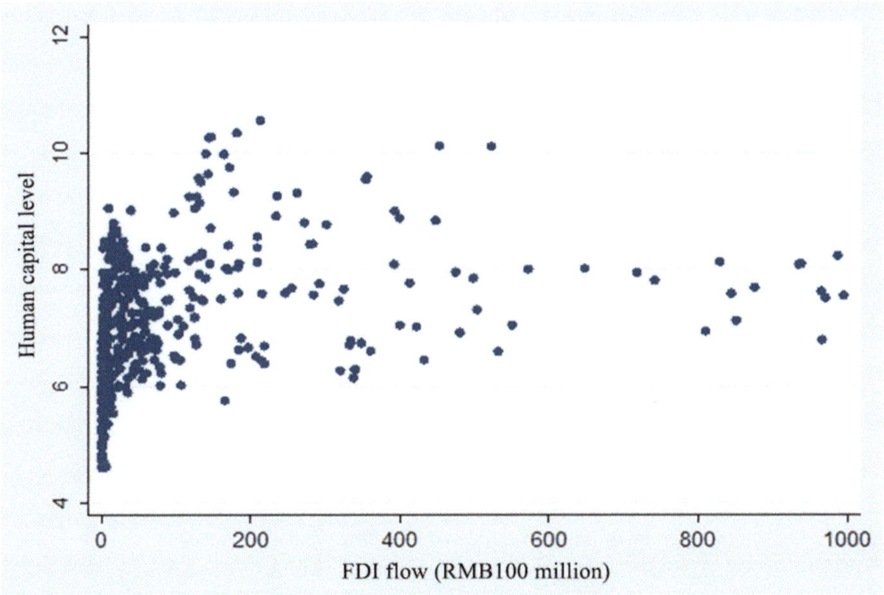

Fig. 3.1 The scatter diagram of human capital level and FDI flow

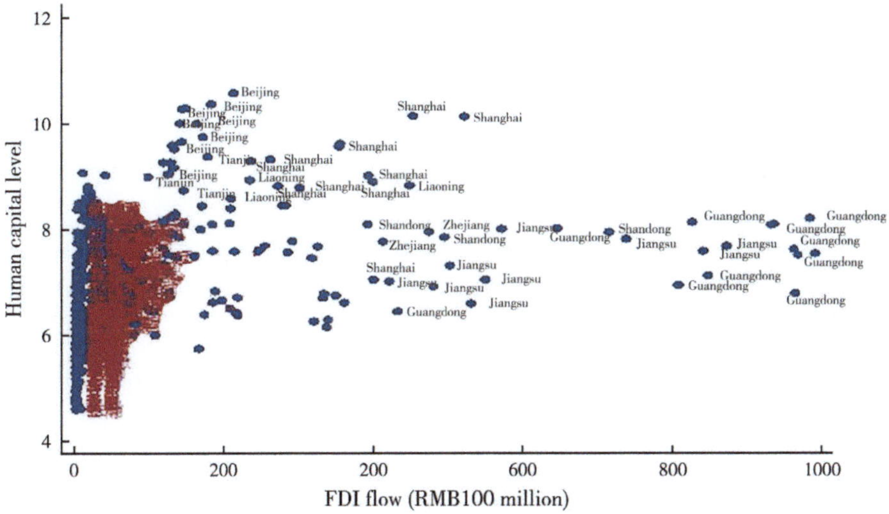

Fig. 3.2 The scatter diagram of human capital level and FDI flow (designated areas)

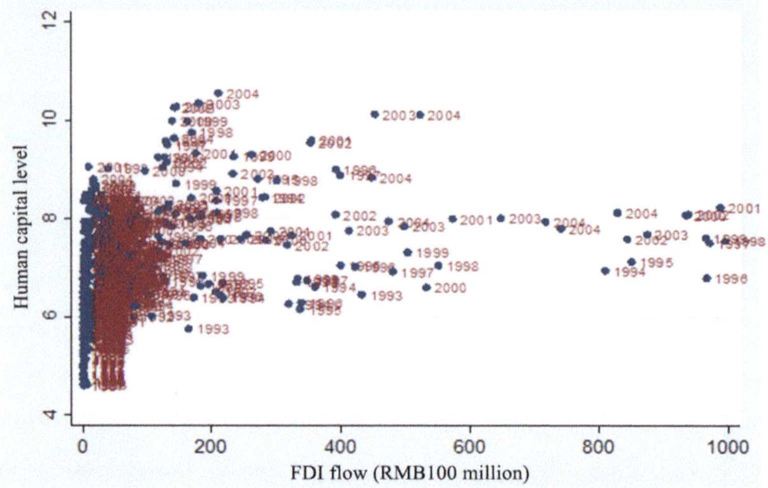

Fig. 3.3 The scatter diagram of human capital and FDI flow (years indicated)

FDI flow reflects the absolute amount. Although the goodness of fit of the model does not rely on the measurement unit of the variables, the absolute amount contains the price level of different regions and years. In other words, the factor of inflation rate shall be considered when using the absolute amount. Here, we use relevant amounts, the proportions of FDI flow converted through exchange rates of the years to regional GDP of the corresponding years, to further investigate the relationship between FDI and human capital level. The relationship between the proportions of FDI to regional GDP of the corresponding years and the human capital level is shown in Figs. 3.4, 3.5 and 3.6:

We have found some interesting changes when remaking a scatter diagram by using the proportions of historical regional FDI to GDP and human capital level. The scatter diagram of regional human capital level and FDI has not significantly changed;

Regions with higher FDI shares are not those regions with higher absolute amount of FDI, and the years with higher FDI shares are mainly between 1993 and 1997;

The relationship between human capital level and FDI continues to be insignificantly positively correlated, but exhibits some common features, and some dispersive features in Figs. 3.1, 3.2 and 3.3 has become relatively concentrated;

The relationship between the human capital level and FDI reflected in the above figures is not very obvious, and these diagrams have heterogeneous characteristics of different regions. In consideration of regional and time changes, we do not use traditional OLS to seek for the relationship between the human capital level and FDI. Rather, we make discussions by using the panel data method.

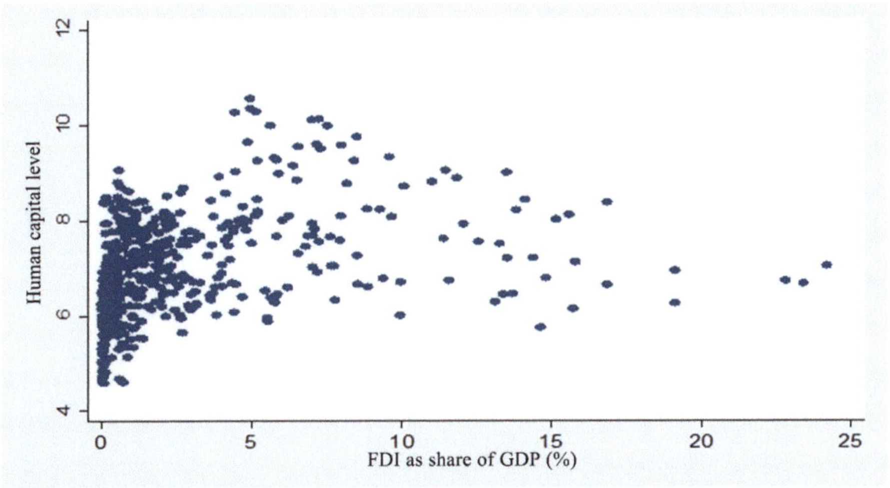

Fig. 3.4 The scatter diagram of FDI as share of GDP and human capital level

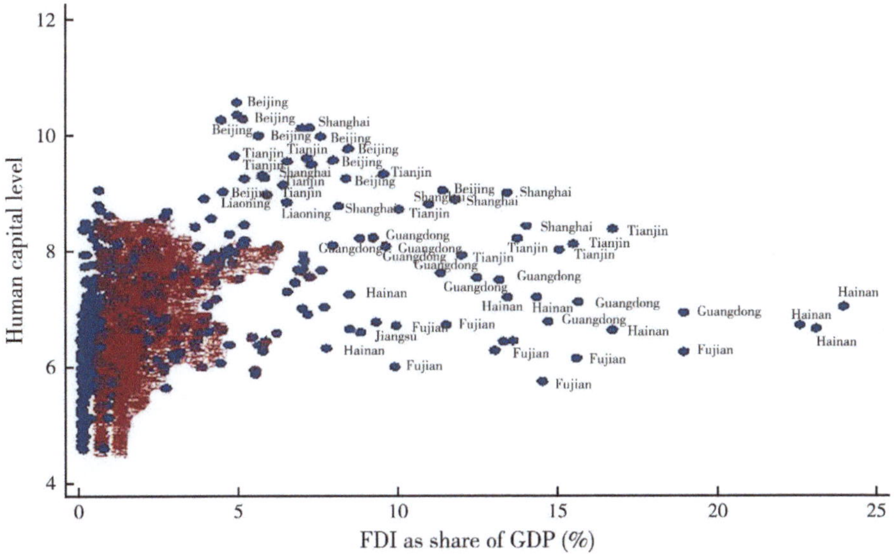

Fig. 3.5 The scatter diagram (designated areas) of FDI as share of GDP and human capital level

3.2.3 Estimation of Results

First of all, we made OLS estimation of Formula (3.1). Table 3.1 lists the regression results of OLS, the regression coefficients of the three types of variables measuring human capital (average schooling, secondary educational level, college educational

Fig. 3.6 The scatter diagram (year indicated) of FDI as share of GDP and human capital level

level) are statistically significant, signifying that human capital is an important factor of FDI inflow for China. However, what cannot be ignored is that R^2 of model 1–4 is merely between 0 and 0.2, less than 0.5, and the goodness of fit cannot meet the need.

Table 3.1 The OLS estimation results of three types of human capital variables and FDI

Explaining variable	Explained variable: FDI			
	1	2	3	4
Edu	1.138345 (7.68)*	1.324457 (6.77)*		
GDPGR		– 0.1370641 (– 2.87)*		0.144839 (0.73)*
Time		– 0.0597688 (– 1.43)*		– 0.5693115 (– 4.19)*
Secondary			0.036078 (1.29)*	0.0824304 (2.92)*
College			0.185721 (2.82)*	0.2228467 (3.54)*
C	– 5.209853 (– 4.96)*	112.8045 (1.37)*	0.2053412 (0.17) *	1136.968 (4.19)*
R^2	0.1050	0.1228	0.0959	0.2049
F	58.92	23.32	8.75	10.5
Prob. > F	0.0000	0.0000	0.0002	0.0000

Note The values in parentheses are t values; the years of data in formulas 3 and 4 are between 1998 and 2004. *indicates that it is significant at the level of 10%

The influence of average schooling above the secondary educational level on FDI is significant at the level of 10 percent. Although OLS estimation indicates that human capital has significant influence on FDI inflow, it is very likely that the goodness of fit is low due to the improper restraint of the estimation model. Meanwhile, the OLS estimation results are not effective as they have heteroscedasticity. We generalize Formula (3.1) below:

$$FDI_{it} = HK_{it} + \beta' CV_{it} + \lambda_{it} + \varepsilon_{it} \tag{3.2}$$

The difference between Formulas (3.2) and (3.1) is that Formula (3.2) is added with individual heterogeneity λ, which does not change over time, but is currently specific in model for an individual region i. While in Formula (3.1), all the regions are the same. In Formula (3.2), namely the fixed effect model we often mention, we assume that regional difference varies with the parameters of regression function.

What is opposite to fixed effect is random effect model, which has common constant term and error term, wherein the ith region is different from the population intercept, that is, regional difference is random. However, as our data are given, it is very hard to judge whether there are random effects. We try to find out inter-regional random effects, Hausman test results, if we keep introducing new variables, significantly reject the original hypothesis and support the hypotheses of fixed effect (see Table 3.2).

Table 3.2 The panel data result of the relationship between human capital level and FDI

Explaining variable	Explained variable: FDI			
	1		2	
	FE	RE	FE	RE
Edu	0.7504147(4.90)	0.7890662 (5.30)*	− 1.861771 (− 2.97)	− 0.2614649 (− 0.57)*
GDPGR			− 0.1288555 (− 3.95)	− 0.1320377 (− 4.01)*
Time			0.3885597 (4.28)	0.1633941 (2.40)*
C	− 2.49624 (− 2.32)	− 2.766611 (− 2.37)	− 759.55 (− 4.29)	− 321.4251 (− 2.42)*
R^2	0.1050	0.1050	0.5224	0.0155
F	20.32		22.26	
Prob. > F	0.0000		0.0000	
LM		1079.79		1106.66
Hausman	1.19		13.93	
H0: RE versus FE	RE		FE	

Note The values within parentheses are t values, and the values within parentheses * are z values

As for Table 3.9, if only average schooling is considered, the following two points can be explained: First, the human capital level has positive influence on FDI inflow. second, if only the simple relationship between human capital and FDI is considered, there is a random effect, i.e., the differences between different regions are random. On the basis of literature researches, we add two variables of GDP growth rate and time trend and only find that the results are opposite to the results when only the variable of human capital level is considered: first, the influence of human capital on FDI has changed, the coefficient has turned from positive to negative, and the effect of economic growth rate on FDI is negatively correlated, but the coefficient of time trend is positive, indicating that other factors have relatively obvious influence on FDI inflows. Second, if we use Hausman test to verify whether the panel data has fixed or random effect, we only find that the fixed effect exists significantly.

The above results may be questionable, whether does human capital play a role in FDI inflows? In order to make a detailed investigation on the specific impacts on the eastern and western regions, we introduce the concepts of regional dummy variable and time dummy variable (see Table 3.3).

By comparing Tables 3.2 and 3.3, we conclude that after the addition of other effect variables such as GDP growth rate representing degree of marketization and the time trend representing other influence factors, the effect of human capital on FDI

Table 3.3 The relationship between FDI and human capital after the introduction of dummy variable

Explaining variable	Explained variable: FDI			
Edu	0.7162609 (4.86)	– 0.643527 (– 1.55)	0.3275286 (1.11)	– 0.1455092 (– 0.34)
GDPGR		– 0.131385 (– 4.01)		– 0.0669692 (– 2.14)
Time		0.2171496 (3.48)		0.1449699 (1.78)
West	0.1168824 (0.12)	– 0.7943154 (– 0.78)		
East	4.194653 (4.58)	4.697619 (4.96)		
D1993–1997			3.200039 (9.17)	2.615008 (6.14)
D1998–2004			0.9438611 (1.83)	0.0357586 (0.05)
C	– 3.9428 (– 3.15)	– 427.6122 (– 3.51)	– 0.6162877 (– 0.32)	– 286.0884 (– 1.79)
R^2	0.3602	0.3652	0.1503	0.0986
Chi2	90.12	90.12	162.41	171.38
Prob. > Chi2	0.0000	0.0000	0.0000	0.0000

Note the values within parentheses are z values

inflow has turned from positive to negative. In addition, we have made the following basic judgments:

In the case of addition of regional dummy variable, the coefficients of both the eastern region and the western region are positive, but the influence of the eastern region on FDI is obvious. After the introduction of GDP growth rate and time trend representing degree of marketization, the coefficient of the variable of human capital level becomes negative. In addition, the coefficient of the eastern region is increasing, while that of the western region turns from positive to negative. It perhaps indicates that, in the eastern region, as the investment climate such as degree of marketization, institutional threshold and infrastructure improves, the human capital level has gradually become an important factor for foreign investors' decisions on investment. Currently, the western region lags far behind the eastern region in terms of market-based development, institutional reform and infrastructure construction, and the effect of human capital on attracting FDI has not yet appeared.

Before the addition of other factors, the coefficient of human capital level is smaller than that of other similar regression models; after the addition of other factors, the coefficient of human capital becomes negative. The coefficients of time dummy variable are positive no matter whether other influence factors are introduced. We believe that China has made greater efforts for its reform and opening up since the Deng Xiaoping's "Southern Tour Speeches" in 1992. Between 1993 and 1997, China, particularly its eastern region, reached a peak season of investment promotion, which is also reflected by the coefficient of D1993–1997 variable in the model. Afterwards, as China kept improving its systems and policies related to investment promotion, its scale of foreign investments steadily grew on the existing basis. It shows that institutional factors were main factors of FDI inflows in the 1990s as China kept deepening its reform and opening up. Since the late 1990s, the effects of human capital level on China's investment promotion have not yet appeared. FDI in China is mostly of the type of processing trade, which does not require a very high human capital level.

We made further analyses by using the two indexes of the proportion of population at the secondary educational level and that of population at the college educational level and above to represent human capital level. Due to the restrictions on acquiring data of proportion of educated population, we adopt the estimation time range of 1998–2004, therefore, we do not consider time dummy variables, and other settings of the model are basically the same as what have been mentioned above. Likewise, we observe some basic features of the data in accordance with the scatter diagram (see Fig. 3.7; Table 3.4).

As is shown in Figs. 3.7 and 3.8, when we measure the human capital level by using secondary educational level and college educational level rather than average schooling, the FDI intensity in the western region is still higher than that in the eastern region. Likewise, the whole diagram does not show a growing tendency of varying with FDI and the human capital level. Further, we investigate the specific relationship between the two on the basis of the empirical results. (see Table 3.4).

The Table 3.4 shows that:

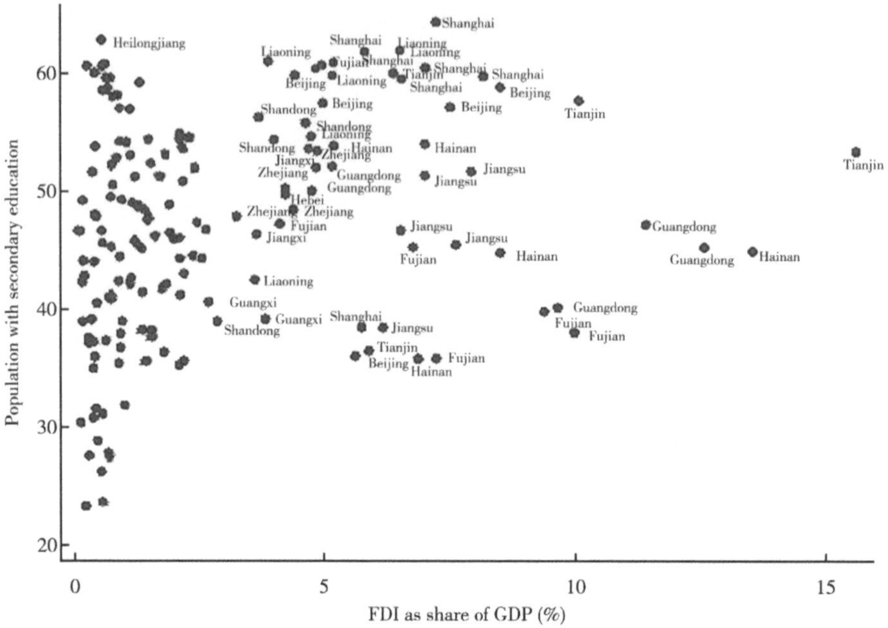

Fig. 3.7 The scatter diagram of the relationship between the population at the secondary educational level and FDI

First, compared with the secondary educational level, the college educational level has a stronger effect on FDI inflows, but generally speaking, the coefficient is small and has little effects on FDI inflow;
Second, in consideration of other factors including degree of marketization and the investment climate, the college educational level is more attractive to FDI inflows. In addition, as the economic development level increases, the higher the level of human capital stock, the stronger its attraction to FDI;
Third, after the introduction of regional difference, the attraction of human capital to FDI weakens. Just as the results of our regional difference analyses made above show, such factors as degree of marketization and investment climate are still the main factors restricting the western region from attracting foreign capital.

We have made the following judgments on the basis of the results and analyses of Tables 3.2, 3.3 and 3.4:

First, if other factors are not considered, the relationship between human capital level and FDI is obviously positively correlated; after the introduction of other influence factors, the effects of human capital level on FDI inflows turn from positive to negative. It means that the effect of human capital level on FDI inflow is not decisive, and even has obvious features such as vulnerability and changeability. In other words, when a foreign investor makes a decision on investment, human

Table 3.4 Panel data results of the relationship between the proportion of educated population and FDI

Explaining variable	Explained variable: FDI					
	1		2		3	
	FE	RE	FE	RE		
Secondary	0.0227784 (1.01)	0.0110565 (0.5)*	0.0581221 (2.34)	0.0642813 (2.72)*	– 0.0005719 (– 0.03)*	0.0476099 (2.06)*
College	– 0.3357477 (– 3.62)	– 0.1484256 (– 1.82)*	– 0.0407001 (– 0.30)	0.1115999 (1.16)*	– 0.130089 (– 1.88)*	0.0121616 (0.16)*
GDPGR			0.1405136 (1.22)	0.1467328 (1.29) *		0.1173833 (1.04)*
Time			– 0.3682926 (– 3.13)	– 0.4713201 (– 4.78) *		– 0.3709252 (– 4.04)*
West					– 0.6704528 (– 0.85)*	– 0.2630164 (– 0.33)*
East					4.613222 (6.07)*	4.104117 (5.37)*
C	3.588355 (4.02)	3.148827 (3.08)*	737.2669 (3.14)	942.3276 (4.79)*	2.001729 (1.83)*	741.2304 (4.05)*
R^2	0.0767	0.0755	0.0829	0.1946	0.5273	0.5822
F	17.54		16.02			
Prob. > F	0.0000		0.0000			
LM		165.26		207.36	62.35	78.38
Hausman	12.76		2.65			
H0: RE versus FE	FE		RE			

Note the values within parentheses are t values, and the values within parentheses * are z values

capital level is a factor that it shall consider, but tends not to be a determining factor.

Second, regional difference is an important influence factor of FDI inflow. Since the policy of reform and opening up was introduced, the eastern region has been a main destination for foreign investors. The human capital level of the western region lags behind that of the eastern region, but the factors such as degree of marketization and investment climate are main factors hindering foreign capital from entering the western region.

Third, at present, the effects of institutional and policy factors on FDI inflows in the eastern region have been gradually weakened, but they remain the main factors hindering the western region from attracting FDI.

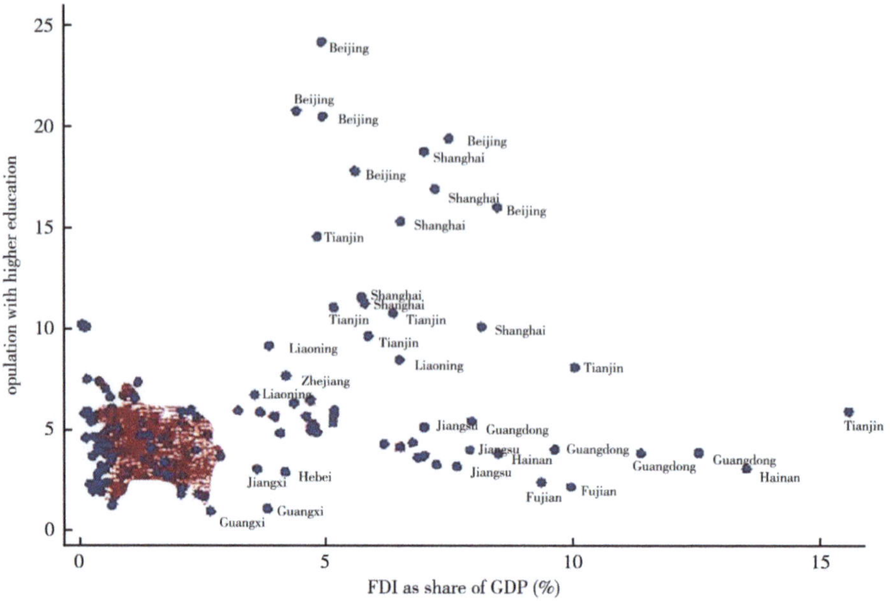

Fig. 3.8 The scatter diagram of the relationship between the population at the higher educational level and FDI

Fourth, the effects of human capital level in attracting FDI in western region will be further reflected as China's economic development and reform deepen.

3.3 Conclusion

There are many influence factors of FDI. What is the position of human capital in these factors? Human capital level is an important variable influencing FDI location selection. However, human capital and FDI complement each other, rather than being mutually independent. Higher-level human capital may make the investment climate of western China more attractive and thereby expanding the scale of foreign capital inflow. In return, the effects of FDI inflow and spillover may promote the development of local human capital and make the investment climate of western China more attractive.[1] Therefore, in the future we have to face such important issues as how to strengthen the development of human resources, increase the human capital level and optimize the human capital structure, and how to attract FDI on a large scale and promote the economic development in western China by strengthening the development of the investment climate including human resources.

Whether it is possible to form a positive interaction mechanism in western China through which human capital accumulation and FDI absorption interact with each

[1] Guo and Chen (2005).

other for common development, the key is that the western regional governments should abide by market rules, establish a management mechanism for talent introduction and retention, and introduce more open and flexible policy on attracting talents, thereby improving the treatment for talents and creating a social environment and an organizational environment that are conducive to the career development of talents. In addition, the governments at all levels in the western region should give serious considerations to increasing spending on education, which is a basic method for increasing the human capital level. In addition to increasing spending on education, we should adjust the areas and structure of educational investment and align the educational plan and the needs of multinational corporations in an appropriate way. Therefore, the following measures may help increase the level of the western region in absorbing foreign capital.

Continue to vigorously develop formal school education. As the Chinese government steadily advances the strategy of large-scale development of the western region, the institutional, infrastructure and market barriers to FDI in the western region will be gradually removed, and human capital will increasingly become an important factor for foreign investors to make decisions on making an investment, while formal school education is the basic approach to accumulating human capital. To foster the basic quality of workers, we should make great efforts to ensure that they have universal access to basic education. So far, great results have been achieved in making nine-year compulsory education universally available in western China and a solid foundation has been laid for promoting the well-rounded development of the people, but there is still a very big gap between the western region and the eastern region. Therefore, we should establish a relatively centralized system for investment in basic education, and ensure the investments in and further popularization of basic education in the western region. On this basis, we should channel great energy into development secondary education and higher education.

Strengthen training of talented personnel receiving junior college education and above and effectively improve the structure of human resources in western China. In western China, the current human capital level is mainly manifested that in the condition that the population at the secondary educational level accounts for the vast majority of the total, increasing the human capital level and optimizing its structure are conducive to FDI absorption and the use of its technology spillover effect. In addition, as the reform of the system of socialist market economy further deepens, the economy grows and the investment climate improves, the human capital level will play an increasingly important role in the introduction of FDI in the future, therefore, we must strengthen training of talented personnel receiving junior college education and above, and work effectively to increase the human resources structure of the western region. The undergraduates and graduate students at colleges and universities in the western region are a central pillar of strength for industrial innovation in the future and have some understanding of the situation there. Therefore, we should adopt policies to help most of them start up their business in the western region, it is of inestimable significance to the introduction of FDI and absorption of its spillover effect in the western region, and even the economic and social development.

Attract a large number of outstanding talents including students returning from overseas, particularly R&D personnel and manufacturing technologists. Without a certain number of talents, it is unrealistic to form aggregation effects and increase the FDI absorptive capacity. Therefore, in addition to fully mobilizing existing local talent resources, we should launch a systematic project for attracting talents at an appropriate time, and first of all attracting a host of outstanding professions who are in urgent need the western region.

Create a favorable investment climate and encourage individuals to start their own business. We should ensure that talents stay with enterprises, and enterprises adapt to the investment climate. The state should improve the investment climate in the western region and attract excellent enterprises by means of systemic building and preferential policies and, give more support to high-tech development zones, incubators and SMEs in the western region in term of policy and fund, and accelerate the establishment of the credit guarantee system and service agencies for SMEs. In order to adapt to the actual situation of different provinces, the central government may even delegate more power to regional governments in the western region, for example, launch the plan on science and technology for people's livelihood, and implement intellectual property policies with a focus on individuals. A scientist or engineer is entitled to signing a contract with his/her employer and other units where he/she take a part-time job on sharing the scientific and technological advances produced on the basis of the material and technical conditions of the employer.

Encourage multinational corporations to train local employers in the western region. Multinational corporations provide local employers with education and training services and carry out activities for innovation in management and system, which are conducive to human capital accumulation and are embodiment of "learn from work". FDI features high technological level and complicated technology and requires higher-level human resources. When employees of FDI enterprises flow to local enterprises or start their own business, the expertise and knowledge they have learned from multinational corporations will spread, which is not only technology spillover but also accumulation of human capital for the western region. As is seen from the experience in the eastern region, many excellent local entrepreneurs and key employees of local enterprises have worked in multinational corporations, and their knowledge learned at and experience accumulated from multinational corporations lay a solid foundation for their career development in the future. Therefore, we should take effective measures to make multinational corporations a school and cradle for human resources in the western region, and make them accumulate human capital for the western region and provide local economic development with a constant stream of talents.

References

Chen, Zhao, Ming Lu, and Yu Jin. 2004. Regional differences in China's human capital and educational development: A Stata estimation. *World Economy* 4.

Guo, Ying, and Feixiang Chen. 2005. The FDI and human capital growth in the developing countries. *International Economics and Trade Research* 2005 (7).

Johanson, J., and F. Wiedersheim-Paul. 1975. The internationalization of the firm: Four Swedish case studies. *Journal of Management Studies* 12: 305–322.

Lai, Mingyong, Qun Bao, Shuijun Peng, and Xin Zhang. 2005. Foreign direct investment and technology spillover: A study based on competitiveness. *Economic Research* 8.

Noorbakhsh, Farhad, and Alberto Paloni. 2001. Human capital and FDI inflows to developing countries: New empirical evidence. *World Development* 29 (9): 1593–1610.

Robert Lucas. 1998. On the mechanics of economic development. *Journal of Monetary Economics* 22(1): 3–42.

Chapter 4
An Analysis of the Impact of Industrial Base on FDI in Western China

At the initial stage of China's introduction of FDI, the main factors causing unbalanced distribution of FDI between the eastern region and the western region are differences in geographical location, preferential policy, and infrastructure, etc. As China further deepens its opening-up, some new factors, particularly industrial factors, increasingly influence multinational corporations' selection of investment areas. Due to the imbalance of China's regional economic development, there is a great gap between the industrial development levels of the western region and the eastern region, and it is mainly reflected in the following three aspects: (1) Difference in industrial level; (2) Difference in industrial structure; (3) Difference in supporting industries. The gap has become one of the important reasons for the expanding imbalanced distribution of FDI in the eastern region and the western region. Therefore, the industrial-level analysis of the issue of difficulties in introduction of foreign capital in the western region is of very important theoretical and practical significance. By analyzing the influence on the introduction of foreign capital in the western region from the three aspects of industrial level difference, industrial structure and industrial agglomeration, this chapter reveals the reasons for the difficulties in the introduction of foreign capital in the western region at the industrial level.

4.1 Impact of Industrial Gap of Western China on FDI

Industrial level difference refers to interstate or inter-regional difference in the stage of industrial development. The existence and changes of interstate industrial level differences are one of the reasons for international industrial transfer. Industrial level difference not only determines the structure of international industrial transfer, but also has an important impact on the flow direction of international industrial transfer. Industrial level difference does not only exist between countries, but also between

© Social Sciences Academic Press 2024

X. Yang et al., *Foreign Direct Investment in Western China, 1994-2004*,
https://doi.org/10.1007/978-981-97-7407-4_4

regions. Due to imbalanced economic development, obvious industrial level differences have formed between different regions of China. Particularly, the industrial level difference between the eastern region and the western region has become very obvious, causing that industrial level difference between them is different from that of foreign countries and further influencing the distribution of international industrial transfer in China. FDI is the carrier of international industrial transfer, so industrial level difference has a significant influence on the introduction of FDI in the western region. In this section we will study this issue.

4.1.1 *Industrial Gap Between the Western Region and the Eastern Region*

The industrial level difference has a significant influence on international industrial transfer. Does the industrial level difference between the western region and the eastern region has the same influence on the distribution of FDI in the western region and the eastern region? Starting from this section we will conduct a study on this issue. We will first of all evaluate the industrial level difference between the western region and the eastern region in this section and analyze the influence of the industrial level difference between the eastern region and the western region on the introduction of FDI in the western region.

4.1.1.1 Measurement of Industrial Gap

Industrial level difference can be measured in various ways. Hollis B. Chenery, on the basis of the relationship between different levels of per capita income and the industrial structure, has put forward the model of six-stage industrialization in correspondence with per capita income level. According to the above method put forward by Hollis B. Chenery, industrial level difference can be measured with GDP per capita. Simon Smith Kuznets put forward the theory of five-stage industrialization by investigating per capita income and the employment structure of labors in different industries. According to the method of Simon Smith Kuznets, industrial level difference can be measured by comprehensive considerations of GDP per capita and employment structure. Hoffmann put forward the theory on four-stage industrial development directly from the proportional relationship of industrial structure. By calculating the Hoffmann's sign we can divide industrialization into different stages. Hoffmann index refers to the proportion of consumer goods industry and capital goods industry in the economy. He believes that compared with the consumer goods industry, the capital goods industry has capital- and technology intensive features. Meanwhile, the large scale of the capital industry means the large scale of intermediate products and the high degree of industrial processing. Therefore, the larger the proportion of the capital goods industry in the economy, the higher the level of the industrialization.

4.1.1.2 Industrial Gap Between the Western Region and the Eastern Region

By calculating the ratio between the manufacturing industries and the primary industries in the western region and the eastern region, we can analyze the industrial level difference between the two regions. The calculation results are shown in Table 4.1.

Table 4.1 compares the indexes of industrial structure in the western region and the eastern region. It shows that there is an obvious industrial level difference between the eastern region and the western region. The average level of the indexes of industrial structure of eastern region reaches 11.27, while that of the western region is merely 1.68, indicating that the eastern region is generally in the upper and middle reaches of the industrial chain, while the western region is generally in the lower reaches of the industrial chain. In the eastern region, Shanghai, Zhejiang, Jiangsu, Guangdong, Beijing and Tianjin have the highest structural indexes, which are 50.53, 13.61, 11.64, 11.46, 12.54, and 8.38, respectively. In the above provinces and municipalities, the manufacturing industry takes up the biggest share while primary industries take very small shares. The structural indexes of Shandong and Fujian are 4.08 and 5.01, respectively, the proportion of manufactured goods is significantly greater than that of primary products. Except for the structural index of Hainan, which is merely 0.83, that of Liaoning and Hebei is 3.58 and 2.36, respectively, greater than that of most

Table 4.1 The comparison between the indexes of industrial structure of the western region and that of the eastern region

Eastern region		Western region	
Beijing	12.54	Shanxi	1.65
Tianjin	8.38	Inner Mongolia	1.31
Hebei	2.36	Guangxi	1.62
Liaoning	3.58	Chongqing	3.46
Shanghai	50.53	Sichuan	1.87
Jiangsu	11.64	Guizhou	1.63
Zhejiang	13.61	Yunnan	1.94
Fujian	5.01	Xizang	0.26
Guangdong	11.46	Shaanxi	1.55
Hainan	0.83	Gansu	2.32
Shandong	4.08	Qinghai	1.01
		Ningxia	2.51
		Xinjiang	0.73
Average	11.27	Average	1.68

Source 2004 economic census

provinces in the western region. In the western region, except for Chongqing, which has a structural index of 3.46 and a relatively developed manufacturing industry, the structural indexes of other provinces and autonomous regions are relatively low. The structural indexes of Sichuan, Gansu, Ningxia, Yunnan, Shaanxi, Guizhou, Guangxi and Shaanxi are higher than 1.5, the proportion of manufactured goods has no obvious advantages compared with that of primary products, and primary industries still take up a relatively large share. The structural indexes of Qinghai, Xinjiang, Xizang and Inner Mongolia are less than 1.5, and rely basically on primary industries.

4.1.2 Impact of the Industrial Gap of Western China on FDI

The main cause of international industrial transfer: developed countries or newly industrialized countries need to adjust their industrial structure due to the relative changes of comparative advantage, so as to evolve into the industrial structure at a higher level and externally transfer the marginal industries whose comparative advantages have lost or will be lost. In the process of outward transfer of the marginal industries, those countries whose advantageous industrial structure is similar with marginal industries have relatively strong abilities to undertake, and receive most international industrial transfers.

The industrial level difference between the eastern region and the western region causes that the abilities of the eastern region and the western region to undertake international industrial transfer vary greatly. The index of the industrial structure of the eastern region has reached 11.27, indicating that the eastern region boasts a highly developed manufacturing industry, precisely matching with (or highly fitting with) the industrial transfers of developed countries and newly industrialized countries to China, and featuring strong abilities and wide scope of industrial transfers. The index of the industrial structure of the western region is merely 1.68, indicating that the manufacturing industry of the western region is still at a relatively low level and the primary industries occupy a relatively large proportion. Structurally, the industrial transfer of developed countries and newly industrialized countries to China has a low matching degree (or a low overlap ratio), and their capacity for receiving international industrial transfer is low. Therefore, industrial level difference is one of the main reasons for the fact that it is hard for the western region to attract FDI.

From Fig. 4.1 we can see the influence of the industrial level difference between the western region and the eastern region on the introduction of FDI in western China. The red curve denotes the comparative advantages of the western region, the yellow curve denotes comparative advantages of the eastern region, and the blue curve indicates comparative advantages of foreign countries investing in China. The differences in curve height and coverage mean the differences in the size of comparative advantages and industrial coverage. The section AB denotes the industrial level difference between the western region and the eastern region, and its existence makes the industrial level difference between the western region and foreign countries investing in China greater than that between the eastern region and foreign countries investing in

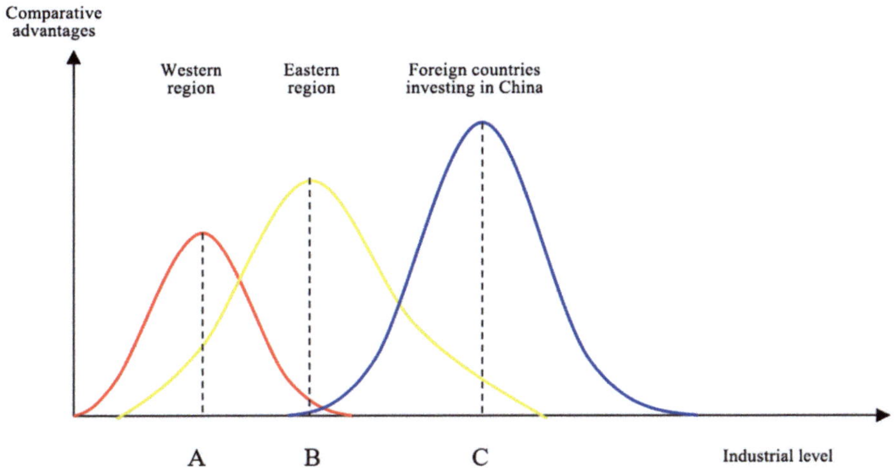

Fig. 4.1 The influence of industrial level differences on the introduction of FDI in western China

China. The section AC denotes the industrial level difference between the western region and foreign countries investing in China, the section BC denotes the industrial level difference between the eastern region and foreign countries investing in China, and the length of the section AC is greater than that of the section BC. From Fig. 4.1 we can see that the comparative advantage curve of the eastern region and that of foreign countries investing in China largely coincide with each other. By contrast, the comparative advantage curve of the western region and that of foreign countries investing in China share small coincidence area, and the section receiving international industrial transfer in the eastern region is greater than that in the western region, therefore, multinational corporations prefer to make investment in the eastern region rather than in the western region.

4.2 Impact of the Industrial Structure of Western China on FDI

The researches on the relationship between the industrial structure of the western region and the introduction of FDI are conducive to deeper analyses of the difficulties in the introduction of FDI in the western region at the industrial level. This section, first of all, analyzes the industrial structure of foreign investments in China, and then studies the relationship between the industrial structure of the western region and the introduction of FDI from the three aspects of dominant industrial structure, advantageous industrial structure and industrial distribution in the industrial chain.

4.2.1 Industrial Distribution of FDI in China

At the initial stage of FDI, China first of all undertook transferred labor-intensive industries, represented by textiles and garment manufacturing, and the investors mainly came from Hong Kong, Macao and Taiwan. As its economy developed rapidly, China entered the stage of heavy and chemical industries, and its comparative advantage changed dynamically. While maintaining the advantages of low costs of production factors such as human resources, China was gradually forming its advantageous manufacturing industry with relatively high technical content and added value. China was entering a development stage with a focus on the processing and assembly manufacturing industry with relatively high technical content and added value. As China enhances the technology, process and management of its manufacturing industry, the gap between China and developed countries was narrowing in terms of product manufacturing. As China increased the advantages of its manufacturing industry and maintained its advantages of low-cost production factors, it has developed stronger ability to receive international industrial transfer and has attracted more and more international manufacturing capacities.

Table 4.2 compares top 15 industries classified by added value of three kinds of foreign-funded industrial enterprises between 1995 and 2003. From which we can see that the industrial structure of foreign investments in China has the following features: First, the industries with fastest-growing added value are mainly equipment manufacturing industries, indicating that capital-intensive and capital-intensive industries have become China's growth areas of foreign investment. Manufacturing of communication equipment, computer and other electronic equipment, transportation equipment manufacturing, manufacture of electrical machinery and equipment, manufacture of raw chemical materials and chemical products and manufacture of instruments and cultural and office supplies were the industries with fastest-growing added value. Second, traditional labor-intensive industries, textiles, textiles, apparel and footwear, leather, fur, feathers (velvet) and their products, beverage production and manufacture of foods still took up greater proportions, but their growth rates have tended to be stable or declined. Third, as is seen from the overall scale, foreign investments in China were mostly concentrated in the industries of manufacturing of light industrial products and equipment in the middle of and the back end of the industrial chain, but were seldom in the mining and metallurgical industries in the front end of the industrial chain.

Table 4.2 Top 15 industries by added value of three kinds of foreign-funded industrial enterprises

1995		2003	
Industry	Added value	Industry	Added value
Manufacturing of communication equipment, computer and other electronic equipment	373.51	Manufacturing of communication equipment, computer and other electronic equipment	2424.52
Transportation equipment manufacturing	189.3	Transportation equipment manufacturing	1291.03
Textiles	182.25	Manufacture of electrical machinery and equipment	713.12
Textiles, apparel and footwear	173.73	Production and supply of electric power and heating power	685.41
Production and supply of electric power and heating power	149.54	Manufacture of raw chemical materials and chemical products	617.81
Manufacture of electrical machinery and equipment	139.31	Textiles	460.74
Manufacture of raw chemical materials and chemical products	128.55	Manufacture of general purpose machinery	436.32
Manufacture of non-metallic mineral products	104.81	Textiles, apparel and footwear	431.78
Leather, fur, feathers (velvet) and their products	103.21	Agricultural and sideline food processing	386.04
Agricultural and sideline food processing	102.37	Plastics manufacturing	336.7
Manufacture of general purpose machinery	96.42	Manufacture of metal products	326.35
Manufacture of metal products	90.56	Leather, fur, feathers (velvet) and their products	299.91
Beverage production	74.99	Manufacture of non-metallic mineral products	295.99
Plastics manufacturing	70.02	Manufacture of instruments and cultural and office supplies	286.03
Manufacture of foods	68.4	Manufacture of foods	275.87

Source China Statistical Yearbook 1996 and China Statistical Yearbook 2004

4.2.2 *Impact of Dominant Industries of Western China on FDI*

4.2.2.1 Dominant Industries: A Comparison of the Western Region and the Eastern Region

A leading industry refers that, in the process of economic development or at different development stages of industrialization, an industry that has an overall impact, occupies a dominant position in the national economic development and can drive the growth of the entire economy through coordination with other industries. It shows that main industries have two important features: First, it takes up a great proportion in the economy, second, it has relatively high industrial relevant effects. In this section, we compare the dominant industrial structure of the western region with that of the eastern region mainly from the perspective of the proportion of various industrial output values to the total industrial output value.

Generally, if the added value of an industry accounts for over 5% of the GDP, it can be considered as a leading industry, and we consider the industry with an output exceeding 5% of the gross industrial output value of a province as the leading industry of the province. Table 4.3 lists the industries of provinces in western region with an output exceeding 5% of the gross industrial output value of the province, from which we can see that most industries in the western region are basic industries, particularly energy, metallurgical and chemical industries. The provinces and autonomous regions with the energy industry including coal mining and washing, petroleum processing and coking, production and supply of electric power and heating power as the main pillar industry: Shanxi, Inner Mongolia, Guizhou, Yunnan, Shanxi, Gansu, Qinghai, Ningxia and Xinjiang. Provinces and autonomous regions with the metallurgical industry involving smelting and pressing of ferrous metals, smelting and pressing of non-ferrous metals as the main pillar industry: Shanxi, Inner Mongolia, Guangxi, Sichuan, Guizhou, Yunnan, Gansu, Qinghai, Ningxia and Xinjiang. Provinces, autonomous regions and municipality directly under the central government with the chemical industry (manufacture of raw chemical materials and chemical products) as the main pillar industry: Shanxi, Guangxi, Chongqing, Sichuan, Guizhou, Yunnan, Qinghai, and Ningxia. In western China, the above three industries are pillar industries in nearly all provinces, except that transportation equipment manufacturing is the pillar industry of Shaanxi, Guangxi, Chongqing, Sichuan and Guizhou, manufacturing of communication equipment, computer and other electronic equipment is the pillar industry of Sichuan and Shaanxi, and manufacture of tobacco is pillar industry of Yunnan and Guizhou. The characteristic of the leading industry in western China is its high dependence on resources. The three major pillar industries, namely the energy industry, the metallurgical industry and the chemical industry depend highly on resources. The energy industry relies on its rich coal, petroleum, natural gas and water resources, the metallurgical industry relies on the rich mineral resources including ferrous metals and non-ferrous metals, the chemical industry relies on various metal and non-metal mineral resources.

Table 4.3 Leading industries of the western region

Shanxi	Inner Mongolia	Guangxi	Chongqing	Sichuan	Guizhou
Coal mining and washing	Smelting and pressing of ferrous metals	Transportation equipment manufacturing	Transportation equipment manufacturing	Smelting and pressing of ferrous metals	Production and supply of electric power and heating power
Smelting and pressing of ferrous metals	Production and supply of electric power and heating power	Agricultural and sideline food processing	Production and supply of electric power and heating power	Production and supply of electric power and heating power	Smelting and pressing of ferrous metals
Petroleum processing and coking	Coal mining and washing	Smelting and pressing of ferrous metals	Manufacture of raw chemical materials and chemical products	Manufacture of raw chemical materials and chemical products	Smelting and pressing of non-ferrous metals
Production and supply of electric power and heating power	Manufacture of foods	Production and supply of electric power and heating power	Smelting and pressing of ferrous metals	Agricultural and sideline food processing	Manufacture of raw chemical materials and chemical products
Manufacture of raw chemical materials and chemical products	Agricultural and sideline food processing	Smelting and pressing of non-ferrous metals		Beverage production	Manufacture of tobacco
Smelting and pressing of non-ferrous metals	Smelting and pressing of non-ferrous metals	Manufacture of raw chemical materials and chemical products		Transportation equipment manufacturing	Transportation equipment manufacturing
	Textiles	Manufacture of nonmetallic minerals		Manufacturing of communication equipment, computer and other electronic equipment	Coal mining and washing

(continued)

Table 4.3 (continued)

Yunnan	Shaanxi	Gansu	Qinghai	Ningxia	Xinjiang
Manufacture of tobacco	Oil and natural gas extraction	Petroleum processing and coking	Production and supply of electric power and heating power	Production and supply of electric power and heating power	Oil and natural gas extraction
Smelting and pressing of non-ferrous metals	Production and supply of electric power and heating power	Smelting and pressing of non-ferrous metals	Oil and natural gas extraction	Smelting and pressing of non-ferrous metals	Petroleum processing and coking
Production and supply of electric power and heating power	Transportation equipment manufacturing	Production and supply of electric power and heating power	Smelting and pressing of non-ferrous metals	Manufacture of raw chemical materials and chemical products	Smelting and pressing of ferrous metals
Smelting and pressing of ferrous metals	Petroleum processing and coking	Smelting and pressing of ferrous metals	Smelting and pressing of ferrous metals	Coal mining and washing	Production and supply of electric power and heating power
Manufacture of raw chemical materials and chemical products	Manufacturing of communication equipment, computer and other electronic equipment	Oil and natural gas extraction	Non-ferrous metals mining and dressing	Petroleum processing and coking	
			Manufacture of raw chemical materials and chemical products	Smelting and pressing of ferrous metals	

Source China Industry Statistical Yearbook 2004

From the comparison between Tables 4.4 and 4.4 we can see that the dominant industrial structure of the eastern region is obviously different from that of the western region, and there are more types of dominant industrial structures in the eastern region than that in the western region. The significant difference lies in manufacturing, which is a pillar industry in many provinces in eastern China. For examples, manufacturing of communication equipment, computer and other electronic equipment is the leading industry of Beijing, Tianjin, Shanghai, Jiangsu, Zhejiang, Fujian and Guangdong, transportation equipment manufacturing is the pillar industry of

Beijing, Tianjin, Liaoning, Shanghai, Jiangsu and Zhejiang, manufacture of general purpose machinery is the pillar industry of Liaoning, Shanghai and Jiangsu, and textiles is the pillar industry of Jiangsu, Fujian and Shandong. In addition, the metallurgical industry and the chemical industry are key industries of eastern China. In general, the dominant industrial structure of the eastern region focuses on various equipment manufacturing industries, which rely mainly on technology and labor and its dependence on resources is relatively low.

4.2.2.2 Impact of the Dominant Industries of Western China on FDI

By making a comprehensive survey on the structure of foreign investments in China's industries and the leading industry in the eastern region and the western region, we can explain the relationship between the dominant industrial structure and introduction of FDI.

Figure 4.2 reflects the matching between the leading industry and the foreign investment structure in the eastern region. The horizontal axis indicates the cumulative percentage of the top 10 industries in the eastern region and the western region in the gross industrial output value of the eastern region, and the vertical axis indicates the cumulative percentage of foreign investments in corresponding industries in the gross industrial output value of China. The higher the degree of matching between the leading industry and the foreign investment structure, the higher proximity of the curve to the 45° line, otherwise, the curve deviates from the 45° line (see the right diagram of Fig. 4.2). The left diagram of Fig. 4.2 is an actual curve calculated based on data. By contrasting the two curves we can see that the curve of the eastern region is very close to the 45° line, while the curve of the western region deviates greatly from the 45° line, indicating that the dominant industrial structure and the foreign investment structure of the eastern region have a high degree of matching, while those of the western region vary greatly.

We can draw the same conclusion by calculating the matching index of the dominant industrial structure and the foreign investment structure between the eastern region and the western region. Assuming that there are m leading industries in the western region, and the proportion of each leading industry to the total industrial output value is r_{w1}, r_{w2},..., r_{wm}, respectively, the proportions of foreign investments in these industries to the industrial investments in China are f_{w1}, f_{w1},..., f_{wm}, respectively, then the matching index of the dominant industrial structure and the foreign investment structure in the western region is $I_w = \sum_{i=1}^{m} r_{w1} f_{w1}$. The higher the value, the higher the matching degree of the dominant industrial structure and the foreign investment structure. In a similar way, the index of eastern region can be calculated. According to China Statistical Yearbook and China Industry Economy Statistical Yearbook 2004, the matching index of the dominant industrial structure and the foreign investment structure in the eastern region is 621.81, and that in the western region is 205.39. It shows that the matching index of the dominant industrial structure and the foreign investment structure in the western region is much lower than that in the eastern region.

Table 4.4 Leading industries of the eastern region

Beijing	Tianjin	Hebei	Liaoning	Shanghai	Jiangsu
Manufacturing of communication equipment, computer and other electronic equipment	Manufacturing of communication equipment, computer and other electronic equipment	Smelting and pressing of ferrous metals	Smelting and pressing of ferrous metals	Manufacturing of communication equipment, computer and other electronic equipment	Manufacturing of communication equipment, computer and other electronic equipment
Transportation equipment manufacturing	Smelting and pressing of ferrous metals	Production and supply of electric power and heating power	Petroleum processing and coking	Transportation equipment manufacturing	Transportation equipment manufacturing
Smelting and pressing of ferrous metals	Transportation equipment manufacturing	Manufacture of raw chemical materials and chemical products	Production and supply of electric power and heating power	Smelting and pressing of ferrous metals	Smelting and pressing of ferrous metals
Manufacture of raw chemical materials and chemical products	Manufacture of raw chemical materials and chemical products		Transportation equipment manufacturing	Manufacture of general purpose machinery	Manufacture of general purpose machinery
Production and supply of electric power and heating power	Oil and natural gas extraction		Manufacture of general purpose machinery	Manufacture of electrical machinery and equipment	Manufacture of electrical machinery and equipment
Petroleum processing and coking			Manufacture of raw chemical materials and chemical products	Manufacture of raw chemical materials and chemical products	Manufacture of raw chemical materials and chemical products

(continued)

Table 4.4 (continued)

Zhejiang	Fujian	Shandong	Guangdong	Hainan
Textiles	Manufacturing of communication equipment, computer and other electronic equipment	Agricultural and sideline food processing	Manufacturing of communication equipment, computer and other electronic equipment	Transportation equipment manufacturing
Manufacture of electrical machinery and equipment	Production and supply of electric power and heating power	Manufacture of raw chemical materials and chemical products	Manufacture of electrical machinery and equipment	Agricultural and sideline food processing
Manufacture of general purpose machinery	Textiles and manufacturing of garments, footwear and hat	Textiles	Production and supply of electric power and heating power	Manufacture of raw chemical materials and chemical products
Manufacturing of communication equipment, computer and other electronic equipment	Manufacture of nonmetallic minerals	Manufacture of nonmetallic minerals	Manufacture of raw chemical materials and chemical products	Production and supply of electric power and heating power
Manufacture of raw chemical materials and chemical products	Textiles	Production and supply of electric power and heating power		Manufacture of pharmaceuticals
Transportation equipment manufacturing		Manufacture of electrical machinery and equipment		Beverage production
Textiles and manufacturing of garments, footwear and hat		Smelting and pressing of ferrous metals		
		Manufacture of general purpose machinery		

Source China Industry Economy Statistical Yearbook 2004

The structure of foreign investments in China reflects to an great extent foreign investors' willingness to make investments in China. If the dominant industrial structure matches with foreign investors' willingness to make investments in a region, it indicates that the region has good conditions for developing these industries and greater ability to attract foreign investments. The dominant industrial structure of the western region is not attractive for foreign investments, which is one of the major reasons for the poor attraction of the western region to FDI.

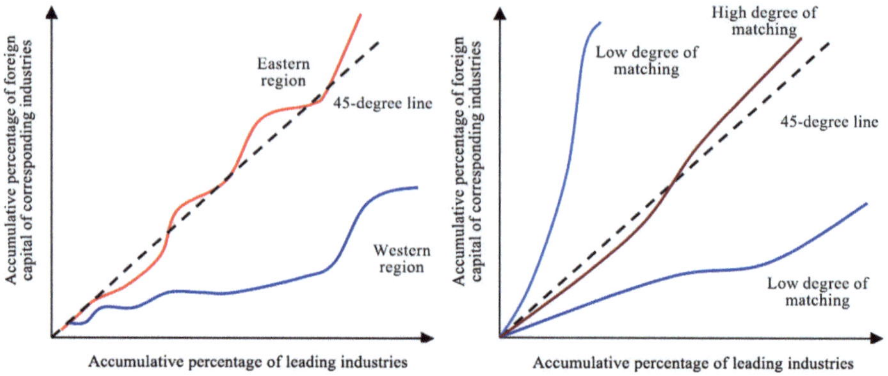

Fig. 4.2 Match between the leading industry and foreign capital. *Note* calculated based on 2004 data of the China Statistical Yearbook and China Industry Statistical Yearbook

4.2.3 Impact of the Advantageous Industries of Western China on FDI

4.2.3.1 Advantageous Industries: A Comparison Between the Western Region and the Eastern Region

The dominant industrial structure is based on a single province, while the advantageous industrial structure is based on horizontal comparison between different provinces. The regional advantageous industrial structure can be reflected by the location quotient (LQ), which can be obtained by measuring the relative degrees of specialization of different industries in different regions. Thus, we can obtain advantageous industrial structures of China's 31 provinces, municipalities and autonomous regions. Industrial categorization is based on relevant national standards of China. Assume that LQ_{ij} is the LQ of industry j in province i then:

$$LQ_{ij} = \frac{V_{ij}/GDP_i}{V_j/GDP}$$

wherein, V_{ij} denotes the added value of industry j of province i, GDP_i denotes the GDP of province i, V_i denotes the added value of China's industry j, GDP indicates China's gross domestic product. If LQ_{ij} is greater than 1, industry j is an advantageous industry of province i. If LQ_{ij} is less than 1, industry j is not an advantageous industry of province i. All industries of province i with LQ_{ij} values greater than 1 constitute the advantageous industrial portfolio of the province. As FDI inflows in China are mainly in the manufacturing industry, we only calculate the LQ of the manufacturing industry.

Tables 4.5 and 4.6 list the LQ of major manufacturing industries of provinces, autonomous regions and municipalities directly under the central governments in the eastern region and western region calculated on the basis of 2004 China Industry Economy Statistical Yearbook, involving a total of 19 manufacturing industries. By comparing Tables 4.5 and 4.6 we can see that there is an obvious gap between the advantageous industrial structure of the western region and that of the eastern region.

First of all, the LQs of most manufacturing industries in the eastern region are higher than that in the western region. Among the 19 manufacturing industries, eastern provinces have on average seven industries with LQ greater than 1, and Beijing, Tianjin, Shanghai, Jiangsu, Zhejiang, Shandong and Guangdong have the most competitive industries. By contrast, in western provinces, there are only a few advantageous industries. Among all the 19 manufacturing industries, on average less than three industries have LQ greater than 1, and in some provinces there is one industry with LQ greater than 1.

Second, in addition to the gap in quantity, the western region and the eastern region vary greatly in type of competitive industries. For example, manufacturing of communication equipment, computer and other electronic equipment is a competitive industry in Beijing, Tianjin, Shanghai, Jiangsu, Fujian and Guangdong, and electrical machinery, equipment, and supplies is a competitive industry in Shanghai, Jiangsu, Zhejiang, Anhui and Guangdong, all of them are in the eastern region. Competitive industries in the western region are mainly manufacture of tobacco (Yunnan, Guizhou), beverage production (Sichuan, Guizhou), food production (Inner Mongolia, Ningxia), petroleum processing, coking and nuclear fuel processing (Shaanxi, Gansu and Xinjiang), and manufacture of pharmaceuticals (Guizhou, Xizang and Shaanxi).

4.2.3.2 Impact of the Advantageous Industries of the Western Region on FDI

In general, the eastern region has great advantages over the western region in labor-intensive manufacturing industries and capital-intensive manufacturing industries, but the western region only has an advantage in manufacturing industries relying highly on particular resources. Competitive industries in the western region are relatively simple and mostly related to local distinctive resources. Western China boasts rich mineral resources and most provinces there have an advantage in processing of mineral resources. The competitive industries of the eastern region are essentially different from that of the western region. The eastern region has an advantage in labor-intensive industries such as textiles and apparel, capital-intensive industries such as mechanical equipment manufacturing, and some capital-intensive industries such as electronic and communication equipment industries.

Figure 4.3 compares the LQ of 19 manufacturing industries in the western region and the eastern region, from it we can see obviously the giant gap between the western region and the eastern region in manufacturing. On the whole, most manufacturing industries in the eastern region have obvious advantages than those in the western region, while the industries which the western region has obvious advantages over the eastern region are merely petroleum processing, coking and nuclear fuel processing,

Table 4.5 Advantageous industries of the western region

Shanxi		Inner Mongolia	
Industry	LQ	Industry	LQ
Petroleum processing, coking and nuclear fuel processing	3.304	Manufacture of foods	2.938
Smelting and pressing of ferrous metals	2.759	Smelting and pressing of ferrous metals	1.609
Smelting and pressing of non-ferrous metals	2.489	Smelting and pressing of non-ferrous metals	1.464
Guangxi		Chongqing	
Industry	LQ	Industry	LQ
Smelting and pressing of non-ferrous metals	1.316	Transportation equipment manufacturing	2.496
Sichuan		Yunnan	
Industry	LQ	Industry	LQ
Beverage production	2.868	Manufacture of tobacco	11.829
		Smelting and pressing of non-ferrous metals	2.194
Shaanxi		Gansu	
Industry	LQ	Industry	LQ
Manufacture of pharmaceuticals	1.949	Smelting and pressing of non-ferrous metals	6.137
Petroleum processing, coking and nuclear fuel processing	1.2	Petroleum processing, coking and nuclear fuel processing	4.346
Manufacture of special purpose machinery	1.186	Manufacture of tobacco	1.038
Ningxia		Guizhou	
Industry	LQ	Industry	LQ
Smelting and pressing of non-ferrous metals	3.765	Manufacture of tobacco	2.981
Textiles, apparel and footwear	2.003	Smelting and pressing of non-ferrous metals	2.743
Manufacture of raw chemical materials and chemical products	1.373	Beverage production	2.461
Manufacture of foods	1.297	Manufacture of pharmaceuticals	1.746
textiles	1.142		
Qinghai		Xinjiang	
Industry	LQ	Industry	LQ
Smelting and pressing of non-ferrous metals	3.709	Petroleum processing, coking and nuclear fuel processing	2.585
Xizang			
Industry	LQ		

(continued)

Table 4.5 (continued)

Shanxi		Inner Mongolia	
Industry	LQ	Industry	LQ
Manufacture of non-metallic mineral products	1.419		
Manufacture of pharmaceuticals	1.13		

Source calculated based on 2004 China Industry Economy Statistical Yearbook and industrial categorization of China's national standards

smelting and pressing of non-ferrous metals, and manufacture of tobacco. These three industries are very typical industries that highly rely on resources.

China is a populous country with fewer resources on a per-person basis. Therefore, the advantageous industrial structure of the eastern region actually reflects the comparative advantage and its changes of China, which fit with marginal industries transferred from developed countries and newly industrialized countries, making the eastern region preferred by multinational corporations. The advantageous industrial structure of the western region indicates that the resources of western region are still an important source of its comparative advantage. Western China has for a long time relied on resources for its industrial development, causing that it lacks an advantageous industrial structure that fits with international industrial transfer, which is one of the reasons for attracting few foreign investment.

4.2.4 Western China's Position on the Industrial Chain and Its Influence on FDI Absorption

4.2.4.1 Position on the Industrial Chain: A Comparison Between the Western Region and the Eastern Region

Industrial chain is a path by which one kind of resource or several kinds of resources keep transferring to downstream industries at several industrial levels through to the consumers. In the industrial chain, except for few industries with products used completely to provide intermediate input or for final consumption, most industrial products can be both consumer goods and immediate input products of other industries. By comparing the proportions of industrial products for intermediate input, we can judge the position of the industry in the industrial chain. Most products of industries at the upper stream of the industrial chain are intermediate input products of other industries, so the proportion of intermediate input products to the total output is relatively large. On the contrary, most products of downstream industries in the industrial chain are consumables, therefore the proportion of intermediate input products to the total output is relatively small. On the basis of the input–output table

Table 4.6 Advantageous industries of the eastern region

Beijing		Tianjin	
Industry	LQ	Industry	LQ
Manufacturing of communication equipment, computer and other electronic equipment	1.811	Manufacturing of communication equipment, computer and other electronic equipment	2.365
Manufacture of pharmaceuticals	1.435	Manufacture of pharmaceuticals	2.034
Manufacture of special purpose machinery	1.357	Manufacture of metal products	1.855
Manufacture of instruments and cultural and office supplies	1.308	Smelting and pressing of ferrous metals	1.642
Manufacture of foods	1.218	Manufacture of raw chemical materials and chemical products	1.602
Transportation equipment manufacturing	1.202	Manufacture of general purpose machinery	1.298
Beverage production	1.196	Petroleum processing, coking and nuclear fuel processing	1.213
		Transportation equipment manufacturing	1.21
		Manufacture of foods	1.197
Shanghai		Jiangsu	
Industry	LQ	Industry	LQ
Transportation equipment manufacturing	3.144	Manufacture of chemical fibers	3.396
Manufacture of general purpose machinery	2.197	Textiles	2.219
Manufacture of instruments and cultural and office supplies	2.062	Manufacture of metal products	1.869
Smelting and pressing of ferrous metals	1.996	Manufacture of general purpose machinery	1.709
Manufacture of metal products	1.73	Manufacturing of communication equipment, computer and other electronic equipment	1.656
Manufacture of tobacco	1.726	Manufacture of raw chemical materials and chemical products	1.52
Petroleum processing, coking and nuclear fuel processing	1.678	Manufacture of electrical machinery and equipment	1.38
Manufacturing of communication equipment, computer and other electronic equipment	1.565	Manufacture of instruments and cultural and office supplies	1.309
Manufacture of electrical machinery and equipment	1.417	Manufacture of special purpose machinery	1.308
Manufacture of foods	1.397	Textiles, apparel and footwear	1.097

(continued)

Table 4.6 (continued)

Beijing		Tianjin	
Industry	LQ	Industry	LQ
Manufacture of special purpose machinery	1.311	Manufacture of pharmaceuticals	1.005
Manufacture of raw chemical materials and chemical products	1.09		
Manufacture of pharmaceuticals	1.004		
Zhejiang		Shandong	
Industry	LQ	Industry	LQ
Manufacture of chemical fibers	2.876	Textiles, apparel and footwear	2.132
textiles	2.224	Manufacture of special purpose machinery	1.787
Manufacture of general purpose machinery	1.708	Textiles	1.533
Manufacture of electrical machinery and equipment	1.533	Manufacture of non-metallic mineral products	1.526
Manufacture of metal products	1.374	Manufacture of general purpose machinery	1.31
Manufacture of instruments and cultural and office supplies	1.265	Manufacture of foods	1.309
Textiles, apparel and footwear	1.221	Manufacture of raw chemical materials and chemical products	1.288
Manufacture of special purpose machinery	1.091	Manufacture of electrical machinery and equipment	1.151
		Manufacture of chemical fibers	1.144
		Petroleum processing, coking and nuclear fuel processing	1.127
Fujian		Guangdong	
Industry	LQ	Industry	LQ
		Manufacturing of communication equipment, computer and other electronic equipment	3.353
Manufacturing of communication equipment, computer and other electronic equipment	1.236	Manufacture of instruments and cultural and office supplies	2.968
Manufacture of chemical fibers	1.223	Manufacture of electrical machinery and equipment	2.191
Manufacture of non-metallic mineral products	1.111	Manufacture of metal products	1.863

(continued)

Table 4.6 (continued)

Beijing		Tianjin	
Industry	LQ	Industry	LQ
Manufacture of instruments and cultural and office supplies	1.098	Textiles, apparel and footwear	1.313
Textiles, apparel and footwear	1.035	Manufacture of foods	1.214
		Manufacture of raw chemical materials and chemical products	1.203
Hainan		Hebei	
Industry	LQ	Industry	LQ
Manufacture of pharmaceuticals	1.507	Smelting and pressing of ferrous metals	2.37
Transportation equipment manufacturing	1.078		

Source Calculated based on 2004 China Industry Economy Statistical Yearbook and industrial categorization of China's national standards

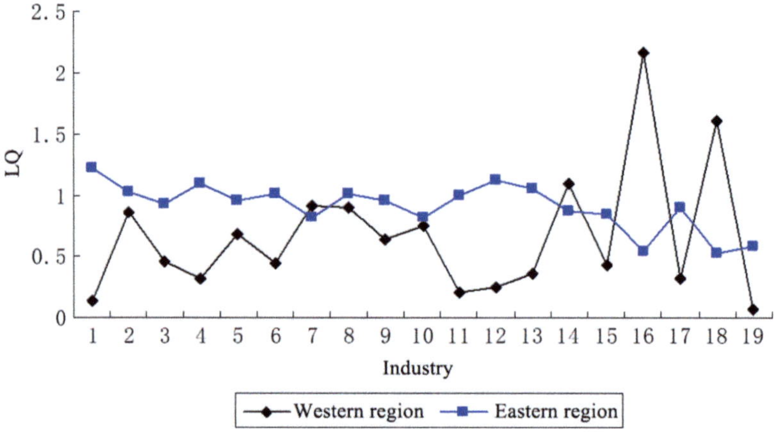

Fig. 4.3 An comparison of LQs of the 19 manufacturing industries in the western region and the eastern region. *Source* Calculated based on 2004 China Industry Economy Statistical Yearbook and industrial categorization of China's national standards

we can calculate the proportion of intermediate products to the total output, thereby judging their positions in the industrial chain.

By using Input–Output Tables of China 2002, we have calculated the proportions of intermediate use of 33 major categories of the mining industry and the manufacturing industry to the total output (see Table 4.7). For convenience, we make the classifications below: if the proportion of intermediate input to the total output of an industry is lower than 0.4, it is deemed as a downstream industry of the industrial chain; if the proportion of intermediate input to the total output of an industry is between 0.4 and 0.7, it is deemed as a midstream industry of the industrial chain; if the proportion of intermediate input to the total output of an industry is higher than 0.7, it is deemed as an upstream industry of the industrial chain. After making appropriate adjustments according to the benchmark, we classify the 32 industries as follows in accordance with the calculation results in Table 4.7:

Downstream industries of the industrial chain: Textiles, apparel and footwear; manufacture of cultural, educational and sporting goods; manufacture of special purpose machinery; manufacture of tobacco; leather, fur, feathers (velvet) and their products; furniture manufacturing; food production.

Midstream industries of the industrial chain: Manufacturing of instrumentation and mechanical equipment for cultural and office use; beverage production; manufacture of electronic and communication equipment; transportation equipment manufacturing; electrical machinery, equipment, and supplies; manufacture of pharmaceuticals; manufacture of general machinery; manufacture of rubber products.

Upstream industries of the industrial chain: Manufacture of metal products; plastics manufacturing; coal mining and washing; manufacture of non-metallic mineral products; manufacture of non-metallic mineral products; wood processing and manufacturing of wood, bamboo, rattan, palm, and grass products; manufacture of raw chemical materials and chemical products; non-metallic mineral mining and dressing; paper making and paper products; smelting and pressing of non-ferrous metals; petroleum processing and coking; printing and reproduction of recorded media; ferrous metals mineral mining and dressing; non-ferrous metals mining and dressing; smelting and pressing of ferrous metals; manufacture of chemical fibers.

On the basis of the classification, we calculate the proportions of the manufacturing industry in the different positions of the industrial chain in the western region and the eastern region, the calculation results are shown in Table 4.8. From which we can see that compared with that of the eastern region, the manufacturing industries of the western region are mostly in the upper stream of the industrial chain, the average proportion of upstream industries to the total has reached 54.38%. In the eastern region, the average proportion of upstream industries has reached 37.48%, indicating that the products from the manufacturing industry in the western region are mostly for providing other industries with immediate input products. In downstream industries and midstream industries, it is lower in the western region than in the eastern region, especially, it varies greatly in midstream industries, the average proportion of midstream industries in the western region to the total is merely 17.81%, and that in the eastern region is 36.96%. As midstream industries are relatively developed, the industries in the eastern region have higher relevancy degree and the driving effects of industries are stronger. In the western region, the exceptional cases are Chongqing and Yunnan, in Chongqing, the proportion of midstream industries to the total has reached 51.47%, indicating that the structure of the manufacturing

Table 4.7 The proportions of intermediate products to the total output of 32 mining and manufacturing industries

Industry	Proportion	Industry	Proportion
Manufacture of chemical fibers	0.99	Manufacture of rubber products	0.68
Smelting and pressing of ferrous metals	0.99	Manufacture of general machinery	0.67
Non-ferrous metals mining and dressing	0.98	Manufacture of pharmaceuticals	0.65
Ferrous metals mineral mining and dressing	0.98	Electrical machinery, equipment, and supplies	0.59
Printing and reproduction of recorded media	0.96	Transportation equipment manufacturing	0.58
Oil and natural gas extraction	0.96	Manufacture of electronic and communication equipment	0.5
Petroleum processing and coking	0.95	Other manufacturing industries	0.47
Smelting and pressing of non-ferrous metals	0.93	Beverage production	0.46
Paper making and paper products	0.92	Manufacturing of instrumentation and mechanical equipment for cultural and office use	0.44
Non-metallic mineral mining and dressing	0.9	Food production	0.43
Manufacture of raw chemical materials and chemical products	0.89	Furniture manufacturing	0.42
Wood processing and manufacturing of wood, bamboo, rattan, palm, and grass products	0.87	Leather, fur, feathers (velvet) and their products	0.34
Manufacture of non-metallic mineral products	0.86	Manufacture of tobacco	0.34
Coal mining and washing	0.86	Manufacture of special purpose machinery	0.32
Plastics manufacturing	0.85	Manufacture of cultural, educational and sporting goods	0.2
Manufacture of metal products	0.74	Textiles, apparel and footwear	0.18

Note Calculated based on Input–Output Tables of China 2002

industry of Chongqing has greater advantages over that of other western provinces and autonomous regions. In Yunnan, the proportion of downstream industries to the total has reached 33.13%, and the main factor for this is the relatively developed tobacco industry.

Table 4.8 The distribution of manufacturing industries in the industrial chain in the western region and the eastern region, %

Western region				Eastern region			
Province/ municipality/ autonomous region	Downstream industries	Midstream industries	Upstream industries	Province/ municipality/ autonomous region	Downstream industries	Midstream industries	Downstream industries
Guangxi	24.81	26.11	40.34	Beijing	10.63	50.13	30.97
Chongqing	12.23	51.47	28.21	Tianjin	9.66	45.00	40.98
Sichuan	17.61	29.00	41.89	Hebei	16.77	13.18	58.98
Guizhou	12.96	20.50	47.80	Liaoning	10.95	23.46	57.07
Yunnan	33.13	7.83	46.34	Shanghai	12.63	53.49	29.69
Xizang	2.02	27.39	55.17	Jiangsu	20.55	37.74	36.61
Shaanxi	11.92	29.00	47.09	Zhejiang	30.90	32.12	33.56
Gansu	9.31	6.49	71.08	Fujian	28.03	33.86	29.47
Qinghai	3.27	4.41	67.23	Shandong	27.18	24.89	41.75
Ningxia	11.89	10.52	54.02	Guangdong	16.16	48.65	26.90
Xinjiang	11.09	4.96	77.45	Hainan	19.82	44.04	26.27
Shanxi	6.20	7.08	78.48				
Inner Mongolia	24.49	6.72	51.86				
Average	13.92	17.81	54.38	Average	18.48	36.96	37.48

Source Calculated based on the manufacturing data of the MacroChina database

4.2.4.2 Impact of Upstream Industrial Concentration on FDI in the Western Region

As is seen from the industrial structure of multinational corporations' investment in China, the investments are mainly concentrated in the middle of the industrial chain. Figure 4.4 is the structural chart of distribution of FDI in the industrial chain, the horizontal axis is arranged in the order of upstream industries, midstream industries and downstream industries, and the vertical axis indicates the proportion of FDI in relevant industries. This shows that FDI inflows in China are concentrated in midstream industries and sparsely distributed in upstream industries and downstream industries, moreover, FDI inflows in downstream industries are higher than those in upstream industries. From Table 4.8 we can see that the proportions of midstream industries and downstream industries in Shanghai, Guangdong, Jiangsu, Zhejiang, Beijing and Tianjin to the total are very large, and they are also regions receiving FDI most in China. In the western region, industries are concentrated in the upstream of the industrial chain, there are few downstream industries attracting FDI, and it is one of the reasons for the difficulties in attracting foreign investments in the western region.

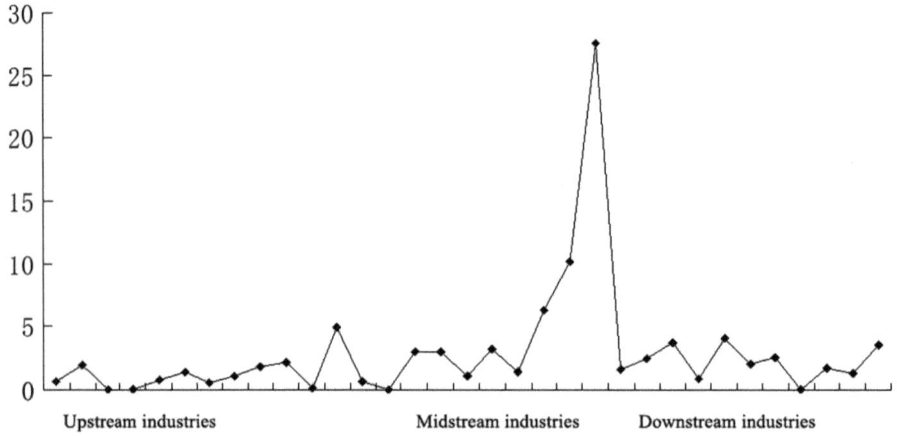

Fig. 4.4 The distribution of FDI in the industrial chain. *Note* Calculated based on China Statistical Yearbook 2004

4.3 Impact of Supporting Industries in Western China on FDI

The industrial level difference of the western region and the eastern region is not only reflected in the difference in industrial structure, but also in the difference in industrial supporting capacity. Through constant optimization and upgrading, relevant supporting industries are concentrated in the eastern region by centering on several core industries. Particularly, due to FDI inflows, the industries in the eastern region remain aligned with international practices and have developed very strong FDI supporting capacity. However, the industrial structure in the western region changes slowly and ages, and fails to form a system of supporting industries with core industries at the center. Therefore, there is a big difference in industrial supporting capacity between the eastern region and the western region. This section analyzes the influence of industrial supporting capacity on the introduction of FDI in the western region.

4.3.1 Industrial Supporting Capacity and Location Selection of FDI

Supporting industry is a concept closely related to industrial chain. Industrial chain is a certain technical and economic correlation, specific logical relationship and spatio-temporal layout relation between different sectors. Under the circumstance of increasingly deepening division of labor based on specialization, the production activities of enterprises become increasingly specialized, and the product production activities are carried cooperatively out by production units in the industrial chain. Industrial supporting capacity is an important factor for attracting investments from multinational corporations. For multinational corporations, investing in locations with better supporting conditions at least have the following benefits: reduction in the investment costs of multinational corporations; reduction in the investment risk of multinational corporations; multinational corporations' rapid approaches to market and production factor.

Industrial supporting radius is used to describe the scope of procurement of an enterprise, and its size and distance have a great impact on the production cost of the enterprise. In the wave of economic globalization, enterprises all over the world have taken part in the global division of labor and global sourcing has gradually become a development trend. Therefore, the supporting radii of many enterprises have extended to overseas. If all supporting producers of an enterprise are in local areas, then the industrial supporting radius is greatly reduced, and the purchase cost is significantly reduced. The size and distance of industrial supporting radius are directly related to transportation cost. By the scope of purchase, supporting industries can be divided into local supporting industries, domestic supporting industries, international supporting industries as well as the composite-type supporting industries consisting of the above three types of supporting industries, corresponding, there are three types of supporting radii, namely local supporting radius, domestic supporting radius and international supporting radius.

4.3.2 A Comparison Between Industrial Supporting Capacity of the Manufacturing Industry in the Western Region and that in the Eastern Region

By analyzing the industries, we choose the top industries to measure the supporting capacity of the western region and that of the eastern region.

Assuming that the industries with greatest intermediate consumption in the industry I are $J_1, J_2, J_3, \ldots J_{10}$, V_{ij} is the gross output of the industry J_j of the province i, then $\sum_{j=1}^{10} V_{ij}$ is the sum of the total output value of the main supporting industries of industry I of the province i, the higher the value, the stronger the supporting capacity of the industry I of the province i. Assuming that there are n provinces, the value of the province with the strongest industrial supporting capacity I is $V_{ma} = \max \sum_{j=1}^{10} V_{ij}\ (i = 1 \cdots n)$, and the supporting capacity of other provinces in relation to the province is $\sum_{j=1}^{10} V_{ij}/V_{ma}\ \ (i = 1 \cdots n)$. By using the indicator, we can compare the supporting capacities of industry I of different provinces. As there are many manufacturing industries, we mainly compare some of representative industries.

4.3.2.1 Equipment Manufacturing Industries

Equipment manufacturing industries refer to all manufacturing industries providing technical equipment for simple reproduction and extended reproduction of all sectors of the national economy, covering the mechanical industry (including manufacture of aerospace products, ships and weapons) and investment products in the electronic industry, manufacture of general purpose machinery, special purpose machinery, aerospace vehicles, railway transportation equipment, vehicles and other transportation equipment, electrical machinery and equipment, communication equipment, computer and other electronic equipment, instrumentation and products for cultural and office use. On the basis of the analysis of the China Input & Output Table for 2002, the supporting industries of main equipment manufacturing industries are shown below:

Manufacture of electronic and communication equipment

Manufacture of electronic and communication equipment, electrical machinery, equipment, and supplies, plastics manufacturing, manufacture of non-metallic mineral products, manufacture of metal products, manufacture of raw chemical materials and chemical products, smelting and pressing of non-ferrous metals, manufacture of general machinery, paper making and paper products, smelting and pressing of ferrous metals.

Transportation equipment manufacturing

Main supporting industries: transportation equipment manufacturing, smelting and pressing of ferrous metals, manufacture of general machinery, manufacture of rubber products, electrical machinery, equipment, and supplies, manufacture of raw chemical materials and chemical products, plastics manufacturing, manufacture of metal products, smelting and pressing of non-ferrous metals, manufacture of electronic and communication equipment.

Manufacture of instrumentation and office supplies

Main supporting industries: Manufacture of electronic and communication equipment, manufacturing of instrumentation and mechanical equipment for cultural and office use, manufacture of raw chemical materials and chemical products, electrical machinery, equipment, and supplies, smelting and pressing of ferrous metals, plastics manufacturing, manufacture of metal products, manufacture of general machinery, manufacture of non-metallic mineral products, smelting and pressing of non-ferrous metals.

Electrical machinery, equipment, and supplies

Main supporting industries: Smelting and pressing of non-ferrous metals, electrical machinery, equipment, and supplies, plastics manufacturing, smelting and pressing of ferrous metals, manufacture of metal products, manufacture of general machinery, manufacture of raw chemical materials and chemical products, manufacture of electronic and communication equipment, paper making and paper products, manufacture of non-metallic mineral products.

Manufacture of instrumentation and products for cultural and office use

Main supporting industries: Manufacture of electronic and communication equipment, manufacturing of instrumentation and mechanical equipment for cultural and office use, manufacture of raw chemical materials and chemical products, electrical machinery, equipment, and supplies, smelting and pressing of ferrous metals, plastics manufacturing, manufacture of metal products, manufacture of general machinery, manufacture of non-metallic mineral products, smelting and pressing of non-ferrous metals.

Industries with the highest degree of superposition: electrical machinery, equipment, and supplies, plastics manufacturing, manufacture of non-metallic mineral products, manufacture of metal products, manufacture of raw chemical materials and chemical products, smelting and pressing of non-ferrous metals, manufacture of general machinery, smelting and pressing of ferrous metals. Based on the calculation method above we can calculate the industrial supporting capacity of equipment manufacturing industries in the western region and the eastern region.

Table 4.9 A comparison between the supporting capacities of equipment manufacturing industries in the western region and the eastern region

Western region		Eastern region	
Chongqing	4.29	Beijing	16.68
Sichuan	12.91	Tianjin	21.27
Guizhou	3.18	Hebei	26.13
Yunnan	5.12	Liaoning	24.5
Xizang	0.03	Shanghai	52.3
Shaanxi	4.11	Jiangsu	91.83
Gansu	4.12	Zhejiang	47.78
Qinghai	0.88	Fujian	18.85
Ningxia	1.35	Shandong	55.79
Xinjiang	1.93	Guangdong	100
Guangxi	4.59	Hainan	0.46
Shanxi	8.66		
Inner Mongolia	4.92		
Average	4.31	Average	41.42

Source China Industry Economy Statistical Yearbook 2004

From Table 4.9 we can see that the provinces in the western region are lack of the supporting capacity for equipment manufacturing industries. Even in Sichuan, which has the best supporting conditions, its supporting capacity is merely 12.91% of that of Guangdong, The supporting capacities of other provinces are very low, less than 10% of that of Guangdong. The supporting capacity of all provinces in eastern China except for Hainan are generally high, particularly, Guangdong, Jiangsu, Shanghai, Zhejiang and Shandong have very strong supporting capacities.

4.3.2.2 Smelting and Pressing of Metals

Smelting and pressing of metals mainly involve smelting and processing of ferrous metals and non-ferrous metals and providing other production sectors with various metallic raw materials.

Smelting and pressing of ferrous metals

Main supporting industries: smelting and pressing of ferrous metals, ferrous metals mineral mining and dressing, petroleum processing and coking, other manufacturing industries, coal mining and washing, manufacture of non-metallic mineral products, manufacture of general machinery, smelting and pressing of non-ferrous metals, manufacture of metal products, manufacture of special purpose machinery.

Smelting and pressing of non-ferrous metals

Main supporting industries: Smelting and pressing of non-ferrous metals, non-ferrous metals mining and dressing, other manufacturing industries, manufacture of raw chemical materials and chemical products, smelting and pressing of ferrous metals, petroleum processing and coking, coal mining and washing, manufacture of general machinery, manufacture of metal products, manufacture of non-metallic mineral products.

By contrasting the main supporting industries of the two industries, we can see that supporting industries of smelting and pressing of metals are basically the same, and the supporting industries are basically the same. We choose these industries to calculate the supporting capacity of the western region and the eastern region.

From Table 4.10 we can see that the western region still lags far behind the eastern region in the supporting capacity for smelting and pressing of metals, but the gap is narrower than that of equipment manufacturing industries. In the western region, Shanxi has the best supporting conditions, and its supporting capacity is 30.45% of Jiangsu, which has the best supporting capacity in the eastern region. Other provinces and autonomous regions in western China with good supporting capacity are Sichuan, Gansu and Inner Mongolia. All provinces in eastern China, particularly Jiangsu, Guangdong, Shanghai, Zhejiang, Shandong, Hebei and Liaoning, have good supporting capacity.

Table 4.10 A comparison of the supporting capacity for smelting and pressing of metals in the western region and the eastern region

Western region		Eastern region	
Chongqing	7.03	Beijing	18.38
Sichuan	19.66	Tianjin	22.70
Guizhou	5.96	Hebei	51.09
Yunnan	9.48	Liaoning	53.90
Xizang	0.11	Shanghai	50.63
Shaanxi	8.48	Jiangsu	100.00
Gansu	11.15	Zhejiang	54.52
Qinghai	1.97	Fujian	15.20
Ningxia	3.09	Shandong	89.57
Xinjiang	7.07	Guangdong	62.23
Shanxi	30.45	Hainan	0.82
Inner Mongolia	11.79		
Guangxi	7.82		
Average	9.54	Average	47.19

Source China Industry Economy Statistical Yearbook 2004

4.3.2.3 Manufacture of Consumer Goods

Manufacture of consumer goods mainly involves textiles, apparel and footwear, food production, beverage production, textiles, leather, fur, feathers (velvet) and their products, manufacture of cultural, educational and sporting goods. These manufacturing industries are close to end consumers, and are mostly labor-intensive industries.

Textiles, apparel and footwear

Main supporting industries: textiles, manufacture of raw chemical materials and chemical products, textiles, apparel and footwear, plastics manufacturing, manufacture of chemical fibers, Leather, fur, feathers (velvet) and their products, paper making and paper products, manufacture of rubber products, printing and reproduction of recorded media.

Food production

Main supporting industries: Food production, plastics manufacturing, manufacture of raw chemical materials and chemical products, paper making and paper products, manufacture of metal products, printing and reproduction of recorded media, coal mining and washing, transportation equipment manufacturing, manufacture of general machinery.

Beverage production

Main supporting industries: Food production, beverage production, paper making and paper products, plastics manufacturing, manufacture of non-metallic mineral products, manufacture of metal products, manufacture of raw chemical materials and chemical products, printing and reproduction of recorded media, coal mining and washing.

Textiles

Main supporting industries: textiles, manufacture of chemical fibers, manufacture of raw chemical materials and chemical products, manufacture of special purpose machinery, paper making and paper products, manufacture of general machinery, plastics manufacturing, coal mining and washing, electrical machinery, equipment, and supplies.

Leather, fur, feathers (velvet) and their products

Main supporting industries: Leather, fur, feathers (velvet) and their products, food production, textiles, manufacture of raw chemical materials and chemical products, plastics manufacturing, manufacture of rubber products, paper making and paper products, textiles, apparel and footwear, manufacture of metal products.

By contrasting the main supporting industries we can see that the supporting industries of manufacture of consumer goods are similar to each other, of which supporting industries needed in most industries are: textiles, manufacture of raw chemical materials and chemical products, plastics manufacturing, manufacture of chemical fibers, paper making and paper products, manufacture of rubber products,

Table 4.11 A comparison of the supporting capacities of manufacture of consumer goods between the western region and the eastern region

Western region		Eastern region	
Chongqing	4.19	Beijing	10.61
Sichuan	11.59	Tianjin	12.08
Guizhou	2.74	Hebei	19.32
Yunnan	3.62	Liaoning	18.12
Xizang	0.01	Shanghai	35.05
Shaanxi	4.43	Jiangsu	100.00
Gansu	2.03	Zhejiang	78.13
Qinghai	0.45	Fujian	15.87
Ningxia	2.00	Shandong	78.06
Xinjiang	2.13	Guangdong	63.23
Shanxi	13.40	Hainan	0.66
Inner Mongolia	5.26		
Guangxi	3.13		
Average	4.23	Average	39.20

Source China Industry Economy Statistical Yearbook 2004

printing and reproduction of recorded media, manufacture of general machinery and coal mining and washing. We use these industries as main supporting industries to compare the supporting capacity of the western region and that of the eastern region.

From Table 4.11 we can see that the western region is poor in its supporting capacity for manufacture of consumer goods, and lags far behind the eastern region. The supporting capacity of many provinces in the western region is less than 5% of Jiangsu, which has the best supporting capacity in the eastern region. The supporting capacities of Shanxi and Sichuan, which are the best in the western region, account for merely 13.4% and 11.59% of that of Jiangsu, respectively. The supporting capacities of provinces in the eastern region vary greatly, and those provinces with good supporting capacity are Jiangsu, Guangdong, Zhejiang and Shandong.

4.4 Conclusion

The western region lags far behind the eastern region in industrial supporting capacity. The gap shows that: first of all, compared with the eastern region, the western region is lack of a relatively complete industrial system, has a relatively simple industrial structure and is lack of an industrial linkage system with the leading industry or competitive industry at the core. By contrast, in the eastern region, there is a relatively complete industrial system and forms an industrial cluster with several industries at the core. Second, the labor is adequately divided based on specialization in the eastern region, but it is not so in the western region, the difference between the western region and the eastern region in industrial supporting capacity is reflected both on the scale and quality of supporting industries.

In the eastern region, thanks to the strong industrial supporting capacity, it is easy for multinational corporations to gain supports from relevant industries and supporting industries, they do neither need to invest in these industries nor purchase relevant and supporting products from other regions, in this way they can quickly start their core production at a relatively low cost. As a result of the inflows of foreign capital, the eastern region has formed a group of specialized manufacturers for foreign-owned enterprises and thus has strong supporting FDI manufacturing capacity. In the western region, the supporting FDI capacity is poor, it is hard for foreign investors to gain relevant supports from supporting industries in the western region, and bulk purchase has to be made from beyond the western region, resulting in high costs of production and operation. As is seen from the structure of foreign investments in China, reduction of production cost is the main cause of foreign investments in China, and local industrial supporting capacity is an important factor needing to be considered by foreign investors when selecting investment locations. To sum up, the lack of industrial supporting capacity in the western region is one of the reasons for difficulties in attracting foreign investments.

As global economic integration keeps deepening, the competitions between multinational corporations have become increasingly fierce, and multinational corporations' strategy of foreign investments has shifted from simple integration to complex integration. Correspondingly, the focus of location selection for foreign investments has shifted from cost reduction to acquisition of strategic assets and enhancement of the core competitiveness. Specifically, the industrial factor is one of the factors to be considered by multinational corporations when selecting the investment location. This paper shows that the gaps of industrial level difference, industrial structure and industrial supporting capacity between the western region and the eastern region are the main cause for the difficulties in absorbing FDI in the western region. Therefore, it is difficult to achieve obvious results in the western region by only using preferential policy to absorb FDI. At present, in many provinces in the western region preferential policies are made on foreign investments, which are on a par with or even stronger than that in the eastern region. However, the attraction of the western region to FDI has not been significantly improved. If the western region continues to absorb FDI by relying on traditional factors (policy and factor costs), then it is very hard to get rid of the difficulty in absorbing FDI. This paper considers that the western region should get rid of the misunderstanding, make intensified efforts to adjust the industrial structure and attract FDI by optimizing and upgrading the industrial structure.

Chapter 5
A Study on Location Issues of the Introduction of FDI in Western China

The decision making on location of FDI is a multi-stage process. In most instances, foreign investors first of all choose the countries to be invested in before determining the region and site where the factory is built. In the process of the development of the theory on FDI location selection, Dunning (1988) summarized the five major types of location factors: market factor (including market size and potential), trade barrier factor, cost factor, investment climate factor and overall conditional factor. The spatial economics that developed in the 1990s embodied the concept of location into geographical location. Spatial distance and transportation cost have become important factors affecting enterprise layout and flows of cross-country direct investments. Spatial economic theory holds that space has an important impact on enterprise's production and operation activities, particularly on the location of enterprise. This chapter mainly analyzes how the location factors of the western region have an impact on the introduction of FDI.

5.1 China's Attractiveness to FDI from Multinational Corporations

Many scholars have always expounded from different perspectives the preferences of multinational corporations for location conditions of the host country and the reasons. At present, the researches on FDI locations are mainly conducted following the three paths (Wei et al. 2001a): (1) Add the analyses of location factors in the FDI theory, and discuss about the influence of national location characteristics on FDI country selection. (2) Use the method of field survey to probe into the decision-making process, influence factors and spatial organization behaviors of location selection for foreign investments. (3) On the basis of the basic fundamental principles of the modern location theory, use various econometric methods to discuss about domestic FDI regional differences or determinant factors of location selection. Next, we will apply

© Social Sciences Academic Press 2024

X. Yang et al., *Foreign Direct Investment in Western China, 1994-2004*,
https://doi.org/10.1007/978-981-97-7407-4_5

the above theory on direct investment from multinational corporations to China's actual situation, study the factors affecting China's FDI regional distribution and analyze the factors of the FDI regional differences between the western region and the eastern region.

From the perspective of spatial distance we analyze the attractiveness of China and other major countries to direct investment. According to the attraction model, outward direct investment flows are highly positively correlated with the economic aggregate of the host country and are negatively correlated with distance. Therefore, we can express this kind of relevance by using outward investment attraction coefficient *K*, which can be expressed as:

$$K' = GDP_j \wedge^2 / D_{ij},$$

wherein GDP_j is the economic aggregate of a host country, D_{ij} denotes the distance between the investing country and the host country. The higher the coefficient of attraction to outward direct investment (*K*), the more likely the investment flow occurs, and higher the flow.

We analyze the location selection of FDI of multinational corporations from potential investing countries and regions all over the world by using the outward investment attraction coefficient (see Table 5.1). The higher the coefficient of attraction to outward direct investment (*K*), the more likely the investment flow occurs, and higher the flow.

Table 5.1 shows that the coefficients of attraction of China to investments from Asian countries such as Japan, South Korea and ASEAN countries are much higher than those to investments from the United States and major capital exporting countries in Europe, and such difference is mainly caused by distance.

5.2 A Comparison of FDI Influencing Factors for FDI Location Selection Between the Western Region and the Eastern Region

The spatial pattern of FDI in China is a gradient distribution model declining from the east to the west (see Table 5.2). The reason for this has been studied by many scholars in recent years. For example, Wei et al. (2001b) have studied foreign investors' motivation of making investments in China by using the questionnaire method (see Table 5.3).

By using the panel data analytical method, Liu (2005) selected the historical statistical data of different provinces (1986–2003), established panel data models of the eastern, central and western regions in different periods, respectively, and made empirical analyses (see Table 5.4) of corresponding factors that are likely to influence FDI location differences.

Table 5.1 The coefficients of China's attraction to FDI from other countries

	American countries					European countries			
	U.S	Canada	Australia	New Zealand	Brazil	Germany	France	Italy	U.K
Distance	4765	4647	4853	5806	9147	4044	4448	4394	4406
Coefficient of attraction	151.36	152.66	150.42	140.83	115.14	159.63	154.89	155.51	155.42
	Asian countries (regions)								
	Russia	Japan	Korea	Singapore	Malaysia	Thailand	Indonesia	Hong Kong	Macao
Distance	3136	1135	519	2407	2341	1772	2804	1090	990
Coefficient of attraction	171.42	204.73	217.76	182.22	183.27	192.8	176.21	205.63	207.66

Source 2004 GDP data from China Statistical Yearbook; the distance refers to the distance of sea transportation, calculated by using the distance calculator in the website www.indo.com

Note when the coefficients of attraction are calculated, the original data have been processed in a standardized and weighted approach

Table 5.2 FDI absorption in the eastern, central and western regions of China by 2003, Unit: percent

	Number of approved foreign-invested enterprises	Accumulated amount of contracted foreign capital	Actual utilization of foreign capital
Proportion in the eastern region	82	86.86	86.27
Proportion in the central region	11.27	7.55	8.93
Proportion in the western region	6.73	5.59	4.8

Source 2004 Report on Foreign Investment in China

Table 5.3 Influencing factors for location selection by foreign investors

Influencing factors	Ranking
Utilization of local cheap labor	1
Expansion and occupation of the market of the Chinese mainland	2
Sufficient supply of raw materials	3
Abundant local natural resources	4
Preferential policy on tax exemption and reduction	5
High ROI	6
China's accession to the WTO	7
Domestic trade and export to a third country	8
Affection and kinship the Chinese mainland	9
After-sale and technological services	10
Reduction of patent royalty	11
Avoidance of foreign exchange risks	12
Avoidance of high tariff barrier	13
Make investments in the Chinese mainland by following suit	14
Collection of commercial intelligence	15

Source Wei and He (2001)

According to Table 5.4, since 1986, the main influence factors for FDI in different periods and regions are FDI concentration effect, labor cost, proportion of the tertiary industry to the total, concentration of industries and infrastructures, policy advantages, market size and scientific and technological R&D spending, etc., and the degrees of influence vary in different periods and in different regions. FDI has very strong effects of capital and industrial concentration. On a long-term basis, regions with complete infrastructure and good environmental conditions for talent training are more attractive for FDI. Accumulative FDI stock plays a more and more important role in location selection of foreign investors through "demonstration effect"

Table 5.4 A comparison of influencing factors for FDI location selection in between 1986 and 2003

No.	1986–1991			1992–2003			1986–2003		
	Eastern	Central	Western	Eastern	Central	Western	Eastern	Central	Western
1	Labor cost (− 1.86)	Labor cost (− 1.72)	Market size (− 4.445)	Market size (− 2.012)	Labor cost (− 1.232)	Labor cost (− 1.604)	Accumulative FDI stock (1.025)	Labor cost (− 1.604)	Proportion of the tertiary industry (− 2.509)
2	Proportion of the tertiary industry (− 1.448)	Market size (1.382)	Labor cost (− 2.289)	Policy advantages (1.63)	Accumulative FDI stock (1.052)	Accumulative FDI stock (1.412)	Market size (− 0.996)	Accumulative FDI stock (1.275)	Labor cost (− 2.263)
3	Accumulative FDI stock (1.426)	Accumulative FDI stock (1.353)	Accumulative FDI stock (1.705)	Proportion of the tertiary industry (0.935)	Proportion of the tertiary industry (− 1.036)	Proportion of the tertiary industry (− 1.228)	Concentration of industries and infrastructures (0.758)	Policy advantages (0.901)	Accumulative FDI stock (1.431)
4	Spending on science and technology (0.274)	Proportion of the tertiary industry (− 0.78)	Proportion of the tertiary industry (− 0.84)	Accumulative FDI stock (0.881)	Policy advantages (0.587)	Concentration of industries and infrastructures (1.064)	Policy advantages (0.751)	Market size (− 0.62)	Policy advantages (0.714)
5	Market size (0.264)	Concentration of industries and infrastructures (0.378)	Spending on science and technology (0.222)	Concentration of industries and infrastructures (0.691)	Market size (− 0.31)	Market size (0.779)	Labor cost (− 0.409)	Proportion of the tertiary industry (0.165)	Spending on science and technology (0.287)

(continued)

Table 5.4 (continued)

No.	1986–1991			1992–2003			1986–2003		
	Eastern	Central	Western	Eastern	Central	Western	Eastern	Central	Western
6	Concentration of industries and infrastructures (0.082)	Spending on science and technology (0.147)	Concentration of industries and infrastructures (− 0.2)	Labor cost (0.39)	Concentration of industries and infrastructures (0.252)	Policy advantages (0.461)	Spending on science and technology (0.145)	Spending on science and technology (0.121)	Concentration of industries and infrastructures (0.187)
7				Spending on science and technology (0.16)	Spending on science and technology (0.112)	Spending on science and technology (− 0.169)	Proportion of the tertiary industry (0.09)	Concentration of industries and infrastructures (0.05)	Market size (0.071)

Source Liu (2005)

and "push effect", namely the aggregation effects of FDI. The more foreign-funded firms in a certain region, the stronger willingness of other foreign investors to make investments in the region. As a high-risk investment behavior with production factors fully involved in, a decision on FDI is quite serious. As it needs to have a comprehensive understanding of the market, regulatory, economic and cultural factors of the host country, FDI usually faces relatively high cost of information seeking, and the implementation of FDI face relatively high transaction cost. Due to such uncertainty and high cost, it is a better choice to adopt a so-called "follow-up" strategy. The very strong positive self-growth effect of FDI has been noticed by scholars. Head and Ries (1996) put forward aggregation effects, Cheng and Kwan (1999) used different estimation methods to obtain self-growth effect. Liang (2004) used relevant and regression calculation results to show that the main role of the site selection model of Japan's investment is industrial concentration effect rather than being based on natural endowments or labor, etc.

At the initial stages for reform and opening-up, it can be said that preferential policy (particularly tax preference) is an important factor attracting foreign investments. The central government's FDI preferential policy, whether in the eastern region, central or western region, had play an important role in the initial stage of introduction of investments, and had particularly a great impact on introduction of foreign capital to the western region in the preliminary stage. But, it has gradually shown a weakening trend on a long-term basis. For example, China has adopted a policy on large-scale development of the western region since 2000, but the effect of the policy on attracting FDI in the western region is not obvious in recent years. It shows that, in the new stages of China's investment promotion and development, all regions should focus on improving environmental conditions including the infrastructures and talent base, etc., rather than excessively competing with each other in terms of preferential policy. After its accession to WTO, China, by relying on its foreign investment policy, has shifted from preferential policy focusing on tax incentive mechanism to rules and policies focusing on fair competition mechanism. The Chinese government is reducing the excessive preferential treatments to foreign investors and giving them national treatments, and is also reducing the restrictions on market access (except for specific industries) and non-national treatment of foreign investors, so as to improve its overall investment climate and promote fair market competitions.

The advantage of low labor cost has been a main factor for capital inflow in the initial stage in different regions in China. Nevertheless, as more multinational corporations and high-quality foreign investments enter China, high-quality foreign investments tend to retain high-quality and excellent talents at a higher cost. Although in the central and western regions the current advantage of low labor cost remains an important reason for attracting FDI, the foreign investments attracted due to the advantage of low labor costs are mostly labor-intensive low-quality foreign investments. To increase the quality of FDI in the central and western regions in the future, it is necessary to increase the labor quality by further optimizing the talent structure, strengthening talent education and training so as to attract high-quality foreign investments.

The proportion of the tertiary industry in the central and western region has negative elasticity in all stages. It had negative elasticity in the eastern region between 1986 and 1991, and positive elasticity between 1992 and 2003, indicating that FDI is mainly concentrated in the secondary industries of different regions. It is the long-term pattern of FDI distribution in China, but has been adjusted to some extent in the eastern region. As the proportion of the tertiary industry in the eastern region increases, the FDI has flowed into the eastern region since 1992. We have enhanced the added value of the first and secondary industries through IT-based renovation and promote more FDI inflows in the industry by raising the proportion of the tertiary industry. It should be the development direction of both the eastern region and the central and western regions, only in this way can we promote the optimization and adjustment of China's industrial structure through FDI inflow.

The elasticity of the spending on science and technology is very low in China's different regions in different stages of introduction of foreign capital. On the one hand, it shows that spending on science and technology has an insignificant impact on China's introduction of foreign capital. On the other hand, it objectively reflects that the technological level of China's FDI inflows is generally not high.

To sum up, the analyses of the location differences of China's use of foreign capital between the western region and the eastern region and their reasons may further explain the key role of location factors in utilization of foreign capital. The western region is not as good as the eastern region in the aspects of geographical location, climatic and natural conditions, economic location, market environment, transportation conditions and communication conditions, making it tend to be marginalized, difficult to gain a favorable condition and less attractive for foreign investments. This is the most fundamental influence factor.

5.3 Location Conditions of Western China

The location selection of FDI is essentially an issue of location selection for investors. The particularity of site selection of FDI relative to general site selection lies in the selection of host country. If the host country is given, we may take no account of country-specific factors affecting FDI, such as trade policy, exchange rate, and national risks, etc., and the attraction of FDI to the western region is an issue of location selection for FDI. The location selection model of Dunning emphasizes that the immovable, natural or acquired endowments of a region are the key to attraction to FDI. In the process of the large-scale development of the western region, the comparative advantages we can use are preferential policies, rich natural resources and low labor cost. From the perspective of modern competitive strategies, preferential policies, natural resources and low labor cost are "low-order" advantages, it is unstable, changeable and can flow to some extent. Although the western region has the advantages of natural resources and labor cost for a long time, it has not actually effectively attract FDI. Next, we will analyze from the perspective of location why multinational corporations do not make direct investments in the western region.

5.3.1 Evaluation of Location Factors in the Western Region

The western region boasts rich natural resources, relatively low-cost labor as well as energy and raw material industries and related industries with a good foundation. However, these advantages are not only relative but also at a "low level". Economic advantage is an integration of multiple factors. The advantages of the central and western China in resources and labor will be weakened or offset by transportation, information and technology infrastructures and the inadequate market mechanism, causing that the comprehensive disadvantage is greater than the comprehensive advantage and it is not attractive to or not attractive enough to foreign investors.

First, the comparative advantages of resources of the western region are quite attractive to foreign investors oriented to production factors. However, the high transportation cost has offset the advantages of low costs of raw materials and labor in the western region. Foreign investors have to spend more on turning the advantages of natural resources in the western region into profits, and fail to achieve higher profitability than in their home country or in the eastern region of China. The western region sustains a great loss due to is its lack of international passageway and sea gate. As there is no convenient sea gate in the western region, the production capacity of high-quality mineral resources has been greatly restricted. In the western region, the backward infrastructures have restricted the entry of foreign capital.

Second, the western region has lots of cheap labors, which are one of its dominant advantages for attracting foreign investments. However, the employed in the western region are less educated and skilled than that in the eastern region, weakening the comparative advantage of the western region. The absolute labor price of the western region is obviously lower than that of the eastern region, but there are few persons who are educated and can be rapidly cultivated into skilled workers. Comparatively, in the eastern region, due to its relatively developed economy and popular basic education, particularly secondary vocational education, it does not cost much and take a long time to train a skilled worker. The per capita wage of the western region is lower than that of the eastern region, but the per capita efficiency wage of the western region is higher than that of the eastern region.

Third, the market demand in the western region is lower than that in eastern region. It is hard to produce local market effects, the market capacity is relatively small, and economic development lacks accumulation effects. In 2004, the per capita income of eastern China was USD1873, while that of western China was USD718, and the per capita income of eastern China is 2.6 times of western China. The effective demand formed by per capita income in the western region is much less than that in the eastern region, and is not enough to attract market-oriented foreign investment projects. There are lots of mountains, deserts and gobi in the western region. The natural barriers formed by geographical conditions also affect the degree of market integration, the market is highly fragmented and segmentary and can hardly form market scale efficiency. There are high marketing costs due to low population density, low per capita income level, strict market segmentation and traditional consumption habits.

Compared with the eastern region, the western region has not much competitive advantages in terms of preferential policy and measures, there are few preferential measures specially for foreign investments in western China. Generally, foreign investors are treated equally with domestic enterprises. For example, "domestic enterprises and foreign-invested enterprises in the western region and are encouraged by the state are entitled to being exempt from paying 15% of their corporate income tax within a certain period. Actually, due to the rights and obligations brought by China's accession to WTO, we cannot simply copy the experience of the coastal areas in eastern China to carry out the strategy of the development of West China, rather, we must get familiar with and adapt to internationally accepted rules and requirements.

5.3.2 Constraints of Special Costs in the Western Region Over FDI

Spatial economic theory shows that spatial cost means transportation cost and time cost. As product and service radii are relatively large, some foreign-owned enterprises need to import a fairly large number of raw materials from overseas and export some of its products, therefore, the convenience of transportation has naturally become one of factors to be considered by foreign investors. Through decades of development, western China (12 provinces, municipality and autonomous regions) has formed an integrated transport network with highway as the mainstay and consisting of railways, highways, inland waterways, airways and underground oil (gas) pipelines. Since the middle of the 1990s, infrastructure construction in the western region has entered a stage of accelerated development, and postal and telecommunication networks with different densities have been established at central cities at all levels and rural areas. On the whole, the infrastructure of the western region lags far behind that of the eastern region. Between 1993 and 2002, the overall infrastructure value of the western region was 0.338 on average, while that the three provinces and municipality (Shanghai, Jiangsu, Zhejiang) was 0.379. Between 2000 and 2002, the infrastructure value of the western region was 0.376, while that of the three provinces and municipality (Shanghai, Jiangsu, Zhejiang) was 0.420.

Transportation infrastructure occupies a decisive position in the infrastructure environment. The developed transportation system is the basic precondition of smooth and efficient flow of people, funds and materials in the process of investment. Multinational companies aim to allocate resources from around the world and promptly respond to the global customer needs, so as to minimize the total cost of the global supply chain. According to statistics, transportation expenses account for 2.88% of the sales revenue (Davis and Drumm 1996), taking the lion's share (about 40%) of the entire logistics fees. Therefore, transport rationalization determines to a great extent logistics rationalization, while the reasonable construction of transportation infrastructure is the precondition of and important guarantee for transport rationalization.

As is seen from transportation conditions, the highway density of the eastern region and that of the western region are 0.3408 km/km^2 and 0.0676 km/km^2, respectively, with a density ratio of 5.04: 1. The railway density of the eastern region and that of the western region are 0.0132 km/km^2 and 0.0025 km/km^2, respectively, with a density ratio of 528:1. Therefore, no matter for highway transportation or railway transportation, the western region lags far behind the eastern region. As is seen from freight capacity, the freight volume of the eastern region accounts for about 50% of the national total, while that of the western region accounts nearly one fifth of the national total. The transportation infrastructure environments of the eastern region and the western region are shown below:

Highway transportation is the dominant mode of transportation in the western region. Among the three modes of transportation in western China, namely highway, railway and waterway, highways account for over 90% of the total. The passenger volume and freight volume of highway transportation account for about 93% and 87% of the aggregate transport volume, respectively, passenger transport turnover and freight transport turnover account for 60% and 32% of the aggregate transport volume, respectively, higher than the national average. As of the end of 2000, in the western region, 554 thousand kilometers of highways have been built and open to traffic, accounting for 39.5% of the total mileage of highways. Specifically, the mileage of highways in the western region was 3677 km, accounting for 22.5% of the total mileage of highways in China. Grade-II and above highways in the western region account for 7.44% of the national total, six percentage points lower than 13.5%, the national average level of China.

As for railway and civil aviation, the western region has harsh geological conditions. Railways were mostly in remote mountains and are very difficult to be built, and railway operations are often encountered by accidents such as debris flow, landslide, flood and snow disaster, etc. In many places, there is even no railway and air services. The transportation services in the western region are inadequate and of poor quality, and railway, civil aviation, water transportation and pipeline transportation generally have problems of scattered distribution and poor economies of scale. From the data in Table 5.5 we can that the western region lags far behind the eastern region in highway which it has certain comparative advantages regionally or in railway, water transportation and aviation, etc. The backward transportation condition of the western region has become a major factor restricting foreign investments.

Table 5.5 An comparison of transportation infrastructures of the eastern region and the western region

	Region	Total	Railway	Highway	Waterway	Aviation
Freight volume (10,000 tons)	Eastern	689,919	64,792	507,142	10,632	198
	Western	247,461	32,695	208,145	3827	40
Passenger volume (10,000 persons)	Eastern	672,135	46,621	612,195	8520	4799
	Western	355,600	15,222	333,170	5407	1766

Source China Statistical Yearbook for Regional Economy (2002)

5.4 Conclusion

FDI is a kind of scarce resource. Attracting FDI is competitive in a global context and between China's western region and its central and eastern regions. The location selection of China's FDI inflows is carried out through full comparison at the provincial, city or lower levels. It is a long-term and integrated process for western China, which is far away from the coast, to overcome regional disadvantages and attract direct investments from multinational corporations. To introduce foreign investments in western China, we should have our eyes on the long-term development and seek for the model of government-driven market development in the short term. To overcome the location disadvantages of the western region, it is imperative to develop competitiveness at some points and create "growth poles", so as to keep strengthening the economic growth through the attraction of the growth poles and driving economic development of neighboring areas through the diffusion effects of growth poles, achieve higher returns to scale, more job opportunities, stronger driving force of scientific and technological progress, and greater economic diffusion effects, and attract inflows of capital and various factors.

References

Cheng, L. K. and Kwan, Y. K. 1999. FDI Stock and its Determinants. In: Wu, Y. (Ed.), Foreign Direct Investment and Economic Growth in China, Chapter 3. Edward Elgar, Cheltenham, 42–56.

Davis, Herbert W, Drumm, William H. 1996. Logistics Costs and Customer Service Levels. Annual Conference Proceedings, Council of Logistics Management, 149–159.

Dunning, J.H. 1988. *Explaining International Production.* Boston: Unwin Hyman.

Head, Keith, and John Ries. 1996. Inter-city competition for foreign investment: Static and dynamic effects of China's incentive areas. *Journal of Urban Economics* 40 (1): 38–60.

Liang, Qi. 2004. Equilibrium and stability of industrial agglomeration. *World Economy* 6.

Liu, Rongtian. 2005. Panel data analysis on regional difference factors of FDI in Eastern, Central and Western China. *The Journal of Quantitative & Technical Economics* 7.

Wei, Houkai, and Canfei He. 2001. Motivation and geographical factors of foreign direct investment in China. *Economic Research* 2.

Wei, Houkai, Canfei He, and Xin Wang. 2001a. Analysis of incentive and geographical factors of FDI in China. *Economic Research* 6.

Wei, Houkai, Canfei He, and Xin Wang. 2001b. Latest theory and research on geographical determinants of foreign investment. *Journal of Shanghai Administration Institute* 4.

Chapter 6
Institutional Factors and the Introduction of FDI in China's Western Region

The reason why institutional changes can fuel economic growth lies in the fact that "new arrangements have typically been profitable to realize potential economies of scale, reduce information costs, spread risk, and internalize externalities."[1] As part of China's opening up policy, utilizing FDI is in itself an institutional change. In "Motivation and geographical factors of foreign direct investment in China," Wei et al. (2002) pointed out that FDI was responsible for nearly 90% of the GDP growth disparity between the developed eastern region and the underdeveloped western region during the period from 1985 to 1999. Not only that, large amounts of funding have been poured into infrastructure in coastal areas, causing the gap in the investment climate and growth potential between the inland and coastal regions to widen. Different investment climate is the main cause of regional disparity in the distribution of inbound FDI. This chapter attempts to answer the following questions: What is the relationship between institutional factors and FDI? What measures could the western region take to effectively improve the institutional environment for the purpose of attracting FDI and promoting balanced regional development?

6.1 Literature Review

Most of the existing theoretical literature on geographical distribution of FDI focuses on economic and physical environmental factors. Only a few studies deal with the role of institutional factors. Jun and Singh (1996) used a panel dataset of 31 developing countries in the period 1970–1993 to analyze the impact of tariffs and trade barriers, export-oriented policies and political risks on FDI, and concluded that they were important factors affecting FDI flows. The United Nations Conference on Trade

[1] Wang (1992).

© Social Sciences Academic Press 2024
X. Yang et al., *Foreign Direct Investment in Western China, 1994-2004*,
https://doi.org/10.1007/978-981-97-7407-4_6

and Development (UNCTAD 1998) has designed a set of location-specific FDI determinants, of which the first and third categories are related to institutions and policies of the host country. The first category is the policy framework for FDI and trade, including rules regarding entry and operations, standards of treatment of foreign affiliates, policies on market functions, stability of rules, and predictability and transparency; the third category is business facilitation, including the host country's investment promotion policies, investment incentives, social amenities, and public sector corruption.

After comprehensively and systematically analyzing the impact of international economic institutional arrangements, economic institutions, legal institutions, and institutions that affect operating costs of businesses on FDI flows, Lu (1999) drew the conclusion that open economies that welcomed foreign investment and provided legal protection for foreign investment can attract more FDI. Wei (2000) cross-sectional study on the factors affecting FDI flows to major economies showed that China attracts less FDI for two main reasons: institutional obstacles and ineffective policy. Wei (2001) used the opacity index to analyze the impact of institutional factors on FDI, and found that transparent and open policies can promote FDI inflows while policy uncertainty would invalidate tax incentives for foreign investment. Most of the existing literature on location determinants of FDI in China also focuses on physical environment. However, there are some exceptions. For example, Pan and Pan (2004) studied the impact of institutional factors on the geographical distribution of FDI. They argued that institutional factors such as the degree of marketization, efficiency of government, frugality of government, protection of property rights, and trade barriers had a significant impact on the regional flow of FDI, and that although preferential policies aided in attracting FDI, the impact of the central government's preferential policies faded over time and with the interference of local governments.

Most of the above studies examine the impact of institutional factors on location choice of FDI across the world. There is currently a lack of academic literature that systematically analyzes the influence of institutional factors on the location choice of FDI within China. The few existing studies on this topic focus on the degree of association between institutional factors and FDI. In this part of research, we comprehensively analyze the correlation and causality between institutional factors and the geographical distribution of FDI in China using a dataset of 30 provinces, municipalities and autonomous regions in China in the period 2001–2003, and present major conclusions and policy implications on this basis.

6.2 Comparative Analysis of Institutional Factors Across Eastern, Central and Western Regions of China

Institutional factors that affect FDI can be divided into four categories: (i) international economic institutions, including trade barriers and economic integration agreements and bilateral investment treaties (BITs) signed by the host country; (ii) legal factors, including legal protection of private property and the effectiveness of the legal system; (iii) economic factors, which mainly include marketization, financial and foreign exchange policies, economic liberalization, economic openness, market access of foreign investors, and stance towards FDI; and (iv) institutional factors that affect the operating costs of businesses, including operational challenges, public sector corruption, efficiency of public administration, black market transactions (market transparency), wage policy, and taxation system.

Since our study focuses on the distribution of FDI across eastern, central and western regions of China, the following is an empirical comparative analysis of ten formal and informal institutions in categories (ii), (iii) and (iv) across the three regions.

6.2.1 Legal Factors

Legal factors are legal and regulatory institutions influencing inbound FDI.

1. **Protection of private property (PRO)**

PRO is the level of protection provided by law for citizens' private property. Given the fact that most FDI is private investment, the protection of foreign investors' private property is a fundamental prerequisite for attracting FDI. Inbound FDI is directly correlated with how well the host country or region protects private property (including intellectual property rights).

The percentage of non-state-owned companies in the total number of companies registered in the host country or region can be used to gauge how well the host country or region protects private property. As we can see from Table 6.1, the percentage of non-state-owned companies in the total number of companies was 81% in the eastern region, with Zhejiang reporting the highest percentage (97%), 69% in the central region, and only 58% in the western region, with Xizang reporting the lowest percentage (39%). The western regions was 23 percentage points lower than the eastern region. In other words, the level of protection of private property in western region was far lower than that in the developed eastern region. It was also lower than that in the central region.

2. **Quality of laws and regulations (REG)**

Here, REG stands for the quality of the legal system of the host country or region. Political stability is a prerequisite to the efficient functioning of market factors. High-quality law and stable policies often result in lower risk cost of FDI entry, which may further translate into increased chance of FDI survival and more inbound FDI.

Both national and local laws and regulations have an impact on FDI. Local regulations may conflict with national regulations. A lack of standardization in law enforcement is a common problem existing at both national and local levels. The western region lags behind other parts of the country in market liberalization and

Table 6.1 Non-state-owned companies as percentage of the total number of companies registered in eastern, central and western regions of China, 2003, Unit: %

Eastern region				Central region				Western region			
Province	Non-state-owned companies (1)	Total number of companies (2)	(1)/(2) (%)	Province	Non-state-owned companies (1)	Total number of companies (2)	(1)/(2) (%)	Province	Non-state-owned companies (1)	Total number of companies (2)	(1)/(2) (%)
Beijing	2657	4019	66	Shanxi	2259	3613	63	Sichuan	4383	5448	80
Tianjin	3716	5341	70	Jilin	1315	2284	58	Chongqing	1671	2241	75
Hebei	6248	7923	79	Heilongjiang	1597	2567	62	Guizhou	1092	2129	51
Liaoning	5508	6842	81	Anhui	3411	4158	82	Yunnan	1052	1995	53
Shanghai	9492	11,098	86	Jiangxi	1980	3051	65	Shaanxi	1258	2493	50
Jiangsu	22,620	23,862	95	Henan	6838	9091	75	Gansu	2178	2884	76
Zhejiang	24,665	25,526	97	Hubei	4654	6271	74	Qinghai	194	400	49
Fujian	8320	9208	90	Hunan	4325	5967	72	Ningxia	264	418	63
Shandong	14,216	16,177	88					Xinjiang	558	1254	44
Guangdong	22,391	24,494	91					Guangxi	1619	2871	56
Hainan	273	619	44					Inner Mongolia	1062	1653	64
Average percentage in eastern region	10,919	12,283	81	Average percentage in central region	3297	4625	69	Average percentage in western region	1394	2162	58

Source China Statistical Yearbook (2004), China Statistics Press

regulation. When it comes to the quality, openness, transparency, and enforcement of regulations and policies, the eastern region performs substantially better than the central and western regions. Many foreign investors have complained about the overwhelming bureaucracy and excessive red tape in the western region. According to some studies, it takes 3–5 months to obtain a business license or conclude a land use right contract in Shanghai, while it may take as long as a year in some western cities. In his analysis of the decline in foreign investment, Ma Yu, an economist at the Research Department of the Ministry of Foreign Trade and Economic Cooperation, said, "Many foreign investors have complained about bureaucracy, policy instability, a lack of transparency and standardization in enforcement, and defective performance or non-performance of contractual obligations in central and western regions. The operations of traditional vehicles of investment such as joint ventures, partnerships and sole proprietorships are hampered by arbitrary fees and corruption. In addition, constitutional and legal limitations make it difficult for foreign investors to invest in China through mergers and acquisitions and other new models that are widely employed around the world. Most of the joint ventures involving state-owned companies are not run and managed in a market-oriented way." Legal institutions are an important factor influencing location selection of foreign investors because they want to keep their ownership advantage for as long as possible. One indicator may reflect different problems. For example, Zhang Changchun et al. use the number of patents granted to measure the level of applied technology; Pan Zhen and Pan Chichun use the proxy measure of property rights protection; it also indicates the amount of support provided by the host country/region for technological innovation during marketization. Therefore, the number of patents granted each year by province, municipalities, and autonomous regions can be used as a proxy measure of the quality of laws and regulations.

Table 6.2 shows that the total number of patents granted in the western region in 2003 stood at 1,192, only 27% of that in the eastern region. There is a lack of standardization in the market in central and western regions. An inefficient legal system has deterred FDI inflows.

Table 6.2 Number of patents granted in eastern, central and western regions, 2003

	National average	Eastern region	Central region	Western region
Invention patents	333	641	250	107
Design patents	2149	5119	541	498
Utility model patents	1927	3774	1399	587

Source China Statistical Yearbook (2004), China Statistics Press

6.2.2 Economic Factors

For purpose of this section, economic factors refer to economic institutions that affect FDI inflows.

Marketization (MAR)

Indicators that can be used to assess the degree of marketization of a region include non-state-owned economic entities' contribution to fixed asset investment, the private sector's contribution to the national total, and regional contribution to national private sector employment. Theoretically, the higher these indicators, the greater the degree of marketization and the more diversified ownership structures of businesses in the economy. Therefore, these indicators are positively correlated with FDI inflows.

Following China's adoption of the reform and opening up policy, SOEs' monopolistic position in the country's economy weakened, and the percentage of non-state-owned economic entities, such as joint-stock companies, collective enterprises, companies funded by foreign investors, private companies, and self-employed individuals, rose quickly. However, the distribution of non-state-owned economic entities is extremely uneven in the country. The proportion of SOEs in the western region is much higher than that in the eastern region. Take the industrial sector for example. In 1978, SOEs contributed to 77.63% of the industrial sector's gross output at the national level, 76.19% in the eastern region, and 83.89% in the western region. In 2003, these numbers dropped to 55%, 37%, and 67%, respectively. The number of the western region was almost twice that of the eastern region. The private sector contributed to 33% of the industrial sector's gross output in the western region. This number was less than two-thirds of the number of the eastern region and far lower than that of the central region and the whole country. In 2003, non-state-owned economic entities accounted for 49% of the country's total fixed asset investment, 59% of total fixed asset investment in the eastern region, and 40% in the western region (see Table 6.3). These numbers show that the western region seriously lagged behind the eastern region in terms of the SOE reform and the development of non-state-owned economic entities. Accelerating the SOE reform will give a major boost to the economy of the western region.

Financial sector liberalization (BAN)

This indicator measures the accessibility of financing to businesses and reflects the stance of the host country or region towards FDI. Financial constraints, especially on foreign banks, can hamper FDI inflows. Stricter financial regulation often translates into a decline in FDI inflows, and vice versa.

There are two types of corporate financing: direct and indirect financing. Before 1997, companies other than SOEs were not allowed to raise money by selling stocks in China, and foreign-owned companies had access to the following four types of loans: loans for fixed asset investment, working capital loans, loans secured by cash in foreign currency, and standby loans. Sources of funding available to businesses that are partially or wholly funded by foreign investors vary across the country. Generally

Table 6.3 Degree of marketization in eastern, central and western regions, 2003, Unit: %

	National average	Eastern region	Central region	Western region
Non-state-owned economic entities' contribution to total fixed asset investment (fixed asset investment of non-state-owned economic entities/total fixed asset investment)	49	59'	47	40
Private sector's contribution to the total output (output of the private sector/the total output)	45	63	39	33
Regional contribution to national private sector employment (regional private sector employment/national private sector employment)	100	66	17	17

Source China Statistical Yearbook (2004), China Statistics Press

speaking, the more readily available financing options are made to foreign-invested enterprises, the lower their likelihood of running into financial difficulties. Therefore, it is possible to gauge the host country or region's degree of liberalization in the financial sector by looking at the availability of financing choices and the amounts of funding provided to foreign-invested companies. However, due to the lack of data for this indicator, we use marketization of capital as a proxy measure of financial market liberalization. As shown in Table 6.4, in 2001, the contribution of SOEs to the total fixed asset investment in the western region was higher than that in the eastern region, and the proportion of the listed companies in the western region was lower than that in the eastern region. The degree of financial sector liberalization in central and western regions is relatively low and corporate financing mainly relies on the state.

Economic openness (OPE)

The more open an economy, the higher the level of FDI inflows. Economic openness is an important indicator for assessing the degree of marketization of the host country/

Table 6.4 Marketization of capital in eastern, central and western regions, 2000, Unit: %

	Nationwide	Eastern region	Central region	Western region
Contribution of SOEs to the total fixed asset investment (fixed asset investment of SOEs/total fixed asset investment)	53.42	46.85	59.64	61.49
Share of listed companies in the region (listed companies in the region/listed companies in the country)	100	59.24	20.34	20.42

Source China Statistical Yearbook (2001), China Statistics Press

region and how interconnected the economy is with other economies. In this section, we use the sum of foreign trade dependence and foreign investment dependence as the measure of economic openness.

The level of economic openness of China's coastal areas is much higher than that of its central and western regions, which is why the central and western regions lag behind the eastern region in economic development. Conversely, economically developed areas also have a high level of economic openness (see Table 6.5). In 2003, economic openness of the 11 eastern coastal provinces and municipalities reached 78%, while the 8 central provinces and 12 western provinces, autonomous regions and municipalities were all less than 15%, less than one-fifth of that of the coastal areas. Guangdong Province had the highest level of openness among them, at 182%, and Gansu Province had a very low level, at 5.1%. Generally speaking, when trade accounts for more than 45% of a region's GDP, the region has a high level of economic openness, and when trade is less than 27% of its GDP, the level of the region's economic openness is low. As we can see from Table 6.6, the levels of economic openness of all the 12 provinces, autonomous regions and municipalities in China's western region were low.

Low levels of economic openness deter FDI. Guangdong outperforms other provinces in terms of trade. In 2003, its trade totaled USD289.22994 billion, accounting for 15% of the country's total trade, followed closely by Jiangsu (6.3%), Shanghai (5.7%), Zhejiang (3.4%), Shandong (2.6%), Fujian (2.0%), Beijing (1.6%), Tianjin (1.5%), and Liaoning (1.5%). These nine coastal provinces and municipalities accounted for 95.9% of China's total trade, leaving the other 22 provinces far behind. The trade of the 12 western provinces, autonomous areas and municipalities was very low. The sum of their trade was less than 2% of the total trade of the country. Among them, Gansu accounted for 0.04% of the country's total trade, Ningxia 0.03%, Qinghai 0.01%, and Xizang 0.008%.

Economic freedom (FRE)

Economic freedom refers to independence of companies from government interference. The higher the degree of economic freedom of the host country or region, the more FDI inflows it can attract, and vice versa. The local government's restrictions on the use of local raw materials and imports of raw materials and equipment by foreign-funded enterprises will inhibit the entry of foreign capital. The proportion of imports by foreign-invested enterprises in a region's total imports reflects the level of independence of foreign-invested enterprises from intervention and control of the local government. It can be used as an indicator to assess the economic freedom of the region. As we can see from Table 6.7, the economic freedom of the eastern region was 3.12 times that of the western region.

1. **Implementation of preferential policies (ATT)**

Implementation of preferential policies reflects the attitude of the government and people of the host country or region to foreign investment. The central government has rolled out a host of preferential policies to further liberalize the economy of the

Table 6.5 Trade, foreign investment and GDP of provinces, autonomous regions and municipalities in China's eastern, central and western regions, 2003

Eastern region				Central region				Western region			
Province	Foreign trade (USD10,000)	FDI (USD10,000)	GDP (RMB10,000)	Province	Foreign trade (USD10,000)	FDI (USD10,000)	GDP (RMB10,000)	Province	Foreign trade (USD10,000)	FDI (USD10,000)	GDP (RMB10,000)
Beijing	3,133,411	219,126	36,631,000	Shanxi	517,926	21,361	24,565,900	Sichuan	577,991	41,231	54,563,200
Tianjin	3,003,040	153,473	24,476,600	Jilin	673,223	19,059	25,226,200	Chongqing	255,927	26,247	22,505,600
Hebei	968,589	109,979	70,985,600	Heilongjiang	621,514	32,180	44,300,000	Guizhou	155,344	4521	13,561,100
Liaoning	2,986,137	282,410	60,025,400	Anhui	567,499	36,720	39,723,800	Yunnan	272,005	8384	24,652,900
Shanghai	1,1051,596	546,849	62,508,100	Jiangxi	295,684	161,202	28,304,600	Shaanxi	190,697	33,190	23,985,800
Jiangsu	12,128,389	1,056,365	124,608,300	Henan	558,253	53,903	70,485,900	Gansu	74,062	2342	13,046,000
Zhejiang	6,631,807	498,055	93,950,000	Hubei	580,831	179,658	54,017,100	Qinghai	22,081	2522	3,902,100
Fujian	3,856,262	259,903	52,321,700	Hunan	469,895	101,835	46,387,300	Ningxia	53,802	1743	3,853,400
Shandong	4,941,117	601,617	1,243,593					Xinjiang	238,643	1534	18,776,100
Guangdong	28,922,994	1,009,335	136,258,700					Guangxi	322,168	41,856	27,351,300
Hainan	191,151	42,125	6,709,300					Inner Mongolia	322,632	8854	21,504,100
Average percentage in eastern region	7,074,045	434,476	60,883,481	Central China average	535,603	75,740	41,626,350	Average percentage in western region	310,669	15,675	20,700,145

Table 6.6 Economic openness of China's eastern, central and western regions, 2003, Unit: %

	Nationwide	Eastern region	Central region	Western region
Trade dependence (sum of exports and imports/GDP)	0.32	0.73	0.12	0.09
Dependence on foreign investment (foreign investment/GDP)	0.02	0.05	0.02	0.005
Economic openness	0.34	0.78	0.14	0.095

Note The GDP data of each region in the table has been adjusted based on national data, and foreign investment is the sum of FDI and indirect investment
Source China Statistical Yearbook (2004), China Statistics Press

western region, improve the investment climate and attract greater foreign investment. Policies directly related to the investment climate include: (i) tax incentives; (ii) policies aimed at opening up more sectors in the western region for foreign investment; (iii) policies aimed at increasing the ways to channel foreign capital into the western region; (iv) policies aimed at easing restrictions on utilization of foreign capital in the western region; and (v) policies encouraging foreign investment in the mining sector. The central government has also rolled out policies closely related to the investment climate: (i) increase the central government's investment in the western region; (ii) improve infrastructure in the western region; (iii) increase transfer payments to the western region; (iv) promote the development of land and mineral resources in the western region; and (v) increase investment in science and technology and attract top talents to the western region. To lure FDI to the western region, the central government has launched a number of preferential policies. However, many studies have demonstrated that these policies' effects are not immediately apparent. Some preferential policies introduced by local governments have weakened the effects of the central government's policies. In addition, because the western region opens up later than other parts of the country, the effects of preferential policies on the western region have dropped over time. Last but not least, many preferential terms and conditions promised to foreign companies during negotiation or under investment agreements have not been fulfilled.

The ratio of the actual amount of FDI to the aggregate contract value of FDI reflects the change in the attitude of foreign investors after inspecting local investment climate. Therefore, we can use this indicator to assess the percentage of fulfilled preferential terms and conditions. In theory, this indicator is positively correlated with FDI inflows. As shown in Table 6.8, the value of this indicator in the western region was 0.53, which is 17 percentage points lower than that in the eastern region. Apparently, the eastern region did much better than the western region in fulfilling promises relating to preferential treatment to foreign investors.

Table 6.7 Economic freedom of China's eastern, central and western regions, 2003, Unit: %

Eastern region				Central region				Western region			
Province	Imports of foreign-invested enterprises (USD10,000) (1)	Total imports of the region (USD10,000) (2)	Economic freedom (%) (1)/(2)	Province	Imports of foreign-invested enterprises (USD10,000) (1)	Total imports of the region (USD10,000) (2)	Economic freedom (%) (1)/(2)	Province	Imports of foreign-invested enterprises (USD10,000) (1)	Total imports of the region (USD10,000) (2)	Economic freedom (%) (1)/(2)
Beijing	668,181	2,137,426	31	Shanxi	14,836	144,412	10	Sichuan	50,518	275,156	18
Tianjin	1,187,149	1,618,109	73	Jilin	229,358	432,167	53	Chongqing	48,058	106,958	45
Hebei	121,032	374,596	32	Heilongjiang	33,935	249,011	14	Guizhou	16,708	74,162	23
Liaoning	782,336	1,481,429	53	Anhui	95,398	290,621	33	Yunnan	12,374	125,044	10
Shanghai	4,115,782	6,468,305	64	Jiangxi	39,509	154,182	26	Shaanxi	37,478	164,772	23
Jiangsu	4,486,335	6,169,718	73	Henan	52,676	225,179	23	Gansu	3412	55,150	6
Zhejiang	888,179	2,193,298	40	Hubei	117,604	324,268	36	Qinghai	116	12,196	1
Fujian	1,020,892	1,509,499	68	Hunan	43,461	253,509	17	Ningxia	4114	20,662	20
Shandong	1,059,014	2,171,717	49					Xinjiang	5397	246,819	2
Guangdong	7,930,449	13,552,002	59					Guangxi	65,976	144,463	46
Hainan	54,925	126,309	43					Inner Mongolia	6024	170,065	4
Average level in eastern region	2,028,570	3,436,583	53	Average level in central region	78,347	259,169	27	Average level in western region	22,743	126,859	17

Source China Statistical Yearbook (2004), China Statistics Press

Table 6.8 Actual value and contract value of FDI of major provinces, autonomous regions, and municipalities, 2003, Unit: USD10,000

Eastern region				Central region				Western region			
Province	FDI: actual value (1)	FDI: contract value (2)	(1)/(2) (%)	Province	FDI: actual value (1)	FDI: contract value (2)	(1)/(2) (%)	Province	FDI: actual value (1)	FDI: contract value (2)	(1)/(2) (%)
Beijing	214,675	327,132	0.66	Shanxi	31,896	48,100	0.66	Sichuan	58,209	114,687	0.51
Tianjin	163,325	351,297	0.46	Jilin	31,808	72,591	0.44	Chongqing	31,112	55,301	0.56
Hebei	111,567	196,502	0.57	Heilongjiang	102,972	139,483	0.74	Guizhou	5626	5626	1.00
Liaoning	558,269	970,243	0.58	Anhui	39,051	102,367	0.38	Yunnan	16,752	54,351	0.31
Shanghai	58.50	110.64	0.53	Jiangxi	161,234	233,094	0.69	Shaanxi	46,600	83,400	0.56
Jiangsu	1,580,214	3,080,743	0.51	Henan	56,100	18,260,000	0.003	Gansu	3887	24,464	0.16
Zhejiang	544,936	1,205,014	0.45	Hubei	155,702	254,523	0.61	Qinghai	1.96	28,584	0.00007
Fujian	499,300	725,100	0.69	Hunan	148,900	207,500	0.72	Ningxia	3170	3354	0.95
Shandong	709,370	1,341,413	0.53					Xinjiang	4005	16,147	0.25
Guangdong	1,557,800	2,178,900	0.71					Guangxi	45,600	67,198	0.68
Hainan	58,062	29,185	1.99					Inner Mongolia	36,805	43,438	0.85
Average level in eastern region	545,761	945,967	0.70	Average level in central region	90,958	2,414,707	0.53	Average level in western region	22,888	45,141	0.53

Source China Statistical Yearbook (2004)

6.2.3 *Institutional Factors that Affect the Operating Costs of Businesses*

Institutional factors that affect the operating costs of businesses at the micro level include:

Administrative efficiency (ADM)

ADM refers to the efficiency with which the government delivers services. An efficient government can effectively serve enterprises, which is conducive to the survival and development of enterprises, while redundancy will undoubtedly lower the efficiency of the government. Theoretically, administrative efficiency is positively correlated with FDI inflows.

The ratio of employees in government bodies and public organizations to GDP can be used as a proxy for measuring the efficiency of a government in operating and delivering services. As we can see from Table 6.9, the number of employees in government bodies in central and western regions was higher than that in the eastern region. The ratio of GDP to the number of employees in government bodies and public organizations was RMB676,900 per person in the western region, lower than the eastern region (RMB1,723,800 per person). Apparently, the efficiency of public administration in the western region is relatively low.

1. **Public integrity (CLE)**

Public integrity means integrity in public administration. FDI tends to flow into countries or regions with higher levels of public integrity. High administrative expenses will cause investors to worry about public integrity, thereby leading to a decrease in FDI inflows.

The ratio of administrative expenditure to government spending can be used as a proxy for measuring the frugality and integrity of a government. As shown

Table 6.9 Administrative efficiency and public integrity of governments in China's eastern, central and western regions, 2003

	National average	Eastern region	Central region	Western region
The ratio of GDP to the number of employees of government bodies and public organizations (RMB10,000 per person)	109.44	172.38	88.15	67.79
Salary of employees of government bodies as a percentage of total government spending (%)	10.33	10	11	10
Government spending as a percentage of GDP (%)	18	15	15	23
Administrative expenditure as a percentage of total government spending (%)	9.67	8	10	11

Source China Statistical Yearbook (2004), China Statistics Press

in Table 6.9, administrative expenditure and government spending in central and western regions were higher than the eastern region in 2003. The government's financial capability in central and western regions is weak. High administrative expenses and government spending will inevitably place additional strain on local businesses and farmers, which is not conducive to local economic growth and institutional reform.

6.2.4 Evolution of Informal Institutions

Informal institutions take the form of customs, morality, ethics, ideology, etc. They are defining features of a society or region. Only in coordination with informal institutions can formal institutions effectively play their due roles. A market economy is a highly efficient formal institution for resource allocation. It is also a concept, a way of thinking and a culture. China must support the equivalent changes in informal institutions, including philosophy, norms, habits, and culture, in order to advance the country's transition to a market economy. Otherwise, they will obstruct the improvement and operation of formal institutions. The economic development of the western region is being hampered by conservatism, inefficient institutions, and a lack of reform progress. The gap between the eastern and western regions is still growing, because social and cultural factors, which are informal institutions, in the western region do not appeal to investors and top talents. The foundation for capital accumulation within the economy is weak. Comparative analysis shows that there are obvious regional disparities in various institutional reforms across the country. All institutional indicators are higher in the east and lower in the west. Central and western regions are lagging behind the eastern region in institutional reforms.

6.3 An Empirical Test of the Correlation Between Institutional Factors and FDI Across Different Regions

6.3.1 Hypothesis and Indicator Variables

Given that FDI location choice is affected by institutional factors, we propose the following hypothesis:

> Institutional factors are important factors affecting FDI location choice, and a good institutional environment will help attract more FDI.

We employ an empirical model to test the above hypothesis with the response and explanatory variables being FDI inflows and institutional factors. Due to the paucity of available data, some explanatory variables, such as financial sector liberalization (BAN) and market access of foreign investors, are not regressively examined. This study focuses on eight institutional factors. The response and explanatory variables in this study are:

FDI: FDI inflows of a certain province, municipality, or autonomous region in a certain year. The unit of measure is USD10,000.
PRO: Measured as the percentage of non-state-owned economic entities in the total number of economic entities registered in the province, municipality, or autonomous region each year. In theory, this indicator is positively correlated with FDI inflows.
REG: Measured as the number of patent approvals in the province, municipality or autonomous region each year. In theory, this indicator is positively correlated with FDI inflows.
MAR: Measured as the percentage of fixed asset investment of non-state-owned economic entities in the total fixed asset investment of the province, municipality or autonomous region each year. In theory, this indicator is positively correlated with FDI inflows.
OPE: Calculated by dividing the aggregate value of imports and exports over a period by the GDP for the same period. In theory, this indicator is positively correlated with FDI inflows.
FRE: Measured as the percentage of imports by foreign-invested enterprises in the total imports of the host province/region. In theory, this indicator is positively correlated with FDI inflows.
ATT: Calculated by dividing the amount of foreign capital actually utilized by the aggregate contract value of FDI in the host province, municipality, or autonomous region each year. In theory, this indicator is positively correlated with FDI inflows.
ADM: Calculated by dividing the number of employees of government bodies and public organizations by the GDP of the host province, municipality, or autonomous region each year. In theory, this indicator is positively correlated with FDI inflows.
CLE: Calculated by dividing administrative expenses by total government spending. In theory, this indicator is negatively correlated with FDI inflows.

6.3.2 *Data, Measurement Methods and Measurement Models*

This study uses cross-sectional data.

1. **Sample regions**

The sample includes 30 provinces, municipalities, and autonomous regions in China. Xizang is excluded from the sample because it received no or very little FDI.

2. **Sample years**

Given the hysteresis of institutional factors, we take the years from 2001 to 2003 as the sample years of the study. This study uses data from the year 2003 on FDI and current variables, data from 2002 on one-year lagged variables, and data from 2001 on two-year lagged variables. All data come from the corresponding issues of *China Statistical Yearbook*, *China Trade Statistical Yearbook*, and *Almanac of China's Economy* and are transformed using the natural logarithm function (see Tables 6.10, 6.11 and 6.12).

3. **Candidate variables**

Table 6.10 FDI (2003) and values of explanatory variables in 2001

	FDI	PRO	REG	MAR	OPE	FRE	ATT	ADM	CLE
Beijing	219,126	0.50	6246	0.51	0.80	0.27	0.65	117.59	0.05
Tianjin	153,473	0.67	1829	0.65	0.82	0.77	1.02	158.63	0.05
Hebei	96,405	0.67	2791	0.59	0.09	0.28	0.83	86.88	0.09
Shanxi	21,361	0.49	1047	0.39	0.15	0.16	0.78	42.89	0.12
Inner Mongolia	8854	0.51	743	0.46	0.12	0.04	0.40	52.58	0.10
Liaoning	282,410	0.63	4448	0.51	0.35	0.57	0.61	125.20	0.07
Jilin	19,059	0.47	1443	0.47	0.14	0.54	0.58	82.96	0.07
Heilongjiang	32,180	0.47	1870	0.45	0.10	0.10	0.90	94.46	0.07
Shanghai	546,849	0.79	5371	0.62	1.01	0.62	0.58	375.06	0.04
Jiangsu	1,056,365	0.89	6158	0.57	0.47	0.70	0.46	212.79	0.09
Zhejiang	498,055	0.94	8312	0.64	0.45	0.38	0.44	203.87	0.10
Anhui	36,720	0.73	1278	0.48	0.09	0.38	0.52	82.67	0.11
Fujian	259,903	0.80	3296	0.63	0.47	0.70	0.78	149.78	0.08
Jiangxi	161,202	0.40	999	0.48	0.07	0.24	0.75	64.18	0.09
Shandong	601,617	0.80	6725	0.58	0.28	0.51	0.52	119.93	0.10
Henan	53,903	0.71	2582	0.51	0.05	0.18	0.74	68.78	0.11
Hubei	156,886	0.60	2204	0.45	0.07	0.34	1.36	91.06	0.09
Hunan	101,835	0.57	2401	0.50	0.06	0.29	0.85	69.27	0.10
Guangdong	782,294	0.87	18,259	0.65	1.40	0.53	1.06	158.92	0.09
Guangxi	41,856	0.41	1099	0.47	0.08	0.30	0.65	66.01	0.10
Hainan	42,125	0.37	303	0.57	0.25	0.51	3.07	69.99	0.10
Chongqing	26,086	0.65	1197	0.55	0.10	0.23	0.58	97.75	0.10
Sichuan	41,231	0.68	3357	0.55	0.06	0.26	0.59	77.30	0.11
Guizhou	4521	0.38	642	0.34	0.07	0.05	0.31	38.89	0.12
Yunnan	8384	0.37	1347	0.37	0.09	0.10	0.22	58.44	0.10
Shaanxi	33,190	0.41	1354	0.38	0.12	0.21	0.48	48.28	0.10
Gansu	2342	0.76	512	0.34	0.07	0.08	0.47	46.43	0.11
Qinghai	2522	0.26	101	0.40	0.07	0.25	0.18	49.34	0.09
Ningxia	1743	0.50	231	0.38	0.18	0.06	0.21	48.13	0.06
Xinjiang	1534	0.32	755	0.50	0.13	0.02	0.16	57.80	0.11

Table 6.11 FDI (2003) and values of explanatory variables in 2002

	FDI	PRO	REG	MAR	OPE	FRE	ATT	ADM	CLE
Beijing	219,126	0.59	6345	0.58	0.69	0.26	0.62	139.68	0.06
Tianjin	153,473	0.69	1827	0.60	0.92	0.78	0.75	170.93	0.05
Hebei	96,405	0.73	3353	0.64	0.09	0.31	0.68	100.04	0.10
Shanxi	21,361	0.56	934	0.49	0.15	0.10	0.83	50.56	0.11
Inner Mongolia	8854	0.53	679	0.48	0.13	0.08	0.92	62.16	0.10
Liaoning	282,410	0.71	4551	0.60	0.36	0.55	0.65	137.14	0.08
Jilin	19,059	0.52	1507	0.58	0.15	0.60	0.50	92.81	0.07
Heilongjiang	32,180	0.52	2083	0.49	0.10	0.16	1.09	110.60	0.08
Shanghai	546,849	0.82	6695	0.67	1.11	0.63	0.48	325.83	0.04
Jiangsu	1,056,365	0.92	7595	0.59	0.58	0.72	0.52	230.62	0.10
Zhejiang	498,055	0.96	10,479	0.68	0.49	0.36	0.46	226.63	0.10
Anhui	36,720	0.77	1419	0.52	0.10	0.36	0.47	87.69	0.11
Fujian	259,903	0.85	4001	0.64	0.54	0.70	0.99	169.03	0.08
Jiangxi	161,202	0.51	1044	0.51	0.07	0.24	0.72	73.59	0.09
Shandong	601,617	0.85	7293	0.65	0.29	0.53	0.66	132.90	0.10
Henan	53,903	0.74	2590	0.53	0.05	0.21	0.54	76.44	0.12
Hubei	156,886	0.66	2209	0.46	0.08	0.32	1.46	103.23	0.10
Hunan	101,835	0.62	2347	0.53	0.06	0.29	1.03	76.97	0.09
Guangdong	782,294	0.89	22,761	0.70	1.59	0.55	0.74	175.67	0.10
Guangxi	41,856	0.45	1054	0.48	0.09	0.42	0.85	86.46	0.10
Hainan	42,125	0.41	199	0.59	0.25	0.54	2.13	77.45	0.10
Chongqing	26,086	0.70	51	0.58	0.08	0.31	0.41	110.13	0.10
Sichuan	41,231	0.73	231	0.58	0.08	0.19	0.65	87.21	0.12
Guizhou	4521	0.42	47	0.34	0.07	0.18	0.29	42.32	0.12
Yunnan	8384	0.41	83	0.41	0.09	0.12	0.43	63.42	0.09
Shaanxi	33,190	0.45	146	0.42	0.11	0.24	0.49	51.41	0.10
Gansu	2342	0.77	71	0.34	0.07	0.07	0.55	48.80	0.11
Qinghai	2522	0.40	14	0.41	0.06	0.11	0.44	55.02	0.09
Ningxia	1743	0.53	22	0.43	0.12	0.24	0.28	50.66	0.06
Xinjiang	1534	0.36	61	0.51	0.16	0.02	0.13	61.24	0.10

We do not know which factors among the eight indicators have an impact on the current-year value of FDI inflows. In order to avoid preconception bias in variable selection, we try to be as comprehensive as possible when it comes to the selection of candidate variables. We select 24 candidate variables, including current, one-year lagged, and two-year lagged ones.

Table 6.12 FDI (2003) and values of explanatory variables in 2003

	FDI	PRO	REG	MAR	OPE	FRE	ATT	ADM	CLE
Beijing	219,126	0.66	8248	0.66	0.71	0.31	0.66	143.09	0.05
Tianjin	153,473	0.70	2505	0.55	1.02	0.73	0.46	205.69	0.06
Hebei	96,405	0.79	3572	0.66	0.11	0.32	0.57	107.72	0.10
Shanxi	21,361	0.63	1175	0.58	0.17	0.10	0.66	60.81	0.11
Inner Mongolia	8854	0.64	817	0.48	0.12	0.04	0.85	73.90	0.10
Liaoning	282,410	0.81	5656	0.66	0.41	0.53	0.58	136.11	0.08
Jilin	19,059	0.58	1690	0.57	0.22	0.53	0.44	91.73	0.08
Heilongjiang	32,180	0.62	2794	0.51	0.12	0.14	0.74	118.45	0.09
Shanghai	546,849	0.86	16,671	0.69	1.46	0.64	0.53	416.72	0.04
Jiangsu	1,056,365	0.95	9840	0.62	0.81	0.73	0.51	31.62	0.10
Zhejiang	498,055	0.97	14,402	0.71	0.58	0.40	0.45	253.92	0.11
Anhui	36,720	0.82	1610	0.58	0.12	0.33	0.38	97.12	0.10
Fujian	259,903	0.90	5377	0.66	0.61	0.68	0.69	185.54	0.08
Jiangxi	161,202	0.65	1238	0.54	0.09	0.26	0.69	78.84	0.09
Shandong	601,617	0.88	9067	0.70	0.33	0.49	0.53	146.31	0.11
Henan	53,903	0.75	2961	0.58	0.07	0.23	0.003	77.12	0.12
Hubei	156,886	0.74	2871	0.54	0.09	0.36	0.61	103.68	0.11
Hunan	101,835	0.72	3175	0.56	0.08	0.17	0.72	77.44	0.10
Guangdong	782,294	0.91	29,235	0.70	1.76	0.59	0.71	185.64	0.10
Guangxi	41,856	0.56	1331	0.52	0.10	0.46	0.68	87.38	0.10
Hainan	42,125	0.44	296	0.67	0.24	0.43	1.99	83.87	0.10
Chongqing	26,086	0.75	2883	0.61	0.09	0.45	0.56	116.61	0.11
Sichuan	41,231	0.80	4051	0.63	0.09	0.18	0.51	89.59	0.13
Guizhou	4521	0.51	723	0.40	0.09	0.23	1.00	48.09	0.13
Yunnan	8384	0.53	1213	0.47	0.09	0.10	0.31	68.10	0.09
Shaanxi	33,190	0.50	1609	0.43	0.07	0.23	0.56	59.81	0.11
Gansu	2342	0.76	474	0.39	0.05	0.06	0.16	50.37	0.10
Qinghai	2522	0.49	90	0.41	0.05	0.01	0.00007	60.03	0.09
Ningxia	1743	0.63	338	0.52	0.12	0.20	0.95	56.67	0.07
Xinjiang	1534	0.44	752	0.51	0.10	0.02	0.25	68.78	0.10

4. **Measurement method**

We use ordinary least squares (OLS) as our estimator. To account for the possibility of heteroscedasticity and multicollinearity in multivariate cross-sectional regression analysis, we logarithmically transform the model and take natural logarithm of all variables, which can reduce skewness of variables without affecting the regression results. We then employ the modified Frisch function (stepwise regression) for regression analysis and special verification.

5. **Measurement model**

We employ the following measurement model:

$$\mathrm{Ln(FDI_i)} = \beta_0 + \beta_1 \mathrm{Ln(X_{it})} + e_i. \tag{6.1}$$

where i (1, 2, …, 30) is the host province, municipality or autonomous region; t (1, 2, …, 8) is the institutional factor variable; $X_{i1}, X_{i2}, \ldots, X_{i8}$ are values of the institutional factor variable of host provinces, municipalities, and autonomous regions; and e_i is the random disturbance term.

$$\begin{aligned}\mathrm{Ln(FDI)} = {} & \beta_0 + \beta_1 \mathrm{Ln(PRO)} + \beta_2 \mathrm{Ln(REG)} \\ & + \beta_3 \mathrm{Ln(MAR)} + \beta_4 \mathrm{Ln(OPE)} + \beta_5 \mathrm{Ln(FRE)} \\ & + \beta_6 \mathrm{Ln(ATT)} + \beta_7 \mathrm{Ln(ADM)} + \beta_8 \mathrm{Ln(CLE)} + e. \end{aligned} \tag{6.2}$$

Variables employed in the two models include current, first-year lagged, and two-year lagged variables.

6.3.3 Econometric Tests and Interpretation of Results

In order to find out which of the 24 candidate variables have a significant impact on FDI, EViews is used to perform regression analysis on model (1). See Tables 6.13, 6.14 and 6.15 for regression analysis results of legal institution variables, economic institution variables, and variables bearing on business operating costs.

1. **The impact of legal institution factors on FDI inflows**

They have the same meaning throughout this study.

As noted in Table 6.13, coefficient estimates of current, one-year lagged, and two-year lagged versions of PRO and REG are all positive and significant at 1%. These robust estimation results are consistent with our theoretical analysis results This suggests that private property protection and the quality of laws and regulations are positively correlated with FDI inflows.

2. **The impact of economic institution factors on FDI inflows**

As noted in Table 6.14, among economic institution factors, MAR and FRE have the most significant impact on FDI inflows. The coefficient estimates of the current, one-year lagged or two-year lagged versions of MAR and FRE are positive and significant at 1%. These robust estimation results are consistent with our assumptions and theoretical analysis results.

Table 6.13 Regression analysis results of legal institution variables

Response variable	Explanatory variable	β_0	β_1	R^2	F	D.W	s.e.
Ln(FDI)	Ln(PRO)	13.05*** (26.61)	5.87*** (5.29)	0.50	27.98***	1.53	1.36
Ln(FDI)	LN(REG)		1.40*** (61.08)	0.73		1.81	0.98
Ln(FDI)	Ln(PRO-1)	13.10*** (25.84)	4.66*** (5.19)	0.49	26.95***	1.48	1.37
Ln(FDI)	LN(REG-1)	5.24*** (9.33)	0.83*** (10.37)	0.79	107.46***	1.54	0.87
Ln(FDI)	Ln(PRO-2)	13.00*** (24.29)	3.75*** (4.69)	0.44	21.98***	1.63	1.44
Ln(FDI)	LN(REG-1)		1.45*** (59.90)	0.72		1.52	1.00

Note

(1) The values in brackets are t values; *, ** and ***denotes the significance level of 10%, 5% and 1%, respectively

(2) (Explanatory variable-1) denotes one-year lagged version of the variable, and (explanatory variable-2) denotes the two-year lagged version of the variable

The coefficient estimates of the current, one-year lagged or two-year lagged versions of OPE are positive, consistent with our assumptions and theoretical analysis results. The values of the current and two-year lagged versions are significant at 1%, whereas the one-year lagged OPE fails to pass the F-test of significance, suggesting it has almost no influence on FDI inflow.

The coefficient estimates of the current, one-year lagged or two-year lagged versions of ATT are positive, which is consistent with our assumptions and theoretical analysis results. Current ATT does not pass the F-test, suggesting it has almost no effect on FDI inflow, whereas two-year lagged ATT and one-year lagged ATT are significant at 1% and 5%, respectively.

The results demonstrate that marketization, economic freedom, economic openness and implementation of preferential policies are positively correlated with FDI inflows.

3. **The impact of business operating costs factors on FDI inflows**

As shown in Table 6.15, the coefficient estimates of current, one-year lagged, and two-year lagged versions of ADM are positive, completely consistent with our previous assumptions and analysis results, and all are significant at 1%, showing good robustness. Comparison of regression coefficients shows two-year lagged ADM has the strongest impact, followed by one-year lagged ADM, and current ADM has the least impact. This proves the hysteresis of institutional factors. The results show that higher administrative efficiency of a country or region's government can lower business operating costs, thereby luring more FDI.

Table 6.14 Regression analysis results of economic institution variables

Response variable	Explanatory variable	β_0	β_1	R^2	F	D.W	s.e.
Ln(FDI)	Ln(MAR)	15.65*** (19.98)	8.41*** (6.44)	0.60	41.52***	1.12	1.22
Ln(FDI)	Ln(OPE)	13.05*** (27.69)	1.32*** (5.54)	0.52	30.67***	1.02	1.33
Ln(FDI)	Ln(FRE)	12.78*** (32.36)	1.35*** (6.12)	0.57	37.44***	1.84	1.26
Ln(FDI)	Ln(ATT)	11.10*** (29.08)	0.28* (1.60)	0.08	2.57	0.92	1.84
Ln(FDI)	Ln(MAR-1)	15.71*** (19.98)	7.61*** (6.49)	0.60	42.14***	1.08	1.21
Ln(FDI)	Ln(OPE-1)	11.69*** (16.43)	0.52* (1.49)	0.07	2.22	1.26	1.86
Ln(FDI)	Ln(FRE-1)	13.11*** (29.77)	1.72*** (6.12)	0.57	37.47***	1.58	1.26
Ln(FDI)	Ln(ATT-1)	11.60*** (26.54)	1.59*** (2.60)	0.19	6.74**	1.13	1.72
Ln(FDI)	Ln(MAR-2)	16.60*** (18.03)	7.37*** (6.10)	0.57	37.15***	1.20	1.26
Ln(FDI)	Ln(OPE-2)	12.96*** (21.51)	1.19*** (4.02)	0.37	16.19***	0.69	1.53
Ln(FDI)	Ln(FRE-2)	13.15*** (33.34)	1.62*** (7.03)	0.64	49.37***	1.44	1.15
Ln(FDI)	Ln(ATT-2)	11.77*** (29.61)	1.72*** (3.54)	0.31	12.50***	1.24	1.60

Table 6.15 Regression analysis results of variables bearing on business operating costs

Response variable	Explanatory variable	β_0	β_1	R^2	F	D.W	s.e.
Ln(FDI)	Ln(ADM)	0	2.36*** (38.83)	0.34		1.56	1.53
Ln(FDI)	Ln(CLE)	0	− 4.51*** (− 29.56)	-0.12		0.90	2.00
Ln(FDI)	Ln(ADM-1)	0	2.38*** (55.98)	0.68		0.93	1.07
Ln(FDI)	Ln(CLE-1)	0	− 4.45*** (− 29.57)	-0.12		0.90	2.00
Ln(FDI)	Ln(ADM-2)	0	2.44*** (54.02)	0.66		0.91	1.11
Ln(FDI)	Ln(CLE-2)	5.57** (1.84)	− 2.15** (− 1.74)	-0.09	3.02	0.73	1.82

The coefficient estimate of CLE is negative, which is consistent with our assumption and theoretical analysis results. With a low R-squared value, the explanatory power of the indicator, whether it be current, one-year lagged or two-year lagged, is very weak. The two-year lagged CLE failed the F-test, poorly indicating the correlation of clean governance with FDI inflows.

4. **Comparative analysis**

In the preceding section, we examined the impact of each institutional factor on FDI. While this can avoid multicollinearity, we must keep in mind that a change in FDI in a country or region is the result of various factors working together. Of all the institutional factors, it is possible that only one or a very few produce a significant impact on the distribution of FDI across regions, while the others play an insignificant role in attracting FDI. However, a high correlation between the variables allows each of them to pass the significance test in the independent regression analysis, which might lead to the false conclusion that every single variable has a significant impact on FDI. The correlation coefficients shown in Table 6.16 indicate a strong correlation between the institutional factors. Now, we will put 24 institutional factors, including current (t), first-order lagged ($t - 1$) and second-order lagged ($t - 2$) variables, into the same equation and apply EViews on Model (2) for stepwise regression, to eliminate mutual interference between the factors and avoid multicollinearity. In this way, the impact of each institutional factor would be compared and the factors affecting FDI more remarkably would be identified.

The following is the stepwise regression procedure:

Apply regression on each explanatory variable with the response variable. Choose the best regression model as the basic model based on economic theory and the outcomes of statistical tests. Usually, the regression equation with the highest R-squared value is selected.

Add other explanatory variables one by one in the basic regression equation and rerun the linear regression model for every variable added. Keep the explanatory variable in the model if the R-squared value increases and other parameters in the regression equation are still statistically significant. Leave out the variable if the R-squared value does not increase. If adding an explanatory variable improves the goodness-of-fit and significantly affect the values or signs of some parameters in the regression equation, it indicates that there is multicollinearity in the model. Compare the explanatory variable with other explanatory variables related to it and retain the one that has a stronger influence on the response variable and leave out the others.

The regression analysis results of model (1) show that the regression equation of FDI and REG(-1) has the highest R-squared value, so we select it as the basic regression model.

$$\mathrm{Ln(FDI)} = 5.24 + 0.83\,\mathrm{LnREG}(-1) \text{ is the basic regression model in this study.}$$

$$(9.33***)(10.37***)$$

$$R^2 = 0.49\ F = 26.95***\ D.W = 1.48.$$

Table 6.16 Correlation matrix of the explanatory variables

	FDI	PRO	REG	MAR	OPE	FRE	ATT	ADM	CLE	PR-1	RE-1	MA-1	OP-1	FR-1	AT-1	AD-1	CL-1
FDI	1.0																
PRO	0.7	1.0															
REG	0.8	0.7	1.0														
MAR	0.6	0.8	0.6	1.0													
OPE	0.7	0.5	0.8	0.5	1.0												
FRE	0.7	0.6	0.5	0.6	0.7	1.0											
ATT	– 0.0	– 0.2	– 0.0	0.2	0.0	0.2	1.0										
ADM	0.4	0.5	0.6	0.9	0.7	0.6	– 0.0	1.0									
CLE	– 0.1	– 0.0	– 0.1	– 0.1	– 0.5	– 0.4	0.0	– 0.6	1.0								
PR-1	0.7	1.0	0.7	0.7	0.6	0.6	– 0.2	0.5	– 0.0	1.0							
RE-1	0.8	0.6	0.9	0.6	0.8	0.5	– 0.0	0.5	– 0.1	0.7	1.0						
MA-1	0.6	0.7	0.7	0.9	0.6	0.7	0.1	0.7	– 0.2	0.7	0.7	1.0					
OP-1	0.7	0.5	0.9	0.5	0.9	0.7	0.0	0.7	– 0.5	0.5	0.8	0.6	1.0				
FR-1	0.6	0.5	0.5	0.6	0.7	0.9	0.2	0.5	– 0.5	0.5	0.5	0.7	0.6	1.0			
AT-1	– 0.0	– 0.0	– 0.0	0.2	– 0.0	0.1	0.7	– 0.0	0.0	– 0.1	– 0.0	0.2	0.0	0.2	1.0		
AD-1	0.8	0.7	0.7	0.7	0.8	0.8	– 0.0	0.8	– 0.5	0.7	0.6	0.7	0.8	0.7	– 0.0	1.0	
CL-1	– 0.1	– 0.0	– 0.1	– 0.2	– 0.5	– 0.4	– 0.0	– 0.6	0.9	– 0.0	– 0.1	– 0.3	– 0.4	– 0.5	0.0	– 0.5	1.0
PR-2	0.7	0.9	0.7	0.7	0.6	0.6	– 0.2	0.5	0.0	0.9	0.7	0.7	0.6	0.5	– 0.1	0.7	– 0.0
RE-2	0.8	0.7	0.9	0.1	0.8	0.5	– 0.0	0.5	0.0	0.7	0.9	0.7	0.8	0.4	– 0.0	0.6	– 0.0
MA-2	0.6	0.6	0.6	0.9	0.7	0.7	0.1	0.7	– 0.2	0.7	0.6	0.9	0.7	0.7	0.2	0.7	– 0.3
OP-2	0.7	0.5	0.9	0.5	0.9	0.7	0.1	0.7	– 0.5	0.5	0.8	0.6	1.0	0.6	0.0	0.8	– 0.5
FR-2	0.6	0.5	0.5	0.7	0.7	0.9	0.1	0.5	– 0.4	0.7	0.5	0.7	0.7	1.0	0.2	0.7	– 0.4

(continued)

Table 6.16 (continued)

	FDI	PRO	REG	MAR	OPE	FRE	ATT	ADM	CLE	PR-1	RE-1	MA-1	OP-1	FR-1	AT-1	AD-1	CL-1
AT-2	0.0	− 0.0	0.0	0.4	0.1	0.3	0.7	0.7	0.0	− 0.0	0.1	0.3	0.1	0.3	0.9	0.0	0.0
AD-2	0.7	0.6	0.7	0.6	0.8	0.7	− 0.1	0.9	− 0.5	0.6	0.6	0.7	0.7	0.7	− 0.1	1.0	− 0.5
CL-2	− 0.2	− 0.2	− 0.2	− 0.2	− 0.5	− 0.5	− 0.0	− 0.6	0.9	− 0.2	− 0.2	− 0.4	− 0.5	− 0.6	− 0.0	− 0.6	0.9

Note Because of limitations of space, only some of the correlation coefficients of the variables are listed

Add REG and perform least-squares regression on FDI, REG(-1) and REG. We get the following regression equation:

$$\begin{aligned}&\mathrm{Ln(FDI)} = 2.99 + 0.53\mathrm{LnREG}(-1) + 0.55\mathrm{LnREG}\\&(2.94***)(3.90***)(2.55***)\\&\mathrm{R}^2 = 0.83\,\mathrm{F} = 67.48***\ \mathrm{D.W} = 1.74.\end{aligned}$$

After adding REG, the R-squared value of the regression equation is significantly improved and other parameters are still significant, so this explanatory variable is kept in the model.

We then add REG(-2) to the model and get the following regression equation:

$$\begin{aligned}&\mathrm{Ln(FDI)} = 3.91 + 0.59\mathrm{LnREG}(-1) + 1.26\mathrm{LnREG} - 0.91\mathrm{LnREG}(-2)\\&(3.05***)(4.09***)(1.94**)(-1.16)\\&\mathrm{R}^2 = 0.84\,\mathrm{F} = 46.03\,\mathrm{D.W} = 1.79.\end{aligned}$$

Although the R-squared value increases, the sign of the coefficient of REG(-2) is not consistent with our economic theoretical analysis results and it fails the significance test. Therefore, this explanatory variable is left out.

After performing the same procedure on other explanatory variables in the regression Eq. (6.1) one by one, we get the final regression equation:

$$\begin{aligned}&\mathrm{Ln(FDI)} = 4.36 + 0.47\mathrm{LnREG(-1)} + 0.91\mathrm{LnADM}(-1)\\&\quad + 0.49\mathrm{LnFRE}(-2) + 0.24\mathrm{LnFRE}\\&(1.72**)(5.06***)(1.81**)(2.43**)(1.39*)\\&\mathrm{R}^2 = 0.91\,\mathrm{F} = 48.55***\ \mathrm{D.W} = 1.72.\end{aligned}$$

This model has a high goodness-of-fit, all parameters pass the significance test, and all of the signs are positive, which is consistent with theoretical expectations. The influence of institutional determinants on FDI inflows can thus be reliably accounted for by the model. $R^2 = 0.91$ means that the changes in the four independent variables LnREG(-1), LnADM(-1), LnFRE(-2), and LnFRE can explain 91% of the changes in the dependent variable Ln(FDI).

(Note: The values in brackets are t values; *, ** and * denotes the significance level of 10%, 5% and 1%, respectively.)**

The results of our econometric test reveal that:

All but one of the eight indicators we tested, public integrity, significantly affect FDI inflows.

Comparative analysis of each variable's regression coefficients shows that marketization (MAR) is the most important determinant of FDI inflows. The coefficient estimates of current, one-year lagged, and two-year lagged MAR are 8.41, 7.61

and 7.37 respectively, far higher than the coefficient values of other variables. The second most important determinant is protection of private property (PRO), followed by administrative efficiency (ADM), economic freedom (FRE), and implementation of preferential policies (ATT). Quality of laws and regulations (REG) and economic openness (OPE) have less influence on FDI inflows.

However, after the removal of the redundant variables, the most important institutional factors bearing on FDI are one-year lagged administrative efficiency (ADM), two-year lagged economic freedom (FRE), one-year lagged quality of laws and regulations (REG) and current economic freedom (FRE). Marketization (MAR) has a strong correlation with economic freedom, with a correlation coefficient of 0.7, so it is excluded from the final regression equation. Economic freedom has a significant role in how marketization influences FDI inflows. Specifically, economic freedom conditions marketization, which in turn affects FDI inflows. Protection of private property (PRO) is strongly correlated with quality of laws and regulations (REG), with a correlation coefficient of 0.6, and quality of laws and regulations can account for the influence of protection of private property on FDI inflows to a large extent. Therefore, protection of private property is also left out from the final regression equation.

The final regression equation shows that an efficient government, a free and open economy, and an efficient legal system are institutional factors that attract FDI.

6.4 Empirical Research on the Relationships Between Regional Institutional Changes and FDI Inflows

For a long period (1979–1992) after the adoption of the reform and opening up policy, China's economic liberalization efforts were focused on eastern coastal areas, including Special Economic Zones, Open Coastal Cities, and Open Coastal Areas, which formed a coastal economic belt. Correspondingly, the coastal economic belt accounted for more than 90% of FDI inflows of China during this period. The influx of FDI boosted the expansion of exports, employment, and capital accumulation, which together powered the economy of eastern coastal areas. The rapid economic growth in turn increased the income of residents in the eastern coastal areas, expanded local market, improved the investment climate, and generated agglomeration economies, thereby luring more FDI. It is a virtuous circle in which FDI and institutional improvement promote each other. The western region was at a disadvantage in the early stage of the economic reform in terms of economic conditions, institutional environment, and location. Compared with the eastern region, it was less competitive in attracting FDI and as a result less motivated to improve its institutional environment. The response lag to institutional changes further exacerbated the situation. The western region has been caught in a vicious cycle where institutional rigidity deters FDI inflow and leads to economic stagnation, which further increases institutional rigidity. As a result, institutional rigidity becomes the main factor restricting the economic development of the western region.

6.4.1 The Impact of FDI Inflows on Institutional Changes

The comparative analysis and the empirical test of the relationships between institutional factors and FDI inflows in China's eastern, central and western regions in the preceding section reveal that a good institutional environment has a strong correlation with FDI inflows. Next, we will theoretically analyze the impact of FDI inflows on institutional changes in the host region.

1. **Local governments are under pressure to speed up institutional reforms**

New Institutional Economics holds that institutional improvement is constrained by factors such as ideological rigidity, conflicts of interest groups, limitations of social sciences, and information asymmetry. Only by giving full play to the state's rational-legal authority, economies of scale, and coercive control in the process of institutional reform can the effects of these deterring factors be eliminated. Only in this way can a virtuous circle take shape. With the influx of FDI, the demand of foreign investors for a fair playing field, an effective legal system, administrative efficiency and government transparency will force local governments to speed up institutional reforms, streamline institutions, boost work efficiency and improve the market mechanism.

2. **Development of the private sector can promote institutional reforms**

According to the theory of institutional economics, the success of an institutional reform ultimately hinges on whether its benefits outweigh its costs. A new institutional arrangement will be put into place if the expected net benefits (to the primary actors) exceed the expected costs. In China, since the benefits from institutional innovation are significantly higher than costs for private enterprises, private enterprises have become a powerful driving force of institutional reform. FDI inflows will strengthen the market mechanism and force the government to cancel various preferential treatment given to SOE to level the playing field and create more development opportunities for the private sector, thereby driving institutional changes.

3. **FDI inflows can drive local enterprises to change their operating model via demonstration effect**

Enterprises are actors in institutional changes, and the reform and innovation of their own management systems, operating models, and marketing strategies will effectively promote institutional changes. FDI inflows affect local businesses via two processes. First, internationally competitive foreign businesses have cutting-edge technologies, standardized operation models, and scientific management. Their operational efficiency is far higher than that of local companies in the Chinese mainland.

They have a positive demonstration effect on local businesses and may motivate them to restructure their corporate institutions. This process is known as induced institutional change. Second, when cooperating with local companies, it is typical for foreign investors to demand their local partners implement market-based changes. This process is known as forced institutional change.

4. **Technical progress drives institutional changes**

Institutional changes can be induced by technological changes. Ruttan points out: "The production of the new knowledge that leads to technical changes is the result of a process of institutional development. And technical changes, in turn, represent a powerful source of demand for institutional change."[2] Foreign investors often bring cutting-edge technologies with them to the host region. Technological progress will drive industrial restructuring, fuel economic liberalization, and boost productivity growth, which in turn drives institutional changes in the host region.

5. **Cultural interactions bring about a change in mindset**

As Douglass C. North put it, even in the most developed economies formal rules represent merely a small (though very important) part of the constraints that give form to one's choices. Also, he noted, "in our daily interaction with others, whether within the family, in external social relations, or in business activities, the governing structure is overwhelmingly defined by codes of conduct, norms of behavior, and conventions."[3] Cooperation and interaction between foreign and local companies may expose local residents to the ideas, concepts, and customs in a different culture, in addition to the market rules and international practices, providing them with better opportunities to embrace the world. All these might encourage the locals to break away from the old mindset and accept new ideas that better fit the market economy and reflect the international trend, which will eventually lead to an improvement in local institutions.

6.4.2 Test of the Causal Relationship Between FDI Inflows and Institutional Improvement

The above is only a theoretical analysis of the spillovers of FDI-related institutions. Next, we will use the Granger causality test to determine whether FDI can cause institutional changes in China.

A causality test verifies whether the change in one variable is the cause of the change in the values of the other variable. We already know that causality is different from correlation. A regression equation cannot be used to determine whether there is a causal relationship between variables. Although sometimes we say that an explanatory variable in the regression equation is the cause of the response variable, the

[2] Ruttan (1978).

[3] North (1978).

causal relationship is actually a priori. In other words, it is determined before we perform the regression. In many cases, the causal relationship between variables is not immediately apparent, or we lack necessary knowledge to recognize the causal relationship between variables. However, it is often our interest to determine the causal relationship between variables. Even if an economic theory claims a causal relationship, it needs to be proved empirically.

The Granger causality test is currently the most widely used method to verify whether there is a causal relationship between two variables. The majority of economic time series variables in real-world situations are non-stationary. Using F-statistics to test two non-stationary variables for causality may result in pseudo-regression issue, thereby rendering findings meaningless. Using a differential model to make them stationary or employing an error correction model are two ways to fix the aforementioned flaw. We employ the VARD model based on order difference data and F-statistics to examine the causal relationship between FDI inflows and institutional factors. According to the above-mentioned correlation test results, we test the casual relationship between administrative efficiency (ADM), economic freedom (FRE), quality of laws and regulations (REG) with FDI respectively. Because economic freedom data for some years are unavailable, economic freedom is proxied by marketization (MAR).

1. **Unit root test of data**

Using the time series data from 1984 to 2003 in Table 6.17 to perform ADF test on FDIt, we get:

$$D\,FDI_t = 247{,}084.4 - 0.043\,FDI_{t-1} + 0.515\,D\,FDI_{t-1}$$

$$\mathrm{t}(1.512)(-0.820)(2.246)$$

$$\mathrm{R}^2 = 0.255\,\mathrm{ADR}^2 = 0.155\,\mathrm{F} = 2.563\,\mathrm{ADF} = -0.820$$

Because ADF = – 0.820, higher than the 1, 5, and 10% critical values, the FDI_t series is non-stationary.

We then test the stationarity of difference series $D\,FDI_t$ to determine the order of integration of FDI_t and get the regression equation:

$$D^2\,FDI_t = -0.480\,D\,FDI_{t-1} + 0.282\,D^2\,FDI_{t-1}$$

$$\mathrm{t}(-2.201)(1.076)$$

$$\mathrm{R}^2 = 0.244\,\mathrm{ADR}^2 = 0.194\,\mathrm{ADF} = -2.201$$

Given that the ADF value is smaller than the 5 and 10% critical values, $D\,FDI_t$ $I \backsim (0)$, so it is concluded that FDI_t $I \backsim (1)$, which means that ADF is a first-order integrated variable.

In the same vein, ADM is a second-order integrated variable, and MAR and REG are first-order integrated variables.

Table 6.17 FDI, REG, PRO, FRE, MAR, and ADM data of China

Year	Indicator			
	FDI	REG	MAR	ADM
1984	125,800		0.35	9.65
1985	166,100		0.34	11.22
1986	187,400	2671	0.34	11.69
1987	231,400	6401	0.39	12.93
1988	319,400	11,292	0.39	15.37
1989	339,200	15,480	0.39	16.55
1990	348,700	112,103	0.34	17.19
1991	436,600	21,178	0.34	19.03
1992	1,100,700	28,311	0.33	23.20
1993	2,751,500	56,882	0.39	33.63
1994	3,376,700	39,777	0.44	45.27
1995	3,752,100	41,248	0.46	56.12
1996	4,172,500	39,725	0.48	62.11
1997	4,525,700	41,419	0.48	68.13
1998	4,546,300	54,994	0.46	71.42
1999	4,031,900	92,101	0.47	74.47
2000	4,071,500	95,236	0.50	81.04
2001	4,687,800	99,278	0.53	88.39
2002	5,274,300	112,103	0.57	97.83
2003	5,350,500	149,588	0.61	102.29

Source Calculated based on relevant data from *China Statistical Yearbook*

Construction of VARD model

Based on the ADF test results, the second-order difference models (6.3) and (6.4) and the first-order difference models (6.5), (6.6), (6.7) and (6.8) are established as follows:

$$D^2FDI_t = a_0 + a_1D^2FDI_{t-1} + a_2D^2ADM_t + a_3D^2ADM_{t-1} + u_t \tag{6.3}$$

$$D^2ADM_t = b_0 + b_1D^2ADM_{t-1} + b_2D^2FDI_t + b_3D^2FDI_{t-1} + v_t \tag{6.4}$$

where

$$D^2FDI_t = DFDI_t - DFDI_{t-1}$$

$$DFDI_t = a_0 + a_1D\,FDI_{t-1} + a_2D\,MAR_t + a_3D\,MAR_{t-1} + u_t \tag{6.5}$$

$$DMAR_t = b_0 + b_1 D\,MAR_{t-1} + b_2 D\,FDI_t + b_3 D\,FDI_{t-1} + v_t \tag{6.6}$$

$$DFDI_t = a_0 + a_1 D\,FDI_{t-1} + a_2 D\,REG_t + a_3 D\,REG_{t-1} + u_t \tag{6.7}$$

$$DREG_t = b_0 + b_1 D\,REG_{t-1} + b_2 DFDI_t + b_3 DFDI_{t-1} + v_t \tag{6.8}$$

The null hypothesis of models (6.3), (6.5), and (6.7) is H_0: $a_2 = a_3 = 0$ means that changes in ADM, MAR and REG are not the cause of FDI inflows.

The null hypothesis of models (6.4), (6.6) and (6.8) is H_0: $b_2 = b_3 = 0$ means that FDI inflow does not cause changes in ADM, MAR, and REG.

We then perform OLS regression on the VAR model of the original model before the differential treatment of the models (6.3–6.8), and the results show that there is a first-order positive correlation in the original model. Therefore, the differential model complies with the fundamental requirements for using ordinary least squares. Adding the data (calculated based on the relevant data of *China Statistical Yearbook* from 1984 to 2003) into each model and using Eviews for estimation, we get the following results:

$$\begin{aligned} & D^2FDI_t = 0.587D^2FDI_{t-1} + 94865.09D^2ADM_t + 19109.80D^2ADM_{t-1} \\ & t \qquad (3.02) \qquad (2.88) \qquad (0.44) \\ & \mathrm{R}^2 = 0.47\ \mathrm{ADR}^2 = 0.40\ \mathrm{D.W} = 2.00 \end{aligned} \tag{6.9}$$

$$\begin{aligned} & D^2ADM_t = 0.110\,D^2ADM_{t-1} + 3.92E - 06D^2FDI_t - 2.81E - 06D^2FDI_{t-1} \\ & t \qquad (0.39) \qquad (2.88) \qquad (-1.98) \\ & \mathrm{R}^2 = 0.40\ \mathrm{ADR}^2 = 0.31\ \mathrm{D.W} = 2.05 \end{aligned} \tag{6.10}$$

$$\begin{aligned} & DFDI_t = 0.468\,D\,FDI_{t-1} + 6688544\,DMAR_t - 1844165\,DMAR_{t-1} \\ & t \qquad (1.81) \qquad (1.76) \qquad (-0.44) \\ & \mathrm{R}^2 = 0.28\ \mathrm{ADR}^2 = 0.19\ \mathrm{D.W} = 1.75 \end{aligned} \tag{6.11}$$

$$\begin{aligned} & DMAR_t = 0.184\,DMAR_{t-1} + 2.55E - 08\,DFDI_t + 1.11E - 08DFDI_{t-1} \\ & \mathrm{t} \qquad (0.71) \qquad (1.76) \qquad (0.64) \\ & \mathrm{R}^2 = 0.29\ \mathrm{ADR}^2 = 0.194\ \mathrm{D.W} = 1.94 \end{aligned} \tag{6.12}$$

$$\begin{aligned} & DFDI_t = 232068.2 + 0.425DFDI_{t-1} - 2.210DREG_t - 4.034DREG_{t-1} \\ & \mathrm{t} \qquad (1.57) \qquad (1.73) \qquad (-0.63) \qquad (-1.12) \\ & \mathrm{R}^2 = 0.28\ \mathrm{ADR}^2 = 0.10\ \mathrm{F} = 1.54\ \mathrm{D.W} = 1.94 \end{aligned} \tag{6.13}$$

$$DREG_t = 16984.12 - 0.505\,DREG_{t-1} - 0.014DFDI_t + 5.58E{-}05DFDI_{t-1}$$
$$\text{t} \quad (1.40) \quad (-1.89) \quad (-0.63) \quad (0.003)$$
$$R^2 = 0.23\ ADR^2 = 0.04\ F = 1.22\ D.W = 2.48 \tag{6.14}$$

Analysis of (6.9)–(6.14), which are the estimation results of models (6.3)–(6.8) shows that: When the significance level $\alpha = 0.10$ and the fitting degree is acceptable, the test result is significant, that is, the hypothesis is rejected with a 90% confidence interval. Therefore, the change of ADM, MAR, and REG is the cause of FDI inflows, and FDI inflow is also the cause of changes in ADM, MAR, and REG. The results of the empirical test show that FDI inflows and institutional change promote each other.

6.5 Conclusion

There is a strong correlation between regional institutional changes and FDI inflows in China. Institutional factors are important factors bearing on FDI agglomeration. Empirical research also shows that institutional factors have a strong correlation with FDI inflow and that FDI inflow responds to institutional factors with a lag. Among the various institutional factors, lagged variables have a significant impact on the current FDI inflows, indicating a lag in the effect of institutional factors on FDI inflows. Institutional determinants have varying degrees of impact on FDI inflows. Among the three types of institutional determinants, the one with the highest level of influence is administrative efficiency, which affect business operating costs, followed by economic freedom and quality of laws and regulations. There is a serious gap in the development of institutional environment between the eastern and western regions. There are obvious regional disparities in various institutional reforms across the country. All institutional indicators are higher in the east and lower in the west. The central and western regions are lagging behind the eastern region in institutional reforms. There is a two-way causal relationship between regional institutional changes and FDI inflows in China. On the one hand, institutional factors are important factors affecting FDI inflow. On the other hand, FDI plays an important role in promoting institutional changes. The serious lag in institutional reforms in the western region has deterred FDI inflows, and the uneven distribution of FDI across the country is an important factor hindering institutional changes in the western region.

References

Jun, K.W., and Harinder Singh. 1996. The determinants of foreign direct investment: New empirical evidence. *Transnational Corporations* 5 (3): 67–105.

Lu, Minghong. 1999. Institutional factors and geographical distribution of international direct investment: An empirical study. *Economic Research* 7.

North, Douglas. 1978. *Structure and Change in Economic History*. Shanghai Joint Publishing.

Pan, Zhen, and Chichun Pan. 2004. Institutions, policies and the location distribution of foreign investments. *Journal of Nanjing Normal University* 3.

Ruttan, V. 1978. *Induced Institutional Change*, Shanghai Joint Publishing.

UNCTAD. 1998. *World Investment Report 1998*. New York: United Nations.

Wang, Dingding. 1992. Theories of institutional innovation. *Economic Research*.

Wei, Shangjin. 2001. The opacity of economic cost: Loss and additional operating costs of foreign direct investments. *Economics (Quarterly)* 1 (1).

Wei, Shang-Jin. 2000. Why does china attract so little foreign direct investment? In *The Role of Foreign Direct Investment in East Asian Economic Development*, ed. by Takatoshi Ito, and Anne O. Krueger. Chicago and London: University of Chicago Press.

Wei, Houkai, Canfei He, and Xin Wang. 2002. *The Decisions and Public Policies on Location of FDI in China*. The Commercial Press.

Chapter 7
FDI Gap and Economic Growth in China's Western Region

Due to the growing influence of multinational corporations in the global economy, most countries or regions regard attracting FDI as one of the most important measures to fuel economic growth. In this chapter, we will look at the FDI gap in China's western region in light of its level of economic development based on the disparity in FDI per unit of GDP between the western and eastern regions and between the western region and the national average level, the impact of FDI on the growth factors and the economic growth function of the western region, loss of opportunities for economic development as a result of the FDI gap, and FDI related goals of the western region in relation to its economic growth goals.

7.1 FDI Gap in the Western Region

A large number of empirical studies have demonstrated a strong correlation between the quantity of FDI flowing into a country or region and the size of the economy in that country or region. Therefore, a unit of GDP should correspond to a certain quantity of inbound FDI. Because the western region lags behind the eastern region and the national average level in terms of economic development, the quantity of FDI flowing into the western region is naturally lower than that of the eastern region and the national average level. So the question we are concerned with is whether there is a FDI gap in the western region in light of its level of economic development.

© Social Sciences Academic Press 2024

X. Yang et al., *Foreign Direct Investment in Western China, 1994-2004*,
https://doi.org/10.1007/978-981-97-7407-4_7

7.1.1 Disparity in Inbound FDI Per Unit of GDP Between Western and Eastern Regions and Between the Western Region and the National Average Level

To determine whether there is a FDI gap in the western region in light of its level of economic development, we must first estimate the disparity in inbound FDI per unit of GDP between western and eastern regions and between the western region and the national average level. By analyzing current FDI trends and the change in inbound FDI per unit of GDP of the western region, we can get a grasp of the disparity in inbound FDI per unit of GDP between western and eastern regions as well as between the western region and the national average level.

1. **Current FDI trends in the western region**

The period from 1990 to 2004 saw a hike in inbound FDI in the western region followed by a gentle decline with some fluctuations. FDI in the western region increased rapidly from USD111 million in 1990 to USD2.311 billion in 1994, with an average annual growth rate of 113.61%, and then decreased at an average annual rate of 2.88% to USD1.744 billion in 2004. Overall, the average annual growth rate over the past 15 years reached 21.74%. The western region's share of the country's inbound FDI is disproportionately low compared to its share of the country's GDP, and this discordance is still growing. As shown in Fig. 7.1, the distance between the two curves have widened since 1994. The disparity between the western region's share of the country's inbound FDI and its contribution to the country's GDP fluctuated upward. In 2004, the western region accounted for only 2.88% of the country's total inbound FDI, more than 18 percentage points lower than its contribution to the country's GDP (20.91%). In 1994, this difference was only 11.25 percentage points (Table 7.1).

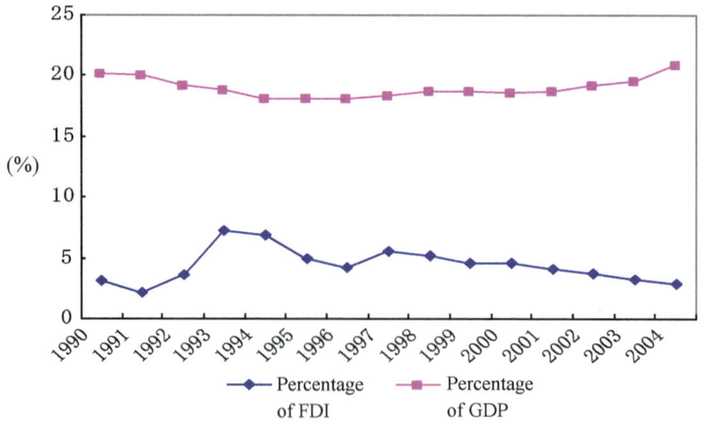

Fig. 7.1 Regional inbound FDI and GDP of western regions, as a percentage of China's total inbound FDI and GDP

Table 7.1 Inbound FDI and GDP of the western region, as a percentage of China's total inbound FDI and GDP (%)

Year	1990	1992	1994	1996
Regional inbound FDI (% of China's total inbound FDI)	3.18	3.59	6.84	4.22
GDP of the western region (% of China's total GDP)	20.20	19.20	18.09	18.11
Gap	17.02	15.61	11.25	13.89
Year	1998	2000	2002	2004
Regional inbound FDI (% of China's total inbound FDI)	5.17	4.55	3.80	2.88
GDP of western regions (% of China's total GDP)	18.70	18.62	19.18	20.91
Gap	13.53	14.07	15.38	18.03

Source Calculated based on relevant data from *China Statistical Yearbook*

2. **Inbound FDI per unit of GDP in the western region**

Inbound FDI per unit of GDP and inbound FDI in the western region are trending in same direction. However, as shown in Fig. 7.2, the increase of inbound FDI per unit of GDP is milder than its drop due to the continuous, rapid growth of GDP. The western region's inbound FDI per RMB100 million of GDP increased rapidly at an average annual rate of 101.91% from RMB141,700 in 1990 to RMB2,355,300 in 1994, followed by a decline, except for fluctuations in 1997 and 1998, at an average annual rate of 14.28%. It dropped to RMB504,300 in 2004 (Table 7.2).

3. **Difference in inbound FDI per unit of GDP between the western region and the national average level**

As we can see from Fig. 7.3, the difference between the western region's inbound FDI per unit of GDP and the national average level rose sharply from RMB757,500 per RMB100 million of GDP in 1990 to RMB3,868,600 per RMB100 million of

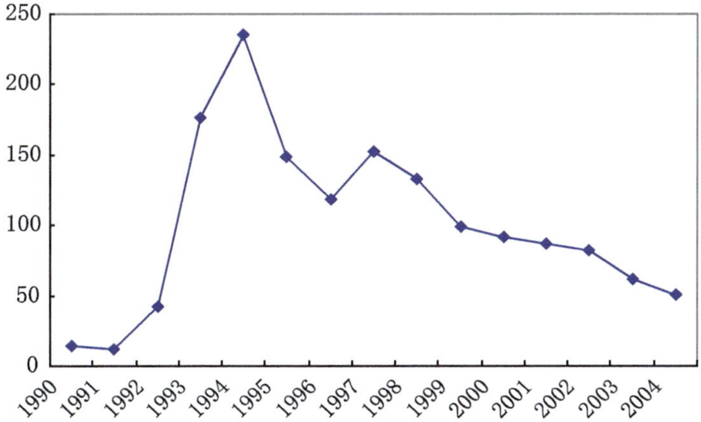

Fig. 7.2 Inbound FDI per unit of GDP in the western region of China

Table 7.2 Inbound FDI per unit of GDP in the western region of China (10,000 yuan/100 million yuan)

Year	1989	1990	1991	1992
Inbound FDI	20.52	14.17	11.57	42.60
Year	1993	1994	1995	1996
Inbound FDI	176.72	235.53	148.01	118.94
Year	1997	1998	1999	2000
Inbound FDI	152.30	132.88	99.04	92.06
Year	2001	2002	2003	2004
Inbound FDI	87.18	82.28	62.13	50.43

Source Calculated based on relevant data from *China Statistical Yearbook*

GDP in 1994, at an average annual rate of 50.33%, and then slowly climbed to RMB3,921,000 per RMB100 million of GDP in 1996, followed by a gentle winding down. It dropped to RMB3,162,000 per RMB100 million of GDP in 2004, at an annual average rate of 2.65% (Table 7.3).

4. **Difference in inbound FDI per unit of GDP between China's western and eastern regions**

As shown in Fig. 7.4 the curve of the difference in inbound FDI per unit of GDP between China's western and eastern regions over the period 1990–2004 starts with a sharp increase and then slopes downwards. The figure rose rapidly from RMB1,201,200 in 1990 to RMB7,705,300 in 1994, at an average annual rate of 59.15%. After 1994, except for the slight fluctuations in 2001 and 2002, the gap embarked on a continuous decline, reaching RMB3,904,100 in 2004, at an average annual rate of 8.15% (Table 7.4).

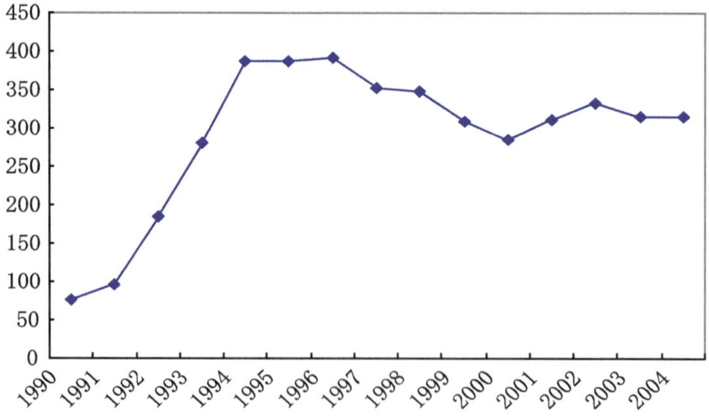

Fig. 7.3 Difference in inbound FDI per unit of GDP between the western region and the national average (RMB10,000/RMB100 million)

Table 7.3 Difference in inbound FDI per unit of GDP between the western region and the national average (10,000 yuan/100 million yuan)

Year	1989	1990	1991	1992
Difference	55.03	75.75	95.94	185.27
Year	1993	1994	1995	1996
Difference	281.04	386.86	387.81	392.10
Year	1997	1998	1999	2000
Difference	351.54	347.55	307.67	284.67
Year	2001	2002	2003	2004
Difference	311.54	332.80	315.13	316.20

Source Calculated based on relevant data from *China Statistical Yearbook*

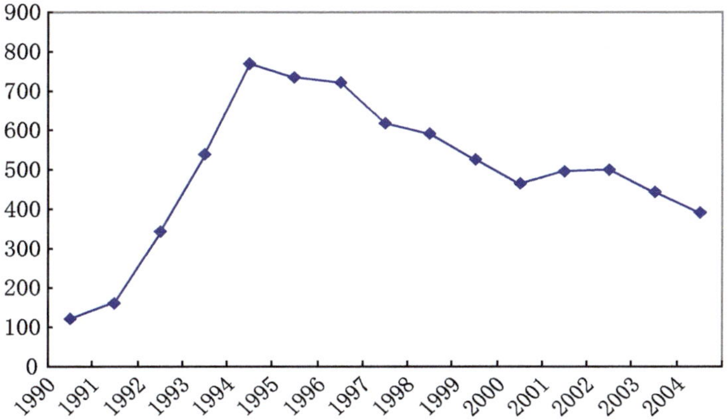

Fig. 7.4 Difference in inbound FDI per unit of GDP between China's western and eastern regions (RMB/RMB100 million)

Table 7.4 Difference in inbound FDI per unit of GDP between China's western and eastern regions (yuan/100,000,000 yuan)

Year	1989	1990	1991	1992
Inbound FDI	94.45	120.12	158.83	343.59
Year	1993	1994	1995	1996
Inbound FDI	537.43	770.53	735.25	722.95
Year	1997	1998	1999	2000
Inbound FDI	615.83	590.72	524.91	463.44
Year	2001	2002	2003	2004
Inbound FDI	495.50	499.85	442.83	390.41

Source Calculated based on relevant data from *China Statistical Yearbook*

Table 7.5 Inbound FDI gap faced by the western region provided that inbound FDI per unit of GDP in the western region reached the national average level, 1990-2004 Unit: USD100 million, %

Year	1990	1992	1994	1996	1998	2000	2002	2004
Target value	7.04	21.13	61.07	75.58	85.00	75.79	101.14	126.78
Gap	5.93	17.18	37.96	57.99	61.49	57.27	81.09	109.34
Percentage gap	84.23	81.31	62.16	76.73	72.34	75.56	80.18	86.24

Source Calculated based on relevant data from *China Statistical Yearbook*

7.1.2 FDI Gap of the Western Region

By assuming that inbound FDI per unit of GDP in the western region was at the same level as the national average and that of the eastern region, we can get the FDI gap in the western region in light of its level of economic development.

1. **FDI gap of the western region provided that inbound FDI per unit of GDP in the western region reached the national average level**

Assuming inbound FDI per unit of GDP in the western region reached the national average level, we can get the FDI gap in the western region relative to the national average level. Provided that inbound FDI of the western region reached RMB89.92 per RMB10,000 of GDP in 1990, the target value of FDI flowing into the western region should be USD704 million, USD593 million higher than the actual quantity of FDI flowing into the western region, which is USD111 million, and the percentage gap[1] would reach 84.23%. In the same vein, we can get the FDI gap of the western region from 1992 to 2004. The results are shown in Table 7.5.

As can be seen from Table 7.5, provided that inbound FDI per unit of GDP of the western region reached the national average level, the FDI gap in the western region would drop first and then rise sharply, forming a U-shaped curve. The figure expands from USD593 million in 1990 to USD10,934 million in 2004, at an average annual rate of 23.14%. The percentage gap drops from 84.23% in 1990 to 72.34% in 1998, and then embarks on a continuous increase, reaching 86.24% in 2004.

2. **FDI gap of the western region provided that inbound FDI per unit of GDP in the western region reached the level of the eastern region**

Assuming that inbound FDI per unit of GDP in the western region reached the level of the eastern region, we can get the FDI gap in the western region relative to the level of the eastern region. Provided that inbound FDI of the western region reached RMB134.29 per RMB10,000 of GDP in 1990, the target value of FDI flowing into the western region should be USD1,052 million, more than nine times the actual quantity of FDI flowing into the western region, which is USD111 million. The gap is USD941 million and the percentage gap reaches 89.45%. In the same vein, we

[1] $Percentagegap = \frac{Gap}{Targetvalue} \times 100\%$

Table 7.6 Inbound FDI gap faced by the western region provided that inbound FDI per unit of GDP in the western region reached the level of the eastern region, 1990–2004, Unit: USD100 million, %

Year	1990	1992	1994	1996	1998	2000	2002	2004
Target value	10.52	35.81	98.72	124.51	128.02	111.76	141.85	152.44
Gap	9.41	31.86	75.61	106.92	104.51	93.24	121.80	135.00
Percentage gap	89.45	88.97	76.59	85.87	81.64	83.43	85.87	88.56

Source Calculated based on relevant data from *China Statistical Yearbook*

can get the inbound FDI gap and the percentage gap of inbound FDI of the western region over the period 1992–2004 by assuming inbound FDI per unit of GDP in the western region reached the level of the eastern region. The results are listed in Table 7.6.

As can be seen from Table 7.6, provided that inbound FDI per unit of GDP of the western region reached the level of the eastern region, the FDI gap in the western region would drop first and then rise sharply, forming a U-shaped curve. The figure expands from USD941 million in 1990 to USD13,500 million in 2004, at an average annual rate of 20.96%. The percentage gap drops from 89.45% in 1990 to 81.64% in 1998, and then embarks on a continuous increase, reaching 88.56% in 2004.

In short, whether the western region's inbound FDI per unit of GDP reached the national average level or the level of the eastern region, the western region would face a large FDI gap (expressed as a dollar amount and percentage). In both scenarios, the FDI gap expressed as a dollar amount is widening; the percentage gap remains high with some fluctuations.

7.2 FDI and Economic Growth in the Western Region

The effect of inbound FDI on the economic growth of the host country is determined by the direct or indirect impact of inbound FDI on various economic factors, especially capital, technologies, trade, and industries. Inbound FDI can directly increase the capital stock of the host country or region, bring cutting-edge technologies and scientific management methods, and generate positive spillovers. It can directly strengthen the trade relationship between the host country or region and other countries and boost foreign trade of the host country or region. It can also directly bring new industries, especially high-tech industries, and reshape the industrial landscape of the host country or region. The direct or indirect impact of FDI on economic factors will eventually be reflected in the changes in the quantity and quality of economic growth.

7.2.1 *The Impact of FDI on Capital Formation in the Western Region*

There are two main ways in which investors can invest funds in a foreign country: starting a company in a foreign country or getting stocks in a business based in a foreign country. In other words, they increase investment in fixed assets in the host country or region. Therefore, the role of FDI in promoting capital formation in the host country/region has been widely regarded as the most important economic benefit for the host country/region. In addition to directly increasing the capital stock of the host region, another two important ways for FDI to promote capital formation in the host region are: (i) making use of the multiplier effect and relationships with upstream and downstream partners to drive local enterprises to increase investment; and (ii) offering follow-on investment and indirect investment.

1. **The impact of inbound FDI on capital formation in the western region**

FDI in fixed assets in the western region[2] increased from RMB14.83 billion in 1995 to RMB45.55 billion in 2004, and the average annual growth rate of the price index of FDI in fixed assets was 11.49%, 5 percentage points lower than the average growth rate of investment in fixed assets in the western region in the same period (16.37%). In the western region, FDI makes up a small fraction of investment in fixed assets. The contribution of FDI to the region's total investment in fixed assets has seen notable fluctuations. Between 1995 and 2004, the contribution of FDI to the total investment in fixed assets dropped from 4.87 to 3.31%. The percentage of FDI in the capital stock in the western region also shows an obvious downward trend. It dropped from 2.59% in 1995 to 1.14% in 2004.

Therefore, despite the fact that inbound FDI can increase the capital stock, accelerate capital formation, and provide capital to finance its development, the impact of FDI on capital formation in the western region is small because the growth of FDI in fixed assets is slow and the ratio of FDI to the total investment in fixed assets in the western region is low. And this direct impact is slowing down.

2. **Change in the capital stock of the western region if the FDI gaps were filled**

(1) Change in capital stock in the western region if its FDI gap relative to the national average level were filled

We use data on inbound FDI gap faced by the western region relative to the national average level (see Table 7.5) and the impact of FDI on capital formulation in the western region (see Table 7.7) to estimate the change in the western region's capital stock if the FDI gap relative to the national average level were filled (see Table 7.8). If the FDI gap were filled, the capital stock in the western region from 2000 to 2004 would increase from RMB1,517,418

[2] The amount of FDI in fixed assets is calculated by adding the investments in fixed asset of foreign investors and investors based in Hong Kong, Macao and Taiwan.

Table 7.7 Impact of FDI on investment in fixed assets and capital stock in the western region, Unit: RMB100 million, %)

Year		1995	2000	2001	2002	2003	2004
FDI in fixed assets	Amount	148.30	188.24	182.39	243.95	291.40	455.50
	Percentage	4.87	3.08	2.55	2.86	2.69	3.31
FDI stocks	Increase[3]	29.54	37.59	35.98	44.05	45.96	54.48
	Percentage	2.59	1.94	1.62	1.58	1.24	1.14

Source Calculated based on relevant data from *China Fixed Assets Investment Statistical Yearbook*

Table 7.8 Change in the western region's capital stock if its FDI gap relative to the national average level were filled Unit: RMB100 million, %

Year	2000	2001	2002	2003	2004
Actual value	15,174.18	17,397.68	20,177.55	23,874.20	28,647.98
Target value	15,290.42	18,726.27	22,355.71	24,557.31	30,989.54
Increase	116.24	1328.59	2178.16	683.11	2341.56
Increase rate	0.77	7.64	10.79	2.86	8.17

Source Calculated based on relevant data from *China Statistical Yearbook* and Tables 7.5 and 7.7

million, RMB1,739,768 million, RMB2,017,755 million, RMB2,387,420 million, and RMB2,864,798 million by 0.77%, 7.64%, 10.79%, 2.86%, and 8.17% respectively to RMB1,529,042 million, RMB1,872,627 million, RMB2,235,571 million, RMB2,455,731 million, and RMB3,098,954 million. The year 2002 would see the largest increase because of the high FDI gap and the enormous impact of FDI on capital formation.

2. Change in capital stock in the western region if its FDI gap relative to the level of the eastern region were filled

We use data on inbound FDI gap faced by the western region relative to the level of the eastern region (see Table 7.6) and the impact of FDI on capital formulation in the western region (see Table 7.7) to estimate the change in the western region's capital stock if the FDI gap relative to the level of the eastern region were filled (see Table 7.9). If the FDI gap were filled, the capital stock in the western region from 2000 to 2004 would increase from RMB1,517,418 million, RMB1,739,768 million, RMB2,017,755 million, RMB2,387,420 million, and RMB2,864,798 million by 1.25%, 8.07%, 11.24%, 3.47 % and 8.80% respectively to RMB1,536,343 million, RMB1,880,218 million, RMB2,244,515 million, RMB2,470,179 million, and RMB3,116,970 million.

[3] We use the depreciation rate of the western region as a proxy measure of the economic depreciation rate of foreign investment in the western region.

Table 7.9 Change in capital stock in the western region if its FDI gap relative to the level of the eastern region were filled, Unit: RMB100 million, %

Year	2000	2001	2002	2003	2004
Actual value	15,174.18	17,397.68	20,177.55	23,874.20	28,647.98
Target value	15,363.43	18,802.18	22,445.15	24,701.79	31,169.70
Increase	189.25	1404.5	2267.60	827.59	2521.72
Percentage	1.25	8.07	11.24	3.47	8.80

Source Calculated based on relevant data from *China Statistical Yearbook* and Tables 7.5 and 7.7

(3) Comparative analysis

First, based on data in Tables 7.5 and 7.6, we can estimate the change in the FDI gap of the western region relative to the national average level and the level of the eastern region. Then, based on data from Tables 7.8 and 7.9, we can estimate the change in capital stock growth in the western region if the FDI gap of the western region relative to the national average level and the level of the eastern region were filled (see Table 7.10). As can be seen from Table 7.10, the change in the FDI gap is greater than the change in capital stock growth. It suggests that inbound FDI has not accelerated capital stock growth in the western region.

In short, filling the FDI gap relative to the national average level and the level of the eastern region would lead to an increase in the capital stock in the western region, but there would be notable fluctuations in the growth. The fluctuations can be accounted for by the magnitude of the FDI gap and the influence of FDI on capital formulation. When the gap and the influence are high, the growth and the growth rate are high. After filling the FDI gap relative to the national average level and the level of the eastern region, the change in the growth and growth rate of the capital stock is not significant. It suggests that the impact of FDI on capital stock growth is not significant.

Table 7.10 Changes in FDI gap and capital stock growth, Unit: %

Year	2000	2001	2002	2003	2004
Percentage change in FDI gap	38.57	37.13	33.42	28.84	19.01
Percentage change in capital stock growth	38.21	5.40	3.94	17.46	7.14

Source Calculated based on relevant data from Tables 7.5, 7.6, 7.8 and 7.9

7.2.2 The Impact of FDI on the Technological Landscape in the Western Region

New growth theory suggests that technological progress plays an extremely important role in boosting economic growth of developing countries. For countries and regions, the key to economic growth lies in technological progress. Empirical research shows that the cost of technology transfer and imitation is lower than the cost of research and development. For many developing countries, technology transfer has become an important way to achieve technological progress. FDI is an important way for the host country or region to gain access to advanced technologies. Although scholars hold different views on the impact of FDI on technological progress including technology research and development capability, there is no doubt about the role of FDI in boosting the efficiency of turning technologies into applications.

1. **The impact of FDI on the technological landscape in the western region**

In the western region, foreign-invested enterprises (FIEs) are more active than other types of enterprises in technology research and development. According to the national economic census data for 2004, the number of FIEs based in the western region reporting scientific and technological activities, R&D activities, product development activities, and existence of affiliated science and technology institutions were 284, 169, 167 and 124, accounting for 16.01%, 9.53%, 9.41% and 6.99% of the total number of FIEs in the western region, respectively, all higher than regional average levels. In 2004, FIEs in the western region employed 15,311 scientists and tech workers, accounting for 3.07% of the total number of people employed at these enterprises, and 6,675 R&D workers, accounting for 43.60% of the total number of scientists and tech workers employed at these enterprises. These two proportions are also higher than the regional average levels (Table 7.11).

FIEs in the secondary sector outperform the regional sector average in terms of the overall labor productivity. From 1999 to 2004, the overall labor productivity of the secondary sector in the western region increased from RMB16,300 per year per person to RMB37,900 per year per person, and that of FIEs in the secondary sector

Table 7.11 Scientific and technological activities of FIEs and all enterprises in the western region, 2004 Unit: %

Scientific and technological activities	Scientific and technological activities	R&D activities	Product development	Affiliated science and technology institutions	Scientists and tech workers employed	R&D personnel
Proportion in FIEs	16.01	9.53	9.41	6.99	3.07	43.60
Proportion in all enterprises	12.88	6.73	6.84	6.06	1.29	42.16

Source Calculated based on national census data (2004)

increased from RMB49,900 per year per person to 108,200 per year per person. The overall labor productivity of the secondary sector excluding FIEs increased from RMB15,700 per year per person to RMB36,700 per year per person, lower than the sectoral values including FIEs. The small but increasing proportion decline indicates that although the influence is small, it is increasing.

The above analysis shows that FIEs have a significant demonstration effect on technological progress in the western region. They have also played an important role in improving the technological efficiency in the region. In other words, inbound FDI has a significant impact on the technological landscape in the western region.

2. **Changes in the overall labor productivity in the western region after filling the FDI gap**

(1) Change in overall labor productivity after filling the western region's FDI gap relative to the national average level

We use data on inbound FDI gap faced by the western region relative to the national average level (see Table 7.5) and the impact of FDI on the overall labor productivity in the western region (see Table 7.12) to estimate the change in the overall labor productivity in the western region if its FDI gap relative to the national average level were filled (see Table 7.13). As shown in Table 7.12, overall labor productivity of FIEs is higher than that of other enterprises. Therefore, if the FDI gap relative to the national average level were filled, the overall labor productivity in the western region from 2000 to 2004 would increase from RMB15,900 per year per person, RMB16,900 per year per person, RMB18,100 per year per person, RMB19,300 per year per person and RMB22,300 per year per person to RMB17,000 per year per person, RMB18,100 per year per person, RMB19,300 per year per person, RMB21,800 per year per person and RMB24,500 per year per person. The percentage increases are 6.92%, 7.10%, 6.63%, 9.55% and 9.87%, respectively.

(2) Change in overall labor productivity in the secondary sector in the western region after filling the western region's FDI gap relative to the level in the eastern region

We use data on inbound FDI gap faced by the western region relative to the level of the eastern region (see Table 7.6) and the impact of FDI on the overall labor productivity

Table 7.12 The impact of FDI on the overall labor productivity of the secondary sector in the western region (constant prices of 1990), Unit: RMB10 thousand per year per person, %

Year	1999	2000	2001	2002	2003	2004
FIEs	3.49	4.07	4.41	4.76	5.79	6.03
Sectoral value (including FIEs)	1.63	1.96	2.35	2.86	3.41	3.79
Sectoral value (excluding FIEs)	1.57	1.89	2.27	2.77	3.29	3.67
Proportion decrease in the sectoral value after excluding FIEs	0.06	0.07	0.08	0.09	0.12	0.12

Source Calculated based on relevant data from *China Statistical Yearbook*

Table 7.13 Overall labor productivity in the western region if its FDI gap relative to the national average level were filled, Unit: RMB10 thousand per year per person, %

Year	2000	2001	2002	2003	2004
Actual value	1.59	1.69	1.81	1.99	2.23
Target value	1.70	1.81	1.93	2.18	2.45
Increase	0.11	0.12	0.12	0.19	0.22
Percentage increase	6.92	7.10	6.63	9.55	9.87

Source Calculated based on relevant data from *China Statistical Yearbook* and Tables 7.5 and 7.12

in the secondary sector in the western region (see Table 7.12) to estimate change in overall labor productivity in the secondary sector in the western region if the FDI gap relative to the level of the eastern region were filled (see Table 7.14). If the FDI gap relative to the level in the eastern region were filled, the overall labor productivity in the secondary sector in the western region from 2000 to 2004 would increase significantly from RMB15,900 per year per person, RMB16,900 per year per person, and RMB18,100 per year per person, RMB19,900 per year per person and RMB22,300 per year per person to RMB18,800 per year per person, RMB20,300 per year per person, RMB21,600 per year per person, RMB24,400 per year per person and RMB26,500 per year per person. The percentage increases are 18.24%, 20.12%, 19.34%, 22.61% and 18.83%, respectively.

(3) Comparative analysis

Based on data in Tables 7.12 and 7.14, we can estimate the change in overall labor productivity in the secondary sector in the western region if the FDI gaps faced by the western region relative to the national average level and the level of the eastern region were filled (see Table 7.15). As can be seen from Table 7.15, the percentage change in the overall labor productivity from 2000 to 2004 is greater than the percentage change in the FDI gap. It suggests that FDI has a significant effect on improving the overall labor productivity.

In short, if the FDI gaps of the western region relative to the national average level and the level of the eastern region were filled, the overall labor productivity in the secondary sector in the western region would significantly increase and the increase

Table 7.14 Overall labor productivity in the secondary sector in the western region if the western region's FDI gap relative to the level in the eastern region were filled, Unit: RMB10 thousand per year per person, %

Year	2000	2001	2002	2003	2004
Actual value	1.59	1.69	1.81	1.99	2.23
Target value	1.88	2.03	2.16	2.44	2.65
Increase	0.29	0.34	0.35	0.45	0.42
Percentage increase	18.24	20.12	19.34	22.61	18.83

Source Calculated based on relevant data from *China Statistical Yearbook* and Tables 7.6 and 7.12

Table 7.15 Comparison between percentage change in the FDI gap and that in the overall labor productivity, Unit: %

Year	2000	2001	2002	2003	2004
Percentage change in FDI gap	38.57	37.13	33.42	28.84	19.01
Percentage change in overall labor productivity	62.07	64.71	65.71	57.78	47.62

Source Calculated based on relevant data from Tables 7.5, 7.6, 7.13 and 7.14

would continue to expand. There is a significant positive correlation between the overall labor productivity and FDI gap in the western region. After filling the FDI gaps relative to the national average level and the level of the eastern region, there are notable changes in both the growth volume and proportion. It suggests that inbound FDI has a significant effect on improving the overall labor productivity in the western region, which is consistent with the theory relating to the impact of FDI on technical efficiency.

7.2.3 The Impact of FDI on Foreign Trade of the Western Region

FDI can directly and indirectly boost foreign trade of the host region. By exporting goods, FIEs can directly contribute to foreign trade growth of the host region. Abundant evidence exists that multinational corporations (MNCs) play an important role in bolstering exports from the host region. Inbound FDI can indirectly boost exports from the host region by driving local enterprises to increase exports. Inbound FDI can increase the competition in the host region, driving local enterprises to strive to expand exports. Local enterprises can strengthen their connections with consumers in foreign markets by establishing relationships with multinational retailers and trading companies. Local procurement and subcontracting arrangements of FIEs in the manufacturing sector can strengthen the link between local businesses and the global market. Many empirical studies show that these effects are sometimes quite significant at the national level.

1. **The impact of FDI on foreign trade in the western region**

From 1995 to 2004, exports from the western region increased from USD8,699 million to USD20,594 million and exports of FIEs in the western region increased from USD533 million to USD2380 million. The contribution of FIEs to the total exports from the western region increased from 6.12 to 11.56%. From 1995 to 2004, imports into the western region increased from USD5,725 million to USD16,137 million and imports of FIEs in the western region increased from USD1,652 million to USD3783 million. The contribution of FIEs to the total imports into the western region increased from 16.52 to 37.83%. From 1995 to 2004, foreign trade (imports plus exports) of the western region increased from USD14,425 million to USD37,631 million and foreign trade of FIEs in the western region increased from USD2185 million to USD6,163 million. The contribution of FIEs to the total foreign trade of the western region increased from 15.15 to 16.78%. The increase in FIEs' share of foreign trade of the western region shows that the impact of FDI on foreign trade in the western region was growing.

2. **Change in foreign trade of the western region if the FDI gaps were filled**

(1) Change in foreign trade of the western region if the FDI gap relative to the national average level were filled

We use data on inbound FDI gap faced by the western region relative to the national average level (see Table 7.5) and the impact of FDI on foreign trade of the western region (see Table 7.16) to estimate the change in the western region's foreign trade if the FDI gap relative to the national average level were filled (see Table 7.17). If the FDI gap were filled, the value of foreign trade of the western region from 2000 to 2004 would increase significantly from USD17,166 million, USD16,837 million, USD20,607 million, USD27,920 million and USD36,731 million to USD24,996 million, USD25,945 million, USD33,566 million, USD49,851 million and USD75,372 million, respectively. The percentage increases are 45.61%, 54.10%, 62.89%, 78.55% and 105.20% respectively.

(2) Change in foreign trade of the western region if the FDI gap relative to the level of the eastern region were filled

Table 7.16 Imports and exports of FIEs in the western region, 1995–2004, Unit: USD100 million, %

Year	1995	2000	2001	2002	2003	2004
Value of exports	5.33	12.37	11.41	13.78	18.19	23.80
Share of total exports	6.12	12.46	12.61	11.70	11.20	11.56
Value of imports	16.52	12.94	14.07	18.27	25.04	37.83
Share of total imports	28.85	17.88	18.06	20.71	21.42	23.44
Value of foreign trade (exports plus imports)	21.85	25.31	25.48	32.06	43.23	61.63
Share of foreign trade	15.15	14.74	15.13	15.56	15.48	16.78

Source Calculated based on relevant data from *China Statistical Yearbook*

Table 7.17 Imports and exports of the western region if the FDI gap relative to the national average level were filled, Unit: USD100 million, %

Year	2000	2001	2002	2003	2004
Actual value	171.66	168.37	206.07	279.20	367.31
Target value	249.96	259.45	335.66	498.51	753.72
Increase	78.30	91.08	129.59	219.31	386.41
Percentage increase	45.61	54.10	62.89	78.55	105.20

Source Calculated based on relevant data from *China Statistical Yearbook* and Tables 7.5 and 7.16

We use data on inbound FDI gap faced by the western region relative to the level of the eastern region (see Table 7.6) and the impact of FDI on foreign trade of the western region (see Table 7.16) to estimate the change in the western region's foreign trade if the FDI gap relative to the level of the eastern region were filled (see Table 7.18). If the FDI gap were filled, the value of foreign trade of the western region from 2000 to 2004 would increase significantly from USD17,166 million, USD16,837 million, USD20,607 million, USD27,920 million and USD36,731 million to USD30,912 million, USD32,320 million, USD41,075 million, USD59,737 million and USD85,440 million. The percentage increases are 80.08%, 91.96%, 99.33%, 113.96% and 132.61% respectively.

Comparative analysis

Based on data in Tables 7.17 and 7.18, we can estimate the percentage change in foreign trade of the western region if the FDI gaps faced by the western region relative to the national average level and the level of the eastern region were filled (see Table 7.19). As can be seen from Table 7.19, the percentage change in foreign trade from 2000 to 2004 is greater than the percentage change in the FDI gap. It suggests that FDI has a significant effect on boosting foreign trade.

In short, if the FDI gaps of the western region relative to the national average level and the level of the eastern region were filled, foreign trade in the western region would significantly increase. There is a significant positive correlation between the growth of foreign trade and FDI gap in the western region. The changes in both the growth volume and proportion are more noticeable than the changes in the FDI gaps of the western region relative to the national average level and the level of the eastern region. It suggests that inbound FDI has a significant effect on boosting foreign trade

Table 7.18 Imports and exports of the western region if the FDI gap relative to the level of the eastern region were filled, Unit: USD100 million, %

Year	2000	2001	2002	2003	2004
Actual value	171.66	168.37	206.07	279.20	367.31
Target value	309.12	323.20	410.75	597.37	854.40
Increase	137.46	154.83	204.68	318.17	487.09
Percentage increase	80.08	91.96	99.33	113.96	132.61

Source Calculated based on relevant data from *China Statistical Yearbook* and Tables 7.6 and 7.16

Table 7.19 Comparison between percentage change in the FDI gap and that in foreign trade in the western region, Unit: %

Year	2000	2001	2002	2003	2004
Percentage change in FDI gap	38.57	37.13	33.42	28.84	19.01
Percentage change in foreign trade	43.04	41.17	36.69	31.07	20.67

Source Calculated based on relevant data from Tables 7.5, 7.6, 7.17 and 7.18

of the western region, which is consistent with the significant impact of FDI on foreign trade.

7.2.4 The Impact of FDI on Industries in the Western Region

FDI directly contributes to the improvement of the industrial structure of the host region primarily via two means: (i) the package of production factors such as capital and technology brought by FDI can change investment distribution in the host region, thereby directly improving the industrial structure of the host region; and (ii) inbound FDI can boost economic growth and income levels of local residents, which can in turn reshape the regional consumption structure, thereby indirectly promoting the improvement of the industrial structure in the host region. Other ways that FDI inflow contributes to investment structure improvement in the host region are through its demonstration effect on local businesses and its influence on local market competition. The bundle of resources brought by FDI, particularly technological assets and market networks can help the host country build emerging industries.

1. **Correlation between FDI and high-tech industries in the western region**

We use value added data of high-tech industries (expressed in 1990s constant price) and inbound FDI in 12 western provinces/municipalities/autonomous regions from 2000 to 2004 and the three most commonly used correlations in statistics to test the correlation between FDI and the development of high-tech industries in the western region (see Table 7.20).

As can be seen from Table 7.20, Pearson's correlation coefficient, Kendall's correlation coefficient and Spearman's correlation coefficient between FDI and the development of high-tech industries in the western region from 2000 to 2004 are statistically significant. It suggests that there is a significant correlation between FDI and the development of high-tech industries in the western region. It also shows that FDI has an obvious impact on the development of high-tech industries in the western region and that the development of high-tech industries in the western region is closely related to FDI. We then use regression analysis to investigate the relationship

Table 7.20 Correlation test results between FDI and the development of high-tech industries in the western region

	FDI-Vadd (2000)	FDI-Vadd (2001)	FDI-Vadd (2002)	FDI-Vadd (2003)	FDI-Vadd (2004)
Pearson	0.646 0.023	0.842 0.001	0.828 0.001	0.752 0.005	0.556 0.060
Kendall	0.687 0.002	0.545 0.014	0.667 0.003	0.727 0.001	0.534 0.016
Spearman	0.830 0.001	0.727 0.007	0.783 0.003	0.867 0.000	0.722 0.008

between FDI and value added of high-tech industries in the western region based on data for the period 2000–2004. The results are as follows:

$$
\begin{aligned}
&V = 10.400 * FDI \\
&(5.732, 0.000) \\
&\mathrm{R} = 0.866\ \mathrm{adjR}^2 = 0.749\ \mathrm{F} = 32.855\ \mathrm{Sig.F} = 0.000 \qquad (7.1)
\end{aligned}
$$

As we can see from the T-value, the R^2 value, and the F-value, the model has a high degree of significance and provides a good fitting. According to the regression model, if an additional USD100 million of FDI flows into the western region, the value added of high-tech industries in the western region will increase by RMB1.04 billion.

2. **Change in value added of high-tech industries in the western region after filling the FDI gaps**

(1) Change in value added of high-tech industries in the western region if the western region's FDI gap relative to the national average level were filled

We use data on inbound FDI gap faced by the western region relative to the national average level (see Table 7.5) and the impact of FDI on the development of high-tech industries in the western region (see model (7.1)) to analyze the change in the value added of high-tech industries in the western region if the FDI gap relative to the national average level were filled (see Table 7.21). If the FDI gap relative to the national average level were filled, the value added of high-tech industries from 2000 to 2004 would increase significantly from RMB28,906 million, RMB32,474 million, RMB37,763 million, RMB40,653 million and RMB48,180 million to RMB78,832 million, RMB91,426 million, RMB105,186 million, RMB108,805 million and RMB131,851 million, respectively. And the percentage increases are 164.45%, 181.54%, 178.54%, 167.64% and 173.66%, respectively. Assuming that value added of other industries remains unchanged, the contribution of high-tech industries to the western region's GDP would increase from 8.62%, 8.43%, 8.52%, 7.51% and 7.38% to 19.97%, 20.58%, 20.60%, 17.85% and 17.90%, respectively.

(2) Change in value added of high-tech industries in the western region if the western region's FDI gap relative to the level of the eastern region were filled

We use data on inbound FDI gap faced by the western region relative to the level of the eastern region (see Table 7.6) and the impact of FDI on the development of high-tech industries in the western region [see model (7.1)] to analyze the change in the value added of high-tech industries in the western region if the FDI gap relative to the level of the eastern region were filled (see Table 7.22). If the FDI gap relative to the level of the eastern region were filled, the value added of high-tech industries from 2000 to 2004 would increase significantly from RMB28,906 million, RMB32,474 million, RMB37,763 million, RMB40,653 million and RMB48,180 million to RMB116,230 million, RMB133,598 million, RMB147,524 million, RMB145,642 million and

Table 7.21 Value added of high-tech industries in the western region if the western region's FDI gap relative to the national average level were filled, Unit: RMB100 million, %

Year		2000	2001	2002	2003	2004
Value added of high-tech industries	Actual value	298.06	324.74	377.63	406.53	481.80
	Target value	788.22	914.26	1051.86	1088.05	1318.51
	Increase	490.16	589.52	674.23	681.52	836.71
	Percentage increase	164.45	181.54	178.54	167.64	173.66
Contribution of high-tech industries to the western region's GDP	Actual value	8.62	8.43	8.52	7.51	7.38
	Target value	19.97	20.58	20.60	17.85	17.90

Source Calculated based on relevant data from *China Statistical Yearbook on High Technology Industries* and Table 7.5

RMB158,538 million, respectively. And the corresponding percentage increases are 289.96%, 311.40%, 290.66%, 258.26% and 229.05%, respectively. Assuming that the value added of other industries remains unchanged, the contribution of high-tech industries to the western region's GDP would increase from 8.62%, 8.43%, 8.52%, 7.51% and 7.38% to 26.89%, 27.47%, 26.68%, 22.53% and 20.77%, respectively.

Comparative analysis

Data on the percentage change in value added of high-tech industries after filling the FDI gaps relative to the national average level and the level of the eastern region are available in Tables 7.21 and 7.22. As can be seen from Table 7.23, the percentage change in value added of high-tech industries from 2000 to 2004 is greater than the percentage change in the FDI gap. It suggests that inbound FDI has a significant effect on the development of high-tech industries in the western region.

Table 7.22 Value added of high-tech industries in the western region if the western region's FDI gap relative to the level of the eastern region were filled, Unit: RMB100 million, %

Year		2000	2001	2002	2003	2004
Value added of high-tech industries	Actual value	298.06	324.74	377.63	406.53	481.80
	Target value	1162.30	1335.98	1475.24	1456.42	1585.38
	Increase	864.24	1011.24	1097.61	1049.89	1103.58
	Percentage increase	289.96	311.40	290.66	258.26	229.05
Contribution of high-tech industries to the western region's GDP	Actual value	8.62	8.43	8.52	7.51	7.38
	Target value	26.89	27.47	26.68	22.53	20.77

Source Calculated based on relevant data from *China Statistical Yearbook on High Technology Industries* and Table 7.6

Table 7.23 Comparison between the percentage change in FDI gap and that in the value added of high-tech industries, Unit: %

Year	2000	2001	2002	2003	2004
Percentage change in FDI gap	38.57	37.13	33.42	28.84	19.01
Percentage change in the value added of high-tech industries	43.28	41.70	38.57	35.09	24.18

Source Calculated based on relevant data from Tables 7.5, 7.6, 7.21 and 7.22

In short, filling the FDI gaps relative to the national average level and the level of the eastern region would lead to an increase in the value added of high-tech industries in the western region, and the increase would expand. The industrial structure improves significantly. The changes in the growth volume and proportion are more noticeable than the changes in the FDI gaps of the western region relative to the national average level and the level of the eastern region. It suggests that inbound FDI has a significant effect on fueling the development of high-tech industries of the western region, which is consistent with the significant impact of FDI on high-tech industries.

7.3 Loss of Opportunities for Economic Development as a Result of the FDI Gap

Because the quantity of FDI flowing into the western region is small, FDI has little effect on economic drivers in the western region, which further leads to loss of opportunities for economic development in terms of both quantity and quality. Before analyzing the extent of the loss, we first need to analyze the influence of various economic drivers on the economic growth of the western region and then study the influence of FDI on the economic growth of the western region. Then, we can draw the conclusion that because the quantity of FDI flowing into the western region is small, the region is losing opportunities for economic growth.

7.3.1 The Economic Growth Function of the Western Region

1. **The economic growth function**

Based on economic drivers in mainstream growth models, we decompose the Solow residual using the Cobb-Douglas production function, and add exports, imports, and technological progress. The economic growth function we get is:

$$GDP = AK^{\alpha}L^{\beta}E^{\lambda}I^{\omega}e^{\phi * T} \tag{7.2}$$

where GDP, K, L, E, I, and T denote output, capital, labor, exports, imports, and technology, respectively. Taking natural logarithms on both sides of Eq. (7.2), we get the economic growth model to be estimated:

$$\begin{aligned}\ln GDP &= A + \alpha * \ln K + \beta * \ln L \\ &\quad + \lambda * \ln E + \omega \ln I + \varphi * T + \varepsilon\end{aligned} \tag{7.3}$$

where A, α, β, λ, ω, φ are parameters to be estimated, and ε is the random error term.

As we already know that there is an obvious correlation among capital, labor, imports, exports, and technology, that is, there is serious multicollinearity[4] in formula (7.3), we use ridge regression to estimate the parameters in the above equation. Our principle for selecting the ridge parameter K is that K should be as small as possible on the basis of ensuring that the ridge trace is stable and that the direction and significance of the regression coefficients of each explanatory variable are consistent with the correlation analysis results.

2. **Data sources and processing**

(1) Data sources

We use data from *China Statistical Yearbook* to calculate GDP, workforce, exports, imports, and labor productivity of the secondary sector. Gross capital stock is calculated by adding investment in this period to the capital stock in the previous period and subtracting the value of assets that have reached the end of their useful life during this period. The gross capital stock in 1989 is estimated based on the net value of fixed assets owned by the state and SOE's contribution to GDP in 1989.

(2) Data processing

Expressing values at constant prices of 1990: The values of indicators related to capital formation, such as GDP, gross capital stock, exports, imports, and labor productivity in the secondary sector, are converted with the corresponding deflator into values at constant prices in 1990.

Logarithmic transformation: Take the natural log of absolute GDP, capital stock, workforce, exports, and imports to obtain the data consistent with the linear estimation outcomes of the growth function model.

Centralization and standardization: Subtract the mean value from datasets of GDP, capital stock, workforce, exports, imports, and labor productivity in the secondary sector and then divide the results by the standard deviation of the corresponding dataset. This process can account for the impact of inconsistent units of measure and help reduce multicollinearity among independent variables, producing outcomes that reflect the changes in the variables.

---

[4] In OLS analysis, because the variance expansion factors are all bigger than 10 and the smallest characteristic roots of X'X are closer to 0, there is still significant multicollinearity among the independent variables even after logarithmic processing. The variance expansion factors are $VIF_1 = 316.0$, $VIF_2 = 14.0$, $VIF_3 = 324.0$, and $VIF_4 = 88.1$ and the characteristic roots are $\lambda_1 = 0.00182$, $\lambda_2 = 0.00347$, $\lambda_3 = 0.0253$, and $\lambda_4 = 0.0855$.

3. **Model fitting and testing**

The minimum K-value that can ensure the ridge trace is stable and that the direction and significance of the regression coefficients of each explanatory variable are consistent with the correlation analysis is 0.08. The results of ridge regression are as follows:

Result 1: Goodness-of-fit. R = 0.9972 $R^2 = 0.9944$ Corrected $R^2 = 0.9922$
Result 2: The overall significance of the equation (see Table 7.24).
Result 3: Significance of regression coefficients (see Table 7.25).

The results of ridge regression show that the model's goodness of fit is 0.9972, which is just 0.0021 lower than that of OLS. Although the F-value has dropped notably, the model still has a high level of significance. The probability of being statistically insignificant is less than 0.0000001. The positive sign of the regression coefficients is consistent with the positive correlation between the explanatory variables and the response variable. The regression coefficients are significantly different from zero, which is consistent with the significant correlation between the explanatory variables and the response variable. Therefore, the ridge regression model not only improves the robustness of the test results but also reflects the real economic changes. The ridge regression equation is as follows:

$$\ln GDP = -0.000013 + 0.396753 * \ln K + 0.058765 * \ln L \\ + 0.142274 * \ln M + 0.401388 * T \quad (7.4)$$

Decentralizing and destandardizing Eq. (7.4), we get the following results:

$$\ln GDP = 1.147184 + 0.229180 * \ln K + 0.409542 * \ln L$$

Table 7.24 Analysis of variance

Statistical value	df	SS	MS	F	Sig.F
Regression	4.000	13.922	3.480	444.5695154	0.0000000
Residual	10.000	0.078	0.008		

Table 7.25 Statistical values of regression coefficients

Statistical value	B	SE (B)	Beta	T = B/SEB	Sig.T
lnK	0.396753	0.025454	0.396748	15.586974	0.000000
lnL	0.058765	0.032389	0.058765	1.814376	0.049844
lnM	0.142274	0.033813	0.142273	4.207740	0.000903
T	0.401388	0.028223	0.401379	14.222065	0.000000
Constant	-0.000013	0.022846	0.000000	-0.000580	0.499774

$$+ 0.086246 * \ln M + 0.315925 * T \tag{7.5}$$

Therefore, the economic growth function for the western region is:

$$GDP = 3.149312 * K^{0.229180} * L^{0.409542} * M^{0.086246} * e^{0.315925*T} \tag{7.6}$$

7.3.2 *FDI Gap and Loss of Opportunities for Economic Growth in the Western Region*

FDI has an impact on many different economic drivers. Some of these drivers only affect the quantity of economic growth, but some not only affect the quantity of economic growth but also the quality of economic growth. Therefore, the existence of the FDI gap in the western region will lead to loss of opportunities for economic development in terms of both quantity and quality.

1. **Loss of growth opportunities**

FDI has a significant impact on economic factors such as capital, imports and exports, and productivity. The estimation results of the loss of economic growth opportunities are different because the FDI gaps of the western region relative to the national average level and the level of eastern region are different.

(1) Loss of economic growth opportunities in the western region based on the FDI gap of the western region relative to the national average level

(i) Capital

We hold other factors constant and employ the economic growth function for the western region (7.6) and data on the impact of FDI on capital stock to calculate regional GDP if the FDI gap of the western region relative to the national average level were filled (see Table 7.26). The existence of the FDI gap gives rise to loss of quantitative growth opportunities associated with capital formation, but the loss is relatively small and continues to decrease. The loss of quantitative growth opportunities in 2000 was the largest, estimated at RMB3.591 billion, accounting for 0.40% of the actual GDP. It dropped to RMB19 million in 2004, accounting for less than one ten-thousandth of the actual GDP.

(ii) Imports and exports

We hold other factors constant and employ the economic growth function for the western region (7.6) and data on the impact of FDI on foreign trade to calculate regional GDP if the FDI gap of the western region relative to the national average

Table 7.26 GDP of the western region if the FDI gap of the western region relative to the national average level were filled (only considering change in capital stock), Unit: RMB100 million, %

Year	2000	2001	2002	2003	2004
Regional GDP	9091.16	9830.06	10870.78	12130.02	14198.81
Increase in regional GDP	35.91	24.55	11.24	4.10	0.19
The ratio of the increase to actual GDP	0.40	0.25	0.10	0.03	0.001

Source Calculated based on relevant data from *China Statistical Yearbook (2005)* and Table 7.8

level were filled (see Table 7.27). The existence of the FDI gap gives rise to loss of quantitative growth opportunities associated with foreign trade. The loss of quantitative growth opportunities associated with foreign trade is significant and fluctuates greatly. The loss from 2000 to 2004 was RMB31,906 million, RMB22,743 million, RMB21,506 million, RMB54,354 million and RMB63,859 million, respectively, all higher than RMB200,00 million, accounting for a large proportion of the actual GDP, with the lowest being close to 2%. It suggests that the loss of quantitative growth opportunities associated with foreign trade as a result of the FDI gap is significant. The disparities in the loss of quantitative growth opportunities associated with foreign trade between years are significant, with the largest being nearly three times the smallest. The fluctuations in this figure are consistent with the fluctuations in the FDI gap, but the fluctuations in this figure are larger than the fluctuations in the FDI gap. This shows that the impact of FDI on economic growth attributable to foreign trade tends to increase.

(iii) Labor productivity

We hold other factors constant and employ the economic growth function for the western region (7.6) and data on the impact of FDI on labor productivity to calculate regional GDP if the FDI gap of the western region relative to the national average level were filled (see Table 7.28). The existence of the FDI gap gives rise to loss of quantitative growth opportunities associated with labor productivity. The loss of quantitative growth opportunities associated with labor productivity is significant and

Table 7.27 GDP of the western region if the FDI gap of the western region relative to the national average level were filled (only changes in foreign trade are considered), Unit: RMB100 million, %

Year	2000	2001	2002	2003	2004
Regional GDP	9,374.31	10,032.94	11,074.61	12,669.45	14,837.21
Increase in regional GDP	319.06	227.43	215.06	543.54	638.59
The ratio of the increase to actual GDP	3.52	2.32	1.98	4.48	4.50

Source Calculated based on relevant data from *China Statistical Yearbook (2005)* and Table 7.17

fluctuates greatly. The loss from 2000 to 2004 was RMB32,903 million, RMB22,880 million, RMB15,467 million, RMB66,828 million, and RMB77,223 million, respectively, with the largest being five times the smallest. The remarkable fluctuations can be largely explained by the significant impact of FDI on economic growth via its influence on labor productivity.

(iv) Total loss of quantitative growth opportunities in the western region if the FDI gap of the western region relative to the national average level were filled

We calculate the total loss of quantitative growth opportunities in the western region based on the FDI gap of the western region relative to the national average level by adding the estimation results of loss associated with capital, foreign trade and labor productivity which we have obtained using the growth function (7.6) (Table 7.29). The existence of the FDI gap gives rise to loss of quantitative growth opportunities associated with various economic factors. The loss is significant and grows with the FDI gap. The ratio of the loss to actual regional GDP is quite high. The loss from 2000 to 2004 was RMB65,500 million, RMB78,720 million, RMB90,114 million, RMB141,088 million, and RMB201,926 million, accounting for 7.23%, 8.03%, 8.30%, 11.64%, and 14.22% of the actual regional GDP respectively. The loss of the economic growth rate was 0.77%, 0.80%, 0.28%, 3.44%, and 2.71% respectively.

Table 7.28 GDP of the western region if the FDI gap of the western region relative to the national average level were filled (only changes in labor productivity are considered), Unit: RMB100 million, %

Year	2000	2001	2002	2003	2004
Regional GDP	9384.28	10,034.31	11,014.22	12,794.19	14,970.85
Increase in regional GDP	329.03	228.80	154.67	668.28	772.23
The ratio of the increase to actual GDP	3.63	2.33	1.42	5.51	5.44

Source Calculated based on relevant data from *China Statistical Yearbook (2005)* and Table 7.13

Table 7.29 GDP of the western region if the FDI gap of the western region relative to the national average level were filled, Unit: RMB100 million, %

Year	2000	2001	2002	2003	2004
Regional GDP	9710.25	10,592.71	11,760.69	13,536.79	16,217.88
Increase in regional GDP	655.00	787.20	901.14	1410.88	2019.26
The ratio of the increase to actual GDP	7.23	8.03	8.30	11.64	14.22
Percentage increase in the growth rate of regional GDP	0.77	0.80	0.28	3.44	2.71

Source Calculated based on relevant data from *China Statistical Yearbook (2005)* and Tables 7.8, 7.13 and 7.17

(2) Loss of quantitative growth opportunities in the western region if its FDI gap relative to the level of the eastern region were filled

(i) Capital

We hold other factors constant and employ the economic growth function for the western region and data on the impact of FDI on capital stock to calculate regional GDP of the western region if the FDI gap of the western region relative to the level of the eastern region were filled (see Table 7.30). The existence of the FDI gap in the western region relative to the level of the eastern region leads to loss of quantitative growth opportunities associated with capital formation, but the loss associated with capital formulation is relatively small and continues to decrease. The percentage of such loss to the actual regional GDP is also quite low. The loss from 2000 to 2004 was RMB4584 million, RMB3367 million, RMB2119 million, RMB2042 million, and RMB1907 million, accounting for only 0.51, 0.34, 0.20, 0.17, and 0.13% of the actual regional GDP. This downward trend indicates that the direct impact of FDI on economic growth by increasing capital stock is declining.

(ii) Imports and exports

We hold other factors constant and employ the economic growth function for the western region and data on the impact of FDI on foreign trade to calculate regional GDP if the FDI gap of the western region relative to the level of the eastern region were filled (see Table 7.31). The existence of the FDI gap gives rise to loss of quantitative growth opportunities associated with foreign trade. This loss is significant, accounting for a relatively large proportion of the actual GDP, and fluctuates greatly. The loss from 2000 to 2004 was RMB46,535 million, RMB39,168 million, RMB38,565 million, RMB72,404 million and RMB78,468 million, respectively, accounting for 5.14%, 3.99%, 3.55%, 5.97%, and 5.53% of the actual regional GDP.

Table 7.30 GDP of the western region if the FDI gap of the western region relative to the level of the eastern region were filled (only changes in capital stock are considered), Unit: RMB100 million, %

Year	2000	2001	2002	2003	2004
Regional GDP	9101.09	9839.18	10,880.74	12,146.33	14,217.69
Increase in regional GDP	45.84	33.67	21.19	20.42	19.07
The ratio of the increase to actual GDP	0.51	0.34	0.20	0.17	0.13

Source Calculated based on relevant data from *China Statistical Yearbook (2005)* and Table 7.9

Table 7.31 GDP of the western region if the FDI gap of the western region relative to the level of the eastern region were filled (only changes in foreign trade are considered), Unit: RMB100 million, %

Year	2000	2001	2002	2003	2004
Regional GDP	9520.60	10,197.19	11,245.20	12,849.96	14,983.30
Increase in regional GDP	465.35	391.68	385.65	724.04	784.68
The ratio of the increase to actual GDP	5.14	3.99	3.55	5.97	5.53

Source Calculated based on relevant data from *China Statistical Yearbook (2005)* and Table 7.18

(iii) Labor productivity

We hold other factors constant and employ the economic growth function for the western region and data on the impact of FDI on labor productivity to calculate regional GDP if the FDI gap of the western region relative to the level of the eastern region were filled (see Table 7.32). The existence of the FDI gap gives rise to loss of quantitative growth opportunities associated with labor productivity. This loss is significant, accounting for a relatively large proportion of the actual GDP, and fluctuates greatly. The loss from 2000 to 2004 was RMB88,491 million, RMB93,651 million, RMB98,937 million, RMB176,371 million and RMB174,357 million respectively, accounting for 9.77%, 9.55%, 9.11%, 14.54%, and 12.28% of the actual regional GDP.

(iv) The total loss of quantitative growth opportunities in the western region if the FDI gap of the western region relative to the level of the eastern region were filled

We calculate the total loss of quantitative growth opportunities in the western region based on the FDI gap of the western region relative to the level of the eastern region by adding the estimation results of loss associated with capital, foreign trade and labor productivity which we have obtained using the growth function (7.6) (Table 7.33). The existence of the FDI gap gives rise to loss of quantitative growth opportunities associated with various economic factors. This loss is significant and grows with the FDI gap. The ratio of the loss to actual regional GDP is quite high. The loss

Table 7.32 GDP of the western region if the FDI gap of the western region relative to the level of the eastern region were filled (only changes in labor productivity are considered), Unit: RMB100 million, %

Year	2000	2001	2002	2003	2004
Regional GDP	9940.16	10,742.03	11,848.92	13,889.62	15,942.19
Increase in regional GDP	884.91	936.51	989.37	1763.71	1743.57
The ratio of the increase to actual GDP	9.77	9.55	9.11	14.54	12.28

Source Calculated based on relevant data from *China Statistical Yearbook (2005)* and Table 7.14

from 2000 to 2004 was RMB140,210 million, RMB173,063 million, RMB199,906 million, RMB279,932 million and RMB326,474 million respectively, accounting for 15.48%, 17.65%, 18.41%, 23.09% and 22.99% of the actual regional GDP. The loss of the economic growth rate was 1.64, 2.03, 0.71, 4.41 and 0.09%.

(3) Comparison analysis

We use data in Tables 7.26, 7.27, 7.28, 7.29, 7.30, 7.31, 7.32 and 7.33 to estimate the percentage change in the loss of quantitative growth opportunities (measured by decline in regional GDP) of the western region if the FDI gaps of the western region relative to the national average level and the level of the eastern region were filled (see Table 7.34). As can be seen from Table 7.34, the percentage change in the loss of quantitative growth opportunities from 2000 to 2004 is greater than the percentage change in the FDI gap. It suggests that the introduction of FDI has a significant effect on accelerating economic growth and the effect is growing

In summary, among the major economic drivers affected by FDI, FDI has the greatest impact on labor productivity, followed by foreign trade and capital. Due to the existence of the FDI gaps in the western region relative to the national average level and the level of the eastern region, there is a loss of opportunity for regional GDP growth that is positively correlated with the FDI gap. The larger the gap, the larger the loss. And the percentage change in the loss is growing.

2. **Loss of qualitative growth opportunities**

Increasing the share of eco-friendly industries and reshaping the industrial structure are the main ways that FDI affects the quality of economic growth in the host region.

Table 7.33 GDP of the western region if the FDI gap of the western region relative to the level of the eastern region were filled, Unit: RMB100 million

Year	2000	2001	2002	2003	2004
Regional GDP	10,457.35	11,536.14	12,858.61	14,925.23	17,463.36
Increase in regional GDP	1402.10	1730.63	1999.06	2799.32	3264.74
The ratio of the increase to actual GDP	15.48	17.65	18.41	23.09	22.99
Percentage increase in the growth rate of regional GDP	1.64	2.03	0.71	4.41	0.09

Source Calculated based on relevant data from *China Statistical Yearbook (2005)* and Tables 7.9, 7.14 and 7.18

Table 7.34 Percentage change in the decline of regional GDP, Unit: %

Year	2000	2001	2002	2003	2004
Percentage change in the decline of regional GDP	53.28	54.51	54.92	49.60	38.15
Percentage change in FDI gap	38.57	37.13	33.42	28.84	19.01

Source Calculated based on relevant data from Tables 7.29 and 7.33

High-tech companies report lower energy consumption, wastewater discharge, waste gas emissions, and solid waste discharge per unit of value added than many traditional industries. In other words, high-tech companies use less energy and cause less pollution than conventional industries for the same amount of GDP growth. During the period from 2000 to 2004, one metric ton of standard coal equivalent of energy consumption could generate a value added of RMB3500 in the secondary sector and RMB19,600 in high-tech industries; similarly, one ton of wastewater, one standard cubic meter of waste gas and one ton of solid waste discharged could generate a value added of RMB2,544,200, RMB2100, and RMB55,222,000, respectively, in the secondary sector and RMB9,032,900, RMB18,500 and RMB938,126,900 in high-tech industries. Compared with other forms of investment, FDI plays a greater role in promoting the development of high-tech industries and can more effectively contribute to qualitative economic growth.

(1) Change in energy consumption and waste emissions in the western region provided that inbound FDI per unit of GDP of the western region reached the national average level

We use data on the FDI gap relative to the national level and the impact of FDI on the development of high-tech industries to estimate the value added of high-tech industries if the FDI gap were filled, and then use data in Table 7.35 to calculate energy consumption for wastewater discharge, waste gas emissions and solid waste discharge of high-tech industries and the secondary sector.[5] The estimation results are listed in Table 7.36. The levels of energy consumption and waste emissions per unit of value added in high-tech industries mainly driven by FDI are much lower than those in the secondary industry (excluding high-tech industries) mainly driven by other types of investment. If the FDI gap relative to the national average level were filled, energy saved in the creation of value added of high-tech industries from 2000 to 2004 would be 11,503,800, 13,835,700, 15,823,800, 15,994,900, and 19,637,100 metric tons of standard coal compared with other secondary industries, respectively. The amount of energy saved accounts for more than 10% of the actual energy consumption in high-tech industries. The ratios of wastewater discharge, waste gas emissions, and solid waste discharge to the actual amount of discharge/emissions are also in the neighborhood of 10%.

(2) Change in energy consumption and waste emissions in the western region provided that inbound FDI per unit of GDP of the western region reached the level of the eastern region

[5] In the process of calculation, we use national energy efficiency and waste emissions data to estimate energy efficiency and waste emissions in the western region. We also assume the distribution of FDI and other types of investment across industries is fixed.

Table 7.35 Growth quality of high-tech industries and the secondary sector[6]

Industry	Energy consumption (RMB10,000 per metric ton of standard coal)	Wastewater discharge (RMB10,000 per ton)	Waste gas discharge (RMB1 per standard cubic meter)	Solid waste discharge (RMB10,000 per ton)
Secondary sector	0.35	254.42	0.21	5522.20
High-tech industries	1.96	903.29	1.85	93,812.69

Source Calculated based on relevant data from *China Statistical Yearbook* from 2001 to 2004

We use data on the FDI gap relative to the level of the eastern region and the impact of FDI on the development of high-tech industries to estimate the value added of high-tech industries if the FDI gap were filled, and then use data in Table 7.35 to calculate energy consumption for wastewater discharge, waste gas emissions and solid waste discharge of high-tech industries and the secondary sector. The estimation results are listed in Table 7.37. If the FDI gap relative to the national average level were filled, energy saved for the value added of high-tech industries from 2000 to 2004 would be 20,283,200, 23,733,200, 25,760,200, 24,640,300, and 25,900,300 metric tons of standard coal compared with other secondary industries. The amount of energy saved in some years accounts for more than 20% of the actual energy consumption in high-tech industries. The ratios of wastewater discharge, waste gas emissions, and solid waste discharge to the actual amount of discharge/emissions are in the neighborhood of 10%.

(3) Comparison analysis

We use data in Tables 7.36 and 7.37 to estimate the percentage change in energy saved and emissions saved in the western region provided that the FDI gaps of the western region relative to the national average level and the level of the eastern region were filled (see Table 7.38). As can be seen from Table 7.38, the percentage change in energy saved and emissions saved from 2000 to 2004 is greater than the percentage change in the FDI gap. It suggests that the introduction of FDI has a significant effect on improving the quality of economic growth. In other words, inbound FDI plays an important role in increasing the contribution of resource-saving, eco-friendly industries to economic growth.

[6] For purpose of this study, high-tech industries include ICT manufacturing, electrical machinery and equipment manufacturing, instrument and office machinery manufacturing, special equipment manufacturing, and pharmaceutical manufacturing.

Table 7.36 Amount of energy and waste emissions that could be saved by high-tech industries provided that inbound FDI per unit of GDP of the western region reached the national average level

Year		2000	2001	2002	2003	2004
Energy consumption	Energy saved (10,000 metric tons of standard coal)	1150.38	1383.57	1582.38	1599.49	1963.71
	The ratio of the amount of energy saved to the actual energy consumption (%)	11.64	12.57	12.50	10.34	10.53
Wastewater	Emissions saved (10,000 metric tons)	13,839.47	16,644.63	19,036.60	19,242.43	23,624.10
	The ratio of the amount of emissions saved to the actual discharge (%)	10.18	10.99	10.93	9.04	9.21
Waste gas	Emissions saved (100 million standard cubic meter)	2069.15	2488.57	2846.17	2876.95	3532.06
	The ratio of the amount of emissions saved to the actual discharge (%)	12.57	13.57	13.49	11.16	11.36
Solid waste	Emissions saved (10,000 metric tons)	835.37	1004.70	1149.07	1161.50	1425.99
	The ratio of the amount of emissions saved to the actual discharge (%)	13.34	14.40	14.32	11.85	12.06

Source Calculated based on relevant data from *China Statistical Yearbook* and Tables 7.21 and 7.35

Table 7.37 Amount of energy and waste emissions that could be saved by high-tech industries provided that inbound FDI per unit of GDP of the western region reached the level of eastern region

Year		2000	2001	2002	2003	2004
Energy consumption	Energy saved (10,000 metric tons of standard coal)	2028.32	2373.32	2576.02	2464.03	2590.03
	The ratio of the amount of energy saved to the actual energy consumption (%)	20.53	21.56	20.34	15.93	13.89
Wastewater	Emissions saved (10,000 metric tons)	24,401.34	28,551.80	30,990.41	29,643.06	31,158.97
	The ratio of the amount of emissions saved to the actual discharge (%)	17.95	18.86	17.79	13.93	12.14
Waste gas	Emissions saved (100 million standard cubic meter)	3648.27	4268.81	4633.41	4431.97	4658.61
	The ratio of the amount of emissions saved to the actual discharge (%)	22.16	23.27	21.95	17.19	14.99
Solid waste	Emissions saved (10,000 metric tons)	1472.90	1723.43	1870.63	1789.30	1880.81
	The ratio of the amount of emissions saved to the actual discharge (%)	23.52	24.71	23.31	18.25	15.91

Source Calculated based on relevant data from *China Statistical Yearbook* and Tables 7.22 and 7.35

Table 7.38 Percentage change in energy saved and emissions saved, Unit: %

Year	2000	2001	2002	2003	2004
Percentage change in energy saved and emissions saved	43.28	41.70	38.57	35.09	24.18
Percentage change in FDI gap	38.57	37.13	33.42	28.84	19.01

Source Calculated based on relevant data from Tables 7.36 and 7.37

7.3.3 Change in the Development Gap Between the Western Region and the National Average Level and Between the Western and the Eastern Regions After Filling the FDI Gap

1. **Change in the development gap between the western region and the national average level after filling the FDI gap**

If the FDI gap of the western region relative to the national average level were filled, the development gap between the western region and the national average level would narrow significantly. In 2004, the disparity between GDP per capita of the western region and the country's GDP per capita was RMB1414.93 per person, and the percentage gap was 27.01%. After filling the FDI gap relative to the national average level, the per capita GDP of the western region would be RMB4368.22 per person, and the gap with the national average level would narrow to RMB871.05, and the percentage gap would drop to 16.63%. The FDI gap contributed to 38.44% of the gap in GDP per capita in 2004. The data from 2000 to 2003 reflect similar changes in the gap (see Table 7.39). The results suggest that the introduction of FDI has an obvious effect of narrowing the development gap between the western region and the national average level.

2. **Change in the development gap between the western and eastern regions after filling the FDI gap**

If the FDI gap of the western region relative to the level of the eastern region were filled, the development gap between the western and eastern regions would narrow significantly. In 2004, the disparity in GDP per capita between the western region and the eastern region was RMB6197.09 per person, and the percentage gap was 61.84%. After filling the FDI gap relative to the level of the eastern region, the per capita GDP of the western region would be RMB4703.68 per person, and the gap with the eastern region would narrow to RMB5317.75, and the percentage gap would

Table 7.39 Comparison of the gap in GDP per capita between the western region and the national average level before and after filling the FDI gap

Year	2000	2001	2002	2003	2004
Actual gap in GDP per capita (RMB1 per person)	1350.57	1421.08	1463.08	1528.89	1414.93
Gap in GDP per capita after filling the FDI gap (RMB1 per person)	1169.60	1205.19	1217.61	1146.72	871.05
Actual percentage gap (%)	35.06	34.56	33.08	31.77	27.01
Percentage gap after filling the FDI gap (%)	30.36	29.31	27.53	23.83	16.63
Percentage change in the gap of GDP per capita (%)	13.40	15.19	16.78	25.00	38.44

Source Calculated based on relevant data from *China Statistical Yearbook* and Table 7.29

Table 7.40 Comparison of the gap in GDP per capita between the western and eastern regions before and after filling the FDI gap

Year	2000	2001	2002	2003	2004
Actual gap in GDP per capita (RMB1 per person)	3847.9	4193.61	4638.05	5329.82	6197.09
Gap in GDP per capita after filling the FDI gap (RMB1 per person)	3460.50	3718.87	4093.34	4571.62	5317.75
Actual percentage gap (%)	60.60	60.92	61.04	61.88	61.84
Percentage gap after filling the FDI gap (%)	54.50	54.02	53.87	53.07	53.06
Percentage change in the gap of GDP per capita (%)	10.07	11.32	11.74	14.23	14.19

Source Calculated based on relevant data from *China Statistical Yearbook* and Table 7.33

drop to 53.06%. The FDI gap contributed to 14.19% of the gap in GDP per capita in 2004. The data from 2000 to 2003 reflect similar changes in the gap (see Table 7.40). The results suggest that the introduction of FDI has an obvious effect of narrowing the development gap between the western and eastern regions.

7.4 Conclusion

1. The period from 1990 to 2004 saw a hike in FDI in the western region followed by a gentle decline with some fluctuations, in contrast with the continuous growth of FDI flowing into the eastern region and that of the whole country. The western region's share of the country's FDI is disproportionately low compared to its share of the country's GDP, and this discordance is still growing. A large number of empirical studies have demonstrated a strong correlation between the quantity of FDI flowing into a region and the size of the regional economy. Due to the difference in the size of economy, there is an FDI gap between the western region and the national average level as well as between the western and eastern regions. Whether the western region's FDI inflow per unit of GDP reached the national average level or the level of the eastern region, the western region would face a large FDI gap (expressed as a dollar amount and percentage). In both scenarios, the FDI gap expressed as a dollar amount is widening; the percentage gap remains high with some fluctuations. It drops first and then rises sharply, forming a U-shaped curve.
2. FDI has a significant impact on capital, technology, imports and exports, and structure, but the degree of influence varies. First, inbound FDI can increase the capital stock, accelerate capital formation, and provide capital to finance its development. But because the growth of FDI in fixed assets is slow and the ratio of FDI to the total investment in fixed assets in the western region is low,

the impact of FDI on capital formation in the western region is small and this direct impact is slowing down. Second, in the western region, foreign-invested enterprises (FIEs) are more active than other types of enterprises in research and development. FIEs have a significant demonstration effect on technological progress in the region. They have also played an important role in improving the technological efficiency in the region. Third, the increase in FIEs' share of foreign trade of the western region shows that the impact of FDI on foreign trade in the western region is growing. Fourth, there is a significant correlation between FDI and value added of high-tech industries in the western region. If an additional USD100 million of FDI flows into the western region, the value added of high-tech industries in the western region will increase by RMB1.04 billion. Inbound FDI can effectively improve the regional industrial structure.

3. Provided that the FDI gap of the western region relative to the national average level and the level of the eastern region were filled, factors such as capital, technology, foreign trade, and industrial structure would change to various extents. First, the change in the FDI gap is greater than the change in capital stock growth. It suggests that inbound FDI would not accelerate capital stock growth in the western region. Second, the labor productivity in the secondary sector in the western region would significantly increases and the increase would continue to expand. There is a significant positive correlation between labor productivity and FDI gap in the western region. Third, foreign trade in the western region would significantly increase. There is a significant positive correlation between the growth of foreign trade and FDI gap in the western region. The change in the increase and percentage increase is more noticeable than the change in the FDI gap of the western region relative to the national average level and the level of the eastern region. It suggests that inbound FDI has a significant effect on boosting foreign trade of the western region. Fourth, the value added of high-tech industries in the western region would increase significantly and the increase would expand. The change in the increase and percentage increase is more noticeable than the change in the FDI gap of the western region relative to the national average level and the level of the eastern region. It suggests that inbound FDI has a significant effect on fueling the development of high-tech industries of the western region.
4. After filling the FDI gap relative to the national and eastern absorption levels, the regional GDP and its growth rate in the western region have increased and improved to varying degrees, and the larger the gap is filled, the greater the increase in GDP, that is, the greater the loss of opportunity growth quantity. And after filling the FDI gap, energy consumption and industrial "three wastes" emissions will be significantly reduced, that is, there is a significant opportunity to improve the quality of growth. Therefore, the FDI gap will cause the economic growth in the west to lose opportunities in terms of growth quantity and growth quality. After filling the FDI gap relative to the national and eastern absorption levels, the gap between the western and national per capita GDP narrowed from

RMB1414.93 per person to RMB871.05 in 2004, and the gap dropped from 27.01 to 16.63%. The gap has narrowed from RMB6197.09 per person to RMB5317.75, and the gap has dropped from 61.84 to 53.06%. Therefore, filling the FDI gap in the west can effectively promote the narrowing of the development gap between the west, the whole country and the east.

Chapter 8
Assessment of the Investment Climate of Western China

The investment climate is the sum of all external factors that affect investment, or more specifically, the cost and benefit for the investors and investees in the process. Western China needs to attract more foreign capital to fuel local economic development and narrow the economic gap between it and the central and eastern regions. A sound investment climate is thus required. In this chapter, by using key success factors (KSF), principal component analysis (PCA) and other methods, as well as statistical software such as SPSS, we conducted a comparative analysis of the investment climate in 12 provinces (autonomous regions, municipalities) in western China. After an in-depth discussion of the differences in investment climate between different parts of the western region, we further analyzed the gap between it and the central and eastern regions. Finally, given the characteristics of FDI from different economies and the spatial differences in the investment climate within the western region, we proposed measures and strategies to make this region a better destination for foreign investors.

8.1 Key MNCs Considerations for Investment in China

8.1.1 MNCs and the Investment Climate of China

In general, the ideal investment climate for multinational companies includes the following elements: developed market economy, advanced technology, sound financial and taxation system, stable exchange rate, sound infrastructure with a clean and good social environment (medical services, educational levels, cultural and living quality, crime rate, and so on.) (Hao 2000). Research shows that cities with good power supply, proximity to seaports, easy transportation and communication, and special preferential policies are the main areas of consideration for foreign investors. Zheng and Geistleger (2001) view the FDI regional differences between China's

© Social Sciences Academic Press 2024

X. Yang et al., *Foreign Direct Investment in Western China, 1994-2004*,
https://doi.org/10.1007/978-981-97-7407-4_8

coastal and inland areas as regional differences in GDP per capita, infrastructure, occupational skill, and bureaucracy. Wei et al. (2001b) discover that cheap labor, convenient transportation conditions, and adjacent target markets are important factors in choosing FDI locations after studying 135 foreign-invested enterprises in Qinhuangdao. By using factor analysis to evaluate the investment climate of various provinces, municipalities and autonomous regions in my country from 1990 to 2000, Lu and Pan (2002) found that the GDP, the proportion of the tertiary industry, the degree of urbanization, labor costs, import restrictions and preferential policies for foreign-funded enterprises have a significant impact on the FDI regional distribution. Sun (2002) concludes that industrial structure, preferential policies, degrees of openness, education, and marketization are factors affecting the choice of FDI locations. Sun and Zhao (2003) suggest environment, policy, structure, and efficiency are factors of the FDI regional differences (Wang 2006).

Based on its 2002–2003 survey of 4000 enterprises in 23 large and medium-sized cities in China, the World Bank released *Improving city competitiveness through the investment climate: ranking 23 Chinese Cities*. The World Bank evaluates the regional investment climate, focusing on important factors that affect the operating performance at the enterprise level. The report categorizes these factors into 10 indicators: infrastructure, local restrictions on market entrance and exit, previously-established skills and technology, labor accessibility, integration of international economy, participation of private sectors, informal payments, taxation, legal efficiency and financing.

In their econometric analysis on the spatial distribution of FDI in China, Broadman and Sun (1997) found that the size of FDI was mainly determined by GDP, infrastructure, education system, and coastal location. Chen (1997b) found that the ratio of efficiency wages (nominal wages divided by average productivity) was significantly negatively correlated with FDI inflows, and FDI inflows were significantly positively correlated with infrastructure. Chen (1997b) also pointed out that a larger economy is more attractive than a smaller economy to FDI. Due to the size and spillover effects of the external economy, a larger economy can provide more opportunities for industry and enterprise development. Coughlin and Segev (2000) found in their study that GNP, average productivity, and coastal location are positive FDI determinants, while average wages and illiteracy rates are negative FDI determinants. Inevitably, the conclusions of these studies are influenced by the variables (factors) and analysis methods they choose.

8.1.2 Key Considerations for Investment in China: Japanese, South Korean, and German Firms

Although having some common requirements on the investment climate, multinational corporations (MNC) from different economies or of different scales and types have their own specific requirements.

8.1.2.1 Japanese MNCs

In the 1980s, Japan's foreign direct investment grew rapidly. Anand and Delios (1996) argue that Japan's FDI in China is out of spatial consideration of easy access to high-productivity resources, including advanced technology, management, and institutionalized knowledge transfer. Anand and Delios (1996) also believe that Japan's FDI in India was motivated by the desire to enter the local market. Guelle (2001) believes that Japanese MNCs investment in China is not "market-seeking" but the inevitable result of post-industrialization. This is consistent with the study of Hatch and Yamamura (1996) that Japan sets East Asian countries as their commodity export destinations. Since 1985, Japan has seen rising production costs domestically. Therefore, cheaper labor costs in China have attracted Japanese companies to invest in and organize production and ultimately sell their goods here (Table 8.1).

Wu Haiying selected four big Japanese manufacturing companies, especially in western China, namely Toyota Motor Corporation, Yamazaki Mazak Corporation, Brother Industries Corporation, and Noritake Corporation, in his research. The research combines on-site visits, questionnaire surveys and panel discussion. The results show that the key factors for these companies in choosing investment areas are as follows: First, lower costs, including labor and land costs. Second, preferential policies and support from the local government. Third, convenient transport, including commodities and personnel. Fourth, huge market potentials. The survey found that companies with different market positioning and products have different preferences in location selection. For example, the Japanese-funded manufacturing companies prefer sound external supporting conditions, such as better infrastructure, institutional environment compatible with the market economy, and industrial supporting capacity (Wu 2006).

8.1.2.2 South Korean MNCs

In the 1980s, South Korean companies began a large scale of foreign direct investment, which is still growing rapidly. From 1999 to 2003, South Korean MNCs added 10,448 foreign branches with 50.2% of these branches in China. While their FDI totalled USD 20 billion, 19.5% of the total is in China and still rising. More than 60% of South Korea's FDI in China is distributed in Northeastern provinces, including Shandong, Liaoning, Tianjin and Jilin.

Using extensive and unique firm-level data analysis on South Korea's direct investment in China, Kang and Lee (2006) found that the spatial distribution of South Korean companies is very uneven, with more than 60% of their branches located in the northeastern provinces. Using the conditional logit model proposed by McFadden (1974), they found that market size, government policies, labor quality, and transportation play are positive spatial determinants for South Korean MNCs in China; on the other hand, such factors as labor costs and proximity to Korea are significantly negative (Table 8.2).

Table 8.1 Distribution of Japan's FDI in China by Province in 1998 (Cassidy 2005)

Province	Total capital stock	Proportion of national total	Number of projects	Proportion of national total	Average project value
	Million yen	%		%	Million yen
Shanghai	621,594	28.7	530	23.1	1173
Guangdong	282,989	13.1	296	12.9	956
Beijing	259,020	12.0	250	10.9	1036
Jiangsu	238,770	11.0	302	13.2	791
Liaoning	205,799	9.5	252	11.0	817
Tianjin	131,966	6.1	130	5.7	1015
Shandong	82,770	3.8	145	6.3	571
Zhejiang	79,424	3.7	99	4.3	802
Hebei	52,681	2.4	42	1.8	1254
Chongqing	46,411	2.1	27	1.2	1719
Fujian	46,029	2.1	49	2.1	939
Anhui	32,708	1.5	11	0.5	2973
Hunan	17,592	0.8	12	0.5	1466
Heilongjiang	9649	0.4	11	0.5	877
Shaanxi	8948	0.4	23	1.0	389
Hubei	8602	0.4	15	0.7	573
Jilin	8484	0.4	17	0.7	499
Henan	8353	0.4	18	0.8	464
Hainan	6743	0.3	9	0.4	749
Sichuan	6644	0.3	16	0.7	415
Inner Mongolia	4779	0.2	8	0.3	597
Guangxi	2790	0.1	6	0.3	465
Yunnan	2666	0.1	3	0.1	889
Jiangxi	1781	0.1	1	0.0	1781
Shanxi	1040	0.0	3	0.1	347
Ningxia	458	0.0	2	0.1	229
Xinjiang	263	0.0	5	0.2	53
Guizhou	221	0.0	1	0.0	221
Other	331	0.0	13	0.6	
Total	2,164,718	100.0	2296	100.0	943

Source Toyo Keizai dataset

Table 8.2 Distribution of South Korea's FDI and FDI projects worldwide and in China by sector, % (Kang and Lee 2006)

		1989–1993		1994–1998		1999–2003	
		Worldwide	China	Worldwide	China	Worldwide	China
Number of investment organization	Primary industry	5.8	3.1	3.0	1.7	1.7	1.3
	Manufacturing	66.5	93.2	69.8	85.8	61.3	85.5
	Service industry	27.8	3.7	27.3	12.5	35.3	13.2
	Total	100.0	100.0	100.0	100.0	100.0	100.0
Total investment	Primary industry	15.9	1.3	4.7	0.7	4.0	0.7
	Manufacturing	50.4	91.5	57.6	80.8	51.6	81.7
	Service industry	33.7	7.0	37.7	18.6	44.4	11.8
	Total	100.0	100.0	100.0	100.0	100.0	100.0

Note Calculated based on the data provided by the Export–Import Bank of Korea, which is responsible for the collection of South Korea's FDI outflow data

8.1.2.3 German Firms

German companies have become one of the most active drivers of global FDI flows, especially with unique advantages in the manufacturing sector in developing countries. Over the past ten years, the growth of Germany's FDI in China has been closely linked to the trade relationship between the two countries. In recent years, German investment in China has grown significantly, especially from 1996 to 1998.

The German companies' investment in China is mainly concentrated in specific regions, with high geographical differences. For example, 39% are in Shanghai, 26.47% in Beijing, 13.5% in Jiangsu, Zhejiang and the eastern coastal provinces of Shandong (of which 77.6% in Jiangsu), and 8.2% in southern coastal provinces, Guangdong and Fujian (of which 77.0% in Guangdong). These accounted for 87.15% of the total. Unlike the distribution of investment from Hong Kong and other Asian countries and regions, German investment is not highly concentrated in southern China but concentrated in Shanghai and some eastern provinces, where there are many major local manufacturing companies. Many German companies' set up their representative offices and holding companies in Beijing.

According to the GIC data, German investment in China is focused on manufacturing and service industries. An analysis based on the numbers of companies by industries shows that 74.7% of companies are in the manufacturing sector and only 25.3% in service industries. Within the manufacturing industry, major investment fields are chemistry (21.75%) and mechanical engineering (74.7%). Within the services sector, 35.6% are in trade and finance, 28.5% in transport and warehousing,

15.7% in accounting and consultation, 10.7% in education and training, 4.2% in design, installation and maintenance, 2.9% in computer software, and 2.4% in law.

According to Bu's survey of German investment in China (2001), 86.3% of the 199 surveyed companies were established between 1994 and 1996. In terms of the lifespan of these companies, the longest is 13 years, the shortest only 7 months, and the average 3.5 years. Chen and Rege (2006) based on the sample data provided by GIC, shows most of the German companies invested in mainland China between 1993 and 1998, with 73.4% of them arriving after 1992. Many German companies planned to carry out long-term business in China, especially those arriving after 1992. However, after 1998, new investment projects from German companies began to decline sharply, which was mainly affected by the financial crisis in Southeast Asia. However, large-scale investments led by large multinational companies continued. Especially in recent years, German MNCs continue to have big investments in China (Table 8.3).

Table 8.3 Distribution and ranking of German firms' investment in China (Chen and Guido 2006)

Province/municipality	GIC data		Survey data	
	%	Ranking	%	Ranking
Beijing	26.47	2	11.00	4
Shanghai	39.00	1	31.00	1
Jiangsu	7.70	3	19.00	2
Shandong	3.58	5	0.00	
Zhejiang	2.23	7	0.00	
Guangdong	6.55	4	11.40	3
Fujian	1.62	8	0.00	
Liaoning	3.17	6	7.70	5
Jilin	1.28	10	0.00	
Tianjin	3.17	6	0.00	
Sichuan	1.35	9	7.70	5
Hubei	1.28	10	3.90	6
Hebei	0.81	11	0.00	
Anhui	0.68	12	0.00	
Other	1.08		1.00	

Note This table is based on the data provided by the Shanghai German Industry and Commerce Mission (GIC) and our questionnaire survey of the Germans in China

8.2 Comparison of Investment Climate in Western Provinces

The spatial determinants of FDI can be divided into the following categories, namely, proximity to the market, labor costs, transportation and other infrastructure, government policies, manufacturing (industry) density, market potential, labor quality, and financial environment. Combining the aforementioned research results and the availability of data, we conducted a comparative analysis of the environment that attracts MNCs direct investment in 12 provinces and regions in western China. By using both qualitative and quantitative methods to study the following factors, we derived a valuable conclusion.

8.2.1 Comparison of Key Factors Affecting the Environment for Foreign Investments

8.2.1.1 City Development and Development Zones

The data from the "China City Yearbook" clearly indicates that how FDI is distributed in various provinces and regions in China are consistent. That is, they are mainly concentrated in large and medium-sized cities as well as various development zones. Therefore, the growth of large and medium-sized cities and development zones affects the competitiveness of these provinces to attract foreign investment. Table 8.4 shows that in the western region, Sichuan and Guangxi have many big cities while many development zones, where the economic benefits are good, are located in Sichuan, Shaanxi, Guangxi and Chongqing. However, the three provinces of Qinghai, Ningxia and Xizang have few (or no) large cities and very few development zones, thus lacking important vehicles to attract FDI. The establishment of economic and technological development zones and high-tech development zones aims to enhance the competitiveness of specific industries and strengthen production capacity and technological research. It is also an important means of extending the coastal opening policy to the inland. In addition, bonded areas, border trade areas and export processing areas are all important windows for opening up and attracting foreign investment. Kang and Lee (2006) believed that the number of development zones of various levels and types in a region reflects a region's policy strength to attract foreign investment. Table 8.5 shows that in terms of foreign investment policy, Shaanxi, Sichuan, and Guangxi are the strongest; Yunnan, Inner Mongolia, and Xinjiang ranked second and followed by Gansu and Guizhou; and Ningxia, Qinghai, and Xizang are the weakest.

Table 8.4 Distribution of large and medium-sized cities in western China, by province

Province/region/ municipality	Number of cities with a population over 1 million in 2003	Number of cities with the GDP exceeding 10 billion in 2004	Note
Inner Mongolia	3	4	
Guangxi	5	4	
Chongqing	1	1	Municipality directly under the Central Government
Sichuan	11	8	One sub-provincial city
Guizhou	1	2	
Yunnan	1	3	
Xizang	0	0	
Shaanxi	1	3	One sub-provincial city
Gansu	2	1	
Qinghai	1	1	
Ningxia	0	1	
Xinjiang	1	2	

Note This table is developed from the data of the China City Yearbook

8.2.1.2 Foreign Trade and Investment

In terms of the size of foreign trade and investment, Sichuan, Shaanxi, Chongqing, Guangxi, Xinjiang, Inner Mongolia and Yunnan have larger ones, followed by Gansu and Guizhou; Ningxia, Qinghai and Xizang have relatively smaller ones (Table 8.6).

Foreign studies found that with other regional factors fixed, regions with a relatively higher stock of foreign investment attract more foreign investment. The data from the China Statistical Yearbook (2001–2005) (as shown in Fig. 8.1) shows that among the 11 western provinces and autonomous regions, Guangxi has the highest cumulative foreign direct investment per capita, reaching USD 48.68, during the five years period from 1999 to 2003; followed by Shaanxi, Chongqing and Sichuan, with USD 42.49, USD 38.32 and USD 26.68, respectively; Guizhou and Xinjiang have the lowest FDI, with a cumulative per capita below USD 5. Chongqing and Guangxi had more than USD 10,000 FDI per square kilometer, at USD 14,589.88 and USD 10,070.93, respectively; Shaanxi and Sichuan ranked third and fourth, respectively; Gansu, Inner Mongolia, Qinghai and Xinjiang have accumulative FDI less than US$1,000 per square kilometre (Fig. 8.2).

Table 8.5 Numbers of development zones in western China, by level and by type

Province/ region/ municipality	National-level					Provincial-level
	High-tech zone	Economic development zone	Border economic cooperation zone	Export processing zone	Tourist resort	Development zone
Inner Mongolia	1	1	2	1	0	1
Guangxi	2	1	1	1	1	3
Chongqing	1	1	0	1	0	1
Sichuan	2	1	0	2	0	10
Guizhou	1	1	0	0	0	7
Yunnan	1	1	3	1	1	3
Xizang	0	1	0	0	0	0
Shaanxi	3	1	0	0	0	1
Gansu	1	1	0	0	0	2
Qinghai	0	1	0	0	0	0
Ningxia	0	1	0	0	0	0
Xinjiang	1	2	3	1	0	1

Note

1. We developed this table based on the data provided by the China Development Zones Association Information Center, and the numbers in the table are incomplete statistics
2. The "high-tech zone" in the table refers to "high-tech development zone"; "economic development zone" refers to "economic and technological development zone"

8.2.1.3 Location and Transportation

Any production naturally requires easy access to highways, rails or ports to streamline operations. Quality infrastructure and a well-developed transportation system can reduce the operational cost, which are conducive to attracting direct investment from export-oriented multinational companies. The better the infrastructure, the more attractive for foreign direct investment, and there is a positive correlation between the two (Hu and Wang 2005) (Table 8.7).

There are three main railway lines (Chengdu-Chongqing Line, Hunan-Chongqing Line, and Sichuan-Guizhou Line) and five branch lines in Chongqing. In 2004, Chongqing had a total length of 718.2 km of railways with 87.59 km in operation per 10,000 km^2, ranking fifth in the western region; the city also has 87.07 km of expressways per 10,000 km^2, ranking first in the western region. Chongqing Port is the largest land–water transportation hub in the upper reaches of the Yangtze River and the southwestern region. Along the Yangtze River, dozens of ports with commercial and cargo terminals have been built, carrying out the river-sea transport from Chongqing to overseas via Shanghai and accommodating thousand-ton ships

Table 8.6 Foreign trade and investment in western China, by province, 2005

Province/region/municipality	Total import and export for the year (USD 100 million)	Export (USD 100 million)	Import (USD 100 million)	Actual FDI (USD 100 million)
Chongqing	42.93	25.21	17.72	5.16
Sichuan	79.00	47.00	32.00	11.00
Guizhou	14.04	8.59	5.45	1.08
Yunnan	47.38	26.42	20.97	1.89
Xizang	2.05	1.65	4.01	…
Shaanxi	45.77	30.76	15.01	6.28
Gansu	26.33	10.91	15.42	0.20
Qinghai	4.13	3.23	0.90	2.66
Ningxia	9.67	6.87	2.80	1.41
Xinjiang	79.42	50.40	29.02	0.47
Inner Mongolia	51.62	20.65	30.97	11.86
Guangxi	51.83	28.77	23.05	3.79

Note This table is developed by the data from the statistical bulletins of the provinces and regions in western China

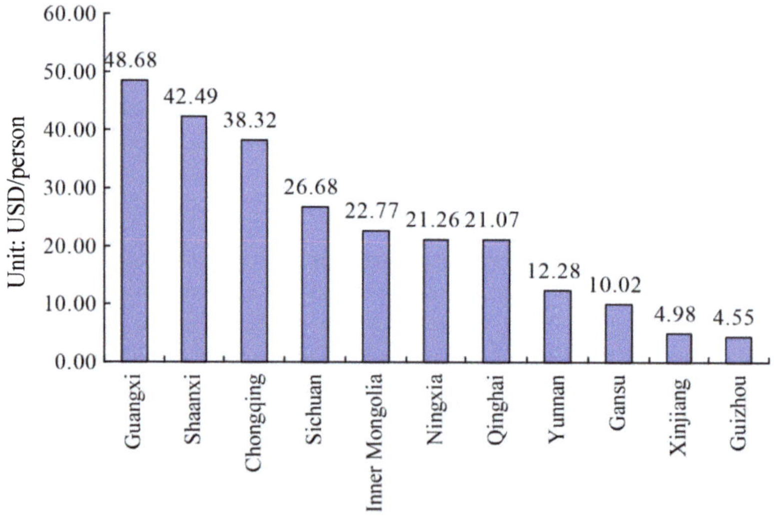

Fig. 8.1 Cumulative foreign direct investment per capita in western China, 1999–2003

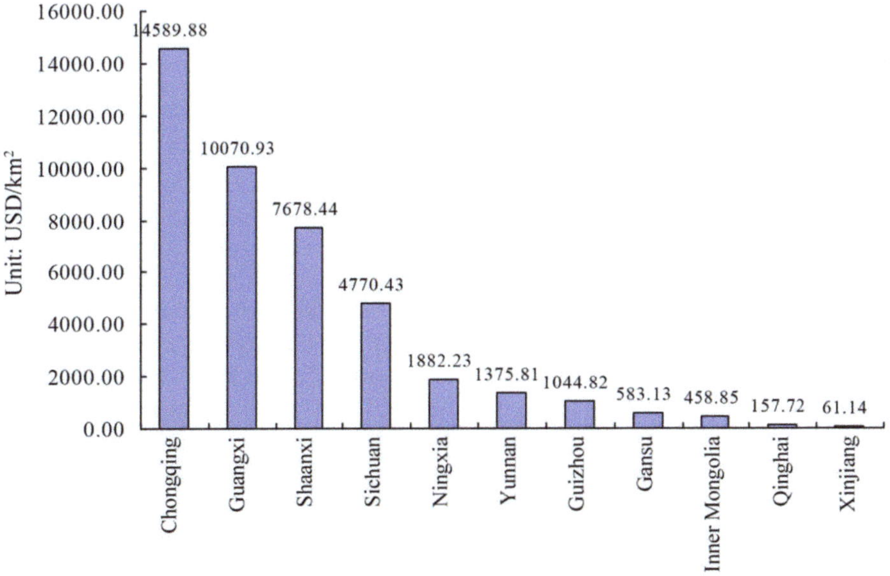

Fig. 8.2 Cumulative foreign direct investment per square kilometer by province, 1999–2003

Table 8.7 Transportation lines in western China in 2004, Unit: km

Province/region/ municipality	Length of transportation lines			Length of transportation lines per 10,000 km^2		
	Railway	Inland waterway	Road	Railway	Inland waterway	Highway
Inner Mongolia	6337.3	2403	75,976	53.57	20.31	4.15
Guangxi	2737.6	5413	59,704	115.85	229.07	48.96
Chongqing	718.2	4103	32,344	87.59	500.37	87.07
Sichuan	2958.0	10,720	113,043	60.61	219.67	36.02
Guizhou	1890.6	3323	46,128	111.21	195.47	24.29
Yunnan	2328.1	2539	167,050	59.09	64.44	32.77
Xizang	…	…	42,203	…	…	…
Shaanxi	3151.2	1066	52,720	153.72	52.00	47.61
Gansu	2295.5	860	40,751	51.01	19.11	15.27
Qinghai	1090.3	329	28,059	15.14	4.57	2.38
Ningxia	791.9	26	12,456	119.26	3.92	82.68
Xinjiang	2763.3	…	86,824	17.27	…	2.69

Note This table is developed by compiling and calculating the data from *China Statistical Yearbook (2005)*

all year round. With more than 4000 km of water transportation, Chongqing can further hold 10,000-ton vessels after the completion of the Three Gorges Project.

The Sichuan Provincial Railway has developed a network composed of 5 main lines (Bao-Chengdu, Xiangyu-Dacheng, Chengdu-Chongqing, Chengkun-Nankun, Neijiang-Kunming, etc.), 8 branch lines and 4 local lines. The network is concentrated in the central and eastern regions. In 2004, Sichuan had a total length of 2958 km of railway in operation, ranking third in the western region. Its expressways are also mainly concentrated in Chengdu and its surrounding areas. Chengdu Expressway, the first expressway in Sichuan, is the main artery between Sichuan Province and Chongqing Municipality. In 2004, Sichuan had 36.02 km of expressway per 10,000 km^2, ranking fifth in the western region. In terms of inland waterway transport, Sichuan ranks third, but the cargo and passenger turnover rates are not large. Chengdu Shuangliu International Airport has become one of the four major airports in China, and there are 10 civil aviation airports in the province.

Shaanxi, located in the middle reaches of the Yellow River and in the hinterland of China, is the nation's gateway to the northwest and a transportation hub connecting the east and central as well as the northwest and southwestern regions. The "New Eurasian Continental Bridge", an international economic channel across Asia and Europe, runs through central Shaanxi, connecting Lianyungang and Rotterdam in the Netherlands. There are 13 railways in Shaanxi, where Xi'an Railway Station is one of the largest railway hubs in Northwest China. In 2004, Shaanxi ranked second in the total railway length of 3151.2 km and first in the length of railway per 10,000 km^2 at 153.72 km. The highways in Shaanxi Province are centered on Xi'an and branched out in four cordial directions. Xi'an Airport is a national first-class airport, with 280 domestic and international air routes connecting 132 cities at home and abroad. In 2004, Shaanxi has the third highest freight turnover at 96.35 billion ton-kilometers, the third highest passenger turnover at 45.03 billion passenger-kilometers, the second highest cargo turnover at 4.7 billion ton-kilometers per 10,000 km^2, and the second highest passenger turnover at 2.197 billion passenger-kilometers per 10,000 km^2 in this region.

The Guangxi railway network connects Guangdong in the east, Yunnan in the west, and Guizhou, Sichuan, Chongqing, Hunan in the north. In 2004, Guangxi had the fifth longest operating railways at 2,737.6 km, the third longest operating railways per 10,000 km^2 at 115.85 km, and the third longest expressways per 10,000 km^2 at 48.96 km in western China. In this region, Guangxi has the second best inland waterway transportation and is the only city with waterway access to the sea. The Beibu Gulf Port, a group of new ports including Fangcheng Port, Qinzhou Port, and Beihai Port, is the maritime gateway of Guangxi and southwest China. Fangcheng Port is one of the 20 major coastal ports of China, facilitating trading and transport activities with 220 ports domestically and globally. According to "China's Coastal Port Planning and Design" promulgated in September 2006, Fangcheng Port was listed as one of the three major national ports in the southwestern coastal area and one of the 24 major coastal ports of the country; Beihai Port and Qinzhou Port were listed as one of the 25 key regional ports of the country. The Beibu Gulf Port in

Guangxi will become the main channel to export goods from southwest China to the Southeast Asian market (Table 8.8).

The Inner Mongolia Autonomous Region is located on the northern border of China, neighboring Mongolia and Russia, with a border line of 4200 km long. Here there are 14 state-owned railway lines, 12 branch lines, and 5 local railways, with an operating length of 6337.3 km and an eighth highest density of 53.57 km per ten thousand square meters in the west. The east–west Jingtong, Jingbao, and Baolan railways run across the region, connecting the northeast, north, and northwest of China. Manzhouli and Erenhot are two large dry ports, connecting Russia and Mongolia and directly reaching European countries. At present, the long-distance transport of goods and passengers has not been realized through inland waterways. In 2004, Inner Mongolia had the ninth longest expressway per 10,000 km^2 at 4.15 km and the eighth highest the cargo turnover per 10,000 km^2 at 881 million ton-km.

Yunnan is located at the southwestern border of China, adjacent to Myanmar in the west, Laos in the south and Vietnam in the southeast, with a total border line of 4061 km. The meter-gauge railway directly connects Kunming and Hanoi of Vietnam. In 2004, the province had 3 standard electric-powered railways and 6 branch lines; the operating length was 2328.1 km, ranking sixth in the west. A highway transportation network has been established with Kunming as the center (hub), connecting the entire province and reaching Sichuan, Guizhou, Guangxi, Xizang as well as neighboring countries such as Burma, Laos, Vietnam and Thailand. In 2004, Yunnan Province had

Table 8.8 Freight and passenger transport per 10,000 km^2 by province in 2004

Province/region/municipality	Freight transport (100 million ton-km)				Passenger transport (100 million passenger-km)			
	Total	Railway	Road	Waterborne transport	Total	Railway	Road	Waterborne transport
Inner Mongolia	11.09	8.81	2.28	…	2.17	0.85	1.31	…
Guangxi	42.25	26.07	9.97	6.21	21.85	4.36	17.38	0.11
Chongqing	63.12	12.82	15.65	34.67	33.62	4.65	27.57	1.40
Sichuan	17.16	11.96	4.73	0.47	13.13	3.49	9.58	0.06
Guizhou	35.94	30.63	4.96	0.35	16.36	7.41	8.87	0.09
Yunnan	16.52	7.20	9.27	0.05	7.05	1.26	5.77	0.02
Xizang	0.19	…	0.19	…	0.12	…	0.12	…
Shaanxi	47.00	37.47	9.52	0.01	21.97	12.46	9.48	0.03
Gansu	19.52	16.63	2.89	…	6.26	4.11	2.14	…
Qinghai	1.91	1.28	0.63	…	0.58	0.26	0.32	…
Ningxia	36.52	26.79	9.73	…	8.95	3.19	5.75	…
Xinjiang	4.55	2.79	1.76	…	1.80	0.64	1.17	…

Note This table is developed by compiling and calculating the data from *China Statistical Yearbook (2005)*

the highest total length of highways at 167,050 km and the sixth longest expressway per 10,000 km^2 at 32.77 km in western China. According to the national statistics, the navigable mileage of Yunnan Water Transport was 2549 km, the cargo throughput of Jinghong Port was 100,000 tons, and the annual cargo throughput of Jinsha River Freight Terminal was 200,000 tons in 2004. Yunan has a total of 10 civil airports, with more than 200 air routes to 92 large and medium-sized cities in China, and 17 air routes to Bangkok, Yangon, Vientiane, Hong Kong and other foreign countries and regions. The planned Kunming Changshui Airport is one of the largest international airports in western China. (Table 8.9).

The Baotou-Lanzhou Railway runs through the northern and central parts of Ningxia and Zhongbao Electrified Railway, the second route from the coast to the northwest, make Ningxia an important part of the "Second Eurasian Continental Bridge". In 2004, Ningxia had the second longest operating railway per 10,000 km^2 at 119.26 km, the second highest expressway length per 10,000 km^2 at 82.68 km, the fourth highest freight turnover per 10,000 km^2 at 3.652 billion ton-km, and the sixth highest passenger turnover per 10,000 km^2 at 895 million passenger-km, in western China.

Gansu is located in the western inland west of China, on the upper reaches of the Yellow River, bordering Shaanxi in the east, Ningxia in the northeast, Qinghai and Xinjiang in the west, Inner Mongolia in the north, and the Mongolian People's Republic. The provincial capital, Lanzhou, is China's geographic center, where the

Table 8.9 Freight and passenger transport by province in 2004

Province/region/municipality	Freight transport (100 million ton-km)				Passenger transport (100 million passenger-km)			
	Total	Railway	Road	Waterborne transport	Total	Railway	Road	Waterborne transport
Inner Mongolia	1311.9	1042.1	269.8	…	256.4	101.1	155.3	…
Guangxi	998.4	616.1	235.6	146.7	516.2	103.0	410.6	2.6
Chongqing	517.6	105.1	128.3	284.3	275.7	38.1	226.1	11.5
Sichuan	837.3	583.6	230.9	22.9	640.6	170.1	467.7	2.8
Guizhou	610.9	520.7	84.3	5.9	278.2	125.9	150.8	1.6
Yunnan	650.8	283.6	365.1	2.1	277.6	49.5	227.2	0.9
Xizang	23.1	…	23.1	…	14.8	…	14.8	…
Shaanxi	963.5	768.1	195.2	0.3	450.3	255.5	194.3	0.6
Gansu	878.3	748.3	130.0	0.1	281.5	185.0	96.3	0.2
Qinghai	137.2	91.9	45.3	…	41.8	18.5	23.2	…
Ningxia	242.5	177.9	64.6	…	59.4	21.2	38.2	…
Xinjiang	727.8	446.3	281.5	…	288.7	101.7	187.0	…

Note This table is developed by compiling and calculating the data from *China Statistical Yearbook (2005)*

Lanxin, Baolan, Longhai, and Lanqing railway lines meet. Since the administrative divisions within the province are long and narrow, all parts of Gansu are not far away from the main railway lines. In 2004, Gansu had the seventh longest operating railway at 2295.5 km, and the ninth longest operating railway per 10,000 km^2 at 51.01 km, the fourth largest cargo throughput at 87.83 billion ton-km, the fifth highest passenger transport at 281.5 100 million people-km, and the eighth longest expressway length per 10,000 km^2 at15.27 km in the west.

Guizhou, located in the transportation hub of Southwest China, is not only an important passage to Yunnan but also a necessary stop from Sichuan, Chongqing and other cities to reach the southwest estuary. Guiyang stands at the intersection of the five major railways including Guizhou-Guizhou, Sichuan-Guizhou, Guizhou-Kunming, Hunan-Guizhou, and Neijiang-Kunming. Of the western provinces in 2004, Guizhou had 1890.6 km of railways in operation, ranking eighth; 111.21 km of railways in operation per 10,000 km^2, ranking fourth; 24.29 km of expressways per 10,000 km^2, ranking seventh; inland waterway transportation ranking fourth. However, its waterborne cargo and passenger turnovers are small. The passenger throughput of Guiyang Longdongbao Airport reached 2.72 million in 2004, ranking 23rd among 140 plus civil airports nationwide.

Xinjiang is located in the hinterland of the Eurasian continent; the geographical center of Asia is located in the suburbs of Urumqi. Xinjiang has a total length of border line of 5600 km, bordering Mongolia in the northeast, Russia, Kazakhstan, Kyrgyzstan, and Tajikistan in the west, and Afghanistan, Pakistan, and India in the southwest. Xinjiang is the province with the longest border line and the most open ports in China. Xinjiang, Qinghai, and Xizang have the lowest density of railway and highway in the western region, and no long-distance waterway transportation systems (Table 8.10).

8.2.1.4 Economic Aggregate and the Three Sectors of the Economy

Based on the preliminary data from the provincial statistical bulletins, Sichuan has the largest economic aggregate and its GDP is nearly twice that of Guangxi, the second largest economy in the west. The economic aggregates of Guizhou and Gansu are very similar while that of Ningxia, Qinghai, and Xizang are relatively small. The GDP of the latter three provinces in 2005 was less than RMB 60 billion, with Xizang less than RMB 30 billion.

In the western region, the industrial structures of Chongqing and Guangxi are "tertiary, industrial (secondary), and primary" type; Xizang also presents a "tertiary, industrial, and primary" type due to the extremely weak foundation of the secondary industry. The other nine provinces present a "secondary, tertiary, primary" type. Table 8.11 shows that the ratios of of industry specialization are higher than 1 in Ningxia, Inner Mongolia, Shaanxi, Gansu, Chongqing, Guizhou and Yunnan, indicating a high degree of industrial concentration; the ratios of tertiary industry specialization are higher than 1 in Xizang, Chongqing, Qinghai, Sichuan, Shaanxi and Guangxi, indicating the concentration of the tertiary industry is high; among

Table 8.10 Value-added of the three sectors in western China in 2005, Unit: RMB 100 million

Province/region/ municipality	Value-added of the primary industry	Value-added of the secondary industry	Value-added of the tertiary industry	GDP
Sichuan	1495.70	3052.70	2836.70	7385.10
Guangxi	902.56	1505.04	1655.70	4063.30
Inner Mongolia	600.09	1685.13	1537.55	3822.77
Shaanxi	418.60	1848.97	1407.18	3674.75
Yunnan	656.18	1449.71	1366.45	3472.34
Chongqing	463.42	1258.32	1347.36	3069.10
Xinjiang	506.00	1195.00	908.00	2609.00
Guizhou	359.18	822.83	759.99	1942.00
Gansu	300.00	836.55	791.59	1928.14
Ningxia	69.78	277.82	251.80	599.40
Qinghai	62.79	264.61	215.80	543.20
Xizang	47.87	59.45	143.28	250.60

Note This table developed by compiling the data from the statistical bulletin (2005) of each province

them, the ratios of industry specialization and the tertiary industry are both greater than 1 in Chongqing and Shaanxi.

A province with a higher density of manufacturers is likely to attract more FDI because foreign investors have more incentive to service existing manufacturers. In the western region, Chongqing, Sichuan, Shaanxi, Yunnan, and Guangxi have relatively high industrial density.

8.2.1.5 Economic Development and Residents' Income Level

According to the data from the China Statistical Yearbook (2005), the GDP per capita of both Inner Mongolia and Xinjiang exceeded RMB 10,000 in 2004; those of Chongqing, Qinghai and Sichuan range between RMB 8000 and RMB 10,000; for Ningxia, Xizang, Shaanxi, Guangxi and Yunnan, they are between RMB 6000 and RMB 8000; those of Gansu and Guizhou are the lowest, below RMB 6000.

Based on the data from the China Statistical Yearbook (2005), we estimated that the per capita income of urban residents in Chongqing was the highest, reaching RMB 9220.96, in 2004; the per capita income of urban residents in Xizang also exceeded RMB 9000; the per capita income exceeded RMB 7500 of urban residents in Yunnan, Guangxi, Inner Mongolia, Sichuan and Xinjiang; those of the other provinces in western China are all above RMB 7000, with the lowest at RMB 7217.87 in Ningxia. In terms of per capita net income of rural households, the highest was that of Inner Mongolia, reaching RMB 2606.37; those of Sichuan and Chongqing exceeded RMB 2500 and above RMB 2000 for Guangxi, Ningxia and Xinjiang. For the rest of the provinces, they were all below RMB 2000, with the lowest at RMB 1721.55 of

Table 8.11 Industrial specialization rate by province in western China

Province/region/municipality	Manufacturing	Tertiary industry	Province	Manufacturing	Tertiary industry	Province	Manufacturing	Tertiary industry
Inner Mongolia	1.08	0.89	Guizhou	1.05	0.94	Gansu	1.07	0.92
Guangxi	0.91	1.02	Yunnan	1.03	0.97	Qinghai	0.99	1.07
Chongqing	1.01	1.09	Xizang	0.21	1.44	Ningxia	1.17	0.93
Sichuan	0.96	1.04	Shaanxi	1.07	1.03	Xinjiang	0.98	0.94

Note This table is developed by using the data of *China Statistical Yearbook (2005)*, with each province as the research area and 12 western provinces as the high-level research area

Guizhou. In terms of the income gap between urban and rural residents, Xizang sees the largest at RMB 7244.76; followed by Yunnan, Chongqing and Guangxi. Ningxia has the smallest gap at RMB 4897.82 (Figs. 8.3 and 8.4).

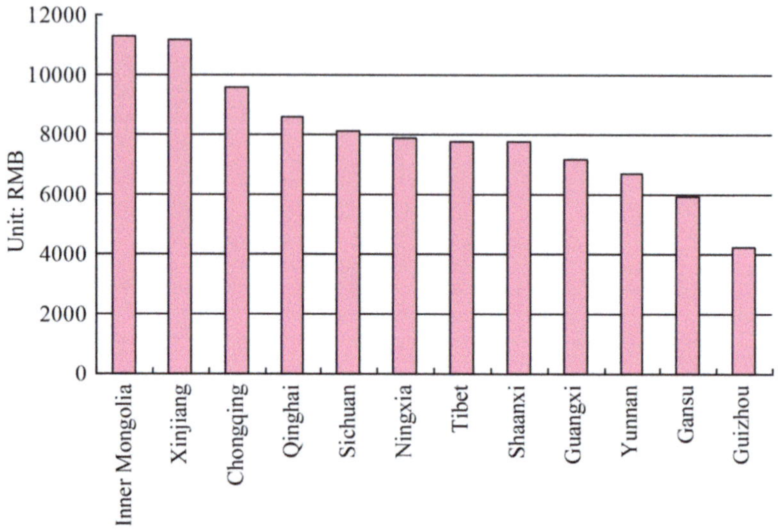

Fig. 8.3 GDP per capita in western China in 2004

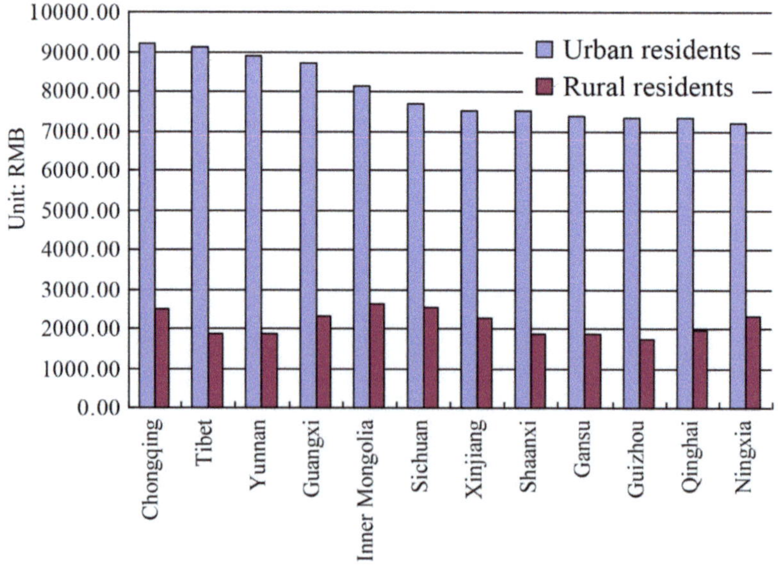

Fig. 8.4 Per capita income in western China in 2004

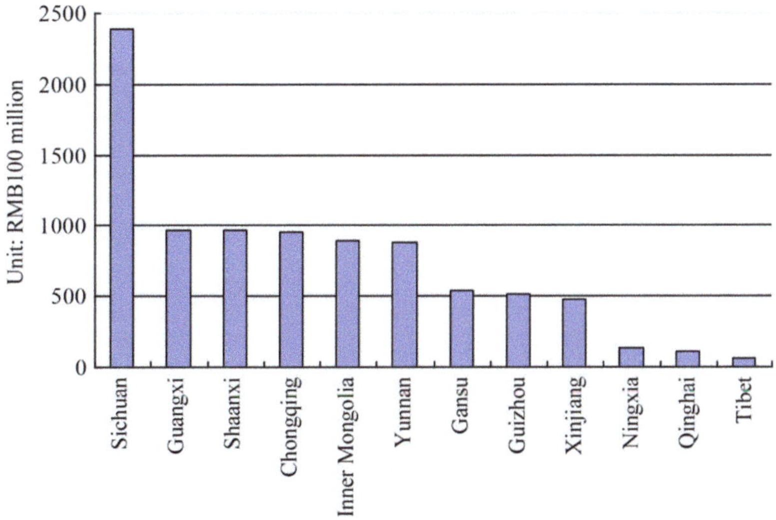

Fig. 8.5 Total retail sales in western China in 2004

8.2.1.6 Market Size

The larger the market size of the host country and the market potential of its surrounding areas, the more competitive it is to attract local market-exploring multinational companies. In Fig. 8.5, we divide the 12 western provinces into four categories by their market size in 2004: the largest is Sichuan, with a total retail sales of nearly RMB 250 billion; the second largest include Guangxi, Shaanxi, Chongqing, Inner Mongolia and Yunnan five provinces with a total retail sales of nearly RMB 250 billion; the third includes Gansu, Guizhou and Xinjiang at around RMB 50 billion; the fourth includes Ningxia, Qinghai, and Xizang below RMB 20 billion. In addition, the surrounding areas of Chongqing, Sichuan, Shaanxi, Inner Mongolia, Guizhou and Ningxia have greater market potential.

8.2.1.7 Education

According to the fifth national census data, for the average education level of the age group of 6+ years among the 12 western provinces and autonomous regions, Inner Mongolia has the highest, reaching 7.76 years of education; followed by Xinjiang, Shaanxi, Guangxi, Chongqing, Sichuan and Ningxia with the average of 7 plus years.; Gansu, Yunnan, Guizhou and Qinghai with 6–7 years; Xizang the lowest, only 3.43 years. For the illiteracy rate of the age group of 15 + years old, Xizang is the highest at 47.25%; followed by Qinghai 25.44%, Guizhou 19.85%; Gansu 19.68%; Ningxia 15.72%, Yunnan 15.44%, and Inner Mongolia over 10%; with the illiteracy rate below 10% includes Sichuan, Shaanxi, Chongqing, Xinjiang and

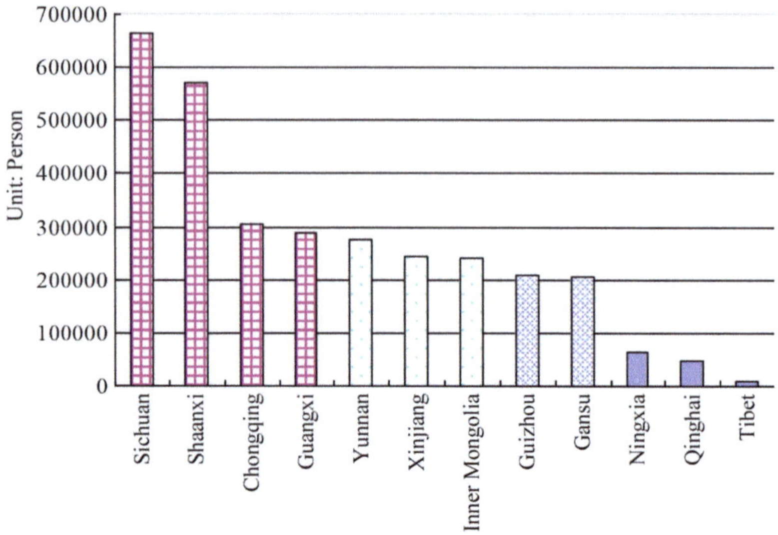

Fig. 8.6 Number of people aged 6 and over with a bachelor's degree or above in western China

Guangxi, of which Guangxi is the lowest at 5.30%. Among these western provinces, Sichuan has the highest number of professional and technical people; followed by Shaanxi, Guangxi and Yunnan; Gansu and Guizhou are very close in total, both ranking in the lower end. In terms of the ratio of professional and technical workers to all types of workers, Xinjiang has the highest share; while Ningxia and Qinghai have a small number of professional and technical workers, both have higher shares among the west (Figs. 8.6 and 8.7).

To sum up, a preliminary conclusion can be drawn that among the 12 western provinces, residents of Shaanxi, Chongqing, Sichuan, Guangxi, Inner Mongolia, and Xinjiang have relatively higher educational attainment; followed by Yunnan and Ningxia and then Gansu and Guizhou; and finally, Qinghai and Xizang.

8.2.1.8 Technological Environment

In terms of the revenue of technology markets in 2004, Chongqing, Yunnan, Sichuan, and Shaanxi are the top ones. It is notable that Guangxi is way below the average; Guizhou, Ningxia and Qinghai have minimal, below RMB 610 million. By the number of high-tech development zones and the profitability of the corporations there, Shaanxi, Chongqing, Sichuan and Guangxi are at the top, while Ningxia, Qinghai, Xizang have not yet established high-tech development zones (Fig. 8.8).

In the 2005 National Statistical Monitoring Report on Scientific and Technological Progress, the National Scientific and Technological Progress Statistical Monitoring and Comprehensive Evaluation Research Group divided the 31 provinces across the

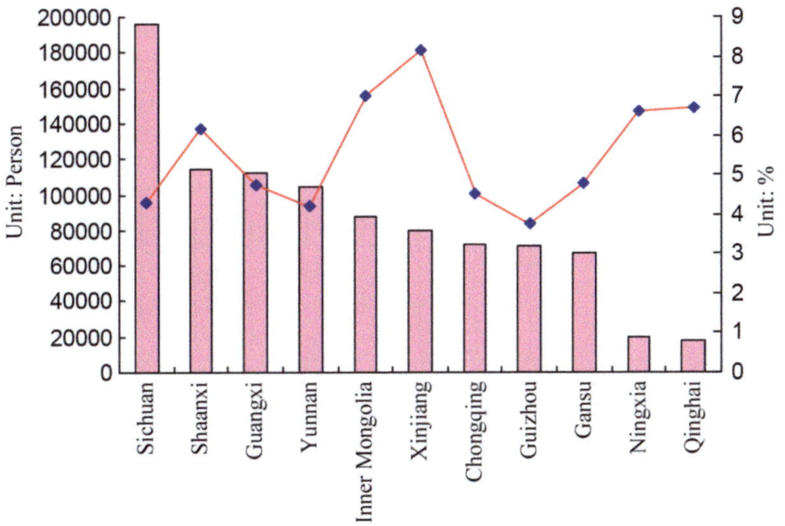

Fig. 8.7 Number of professional and technical personnel in western China and the percentage in each occupation

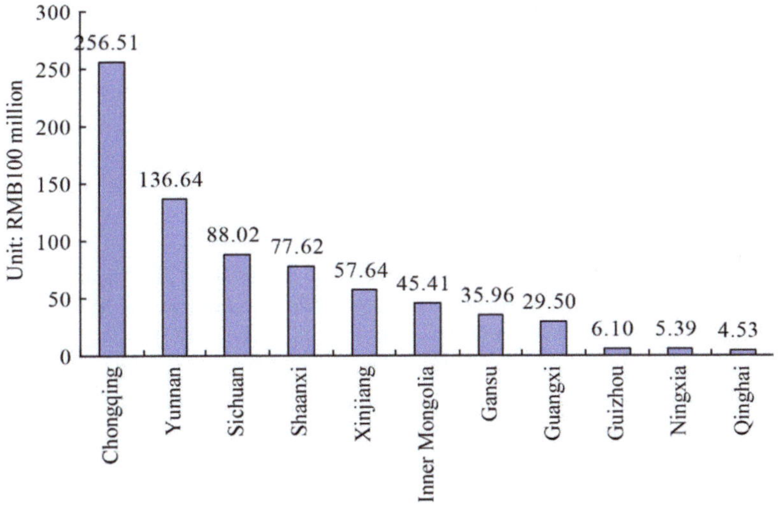

Fig. 8.8 Cumulative turnover of technology market in western China, 1998–2004

country into six categories according to the comprehensive scientific and technological progress level index. Based on this matrix, Shaanxi and Chongqing belong to the third category; Sichuan, Xinjiang, Gansu and Inner Mongolia the fourth; Qinghai, Guangxi, Ningxia, Guizhou and Yunnan the fifth category; Xizang belongs to the sixth category. In terms of the environmental index of scientific and technological

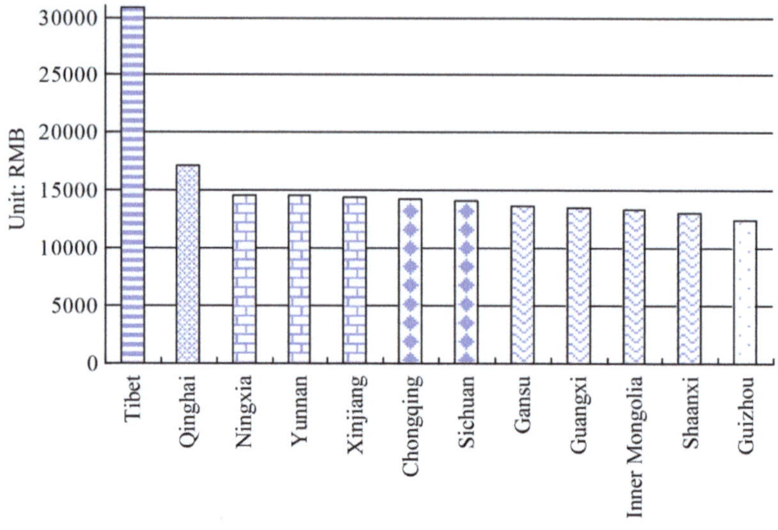

Fig. 8.9 Average annual wages in 2004

progress, Shaanxi ranks in the top 10, which is higher than the national average. In terms of the investment index of scientific and technological activities, Shaanxi ranks in the top 8, which is higher than the national level. In terms of the output index of scientific and technological activities, Chongqing ranks in the top 4, which is higher than the national level.

8.2.1.9 Labor Costs

According to the data from the China Statistical Yearbook (2005), among the 12 western provinces and autonomous regions in 2004, Xizang had the highest average salary, exceeding RMB 30,000; followed by Qinghai at RMB 17,229; Ningxia, Yunnan, Xinjiang, Chongqing and Chengdu around RMB 14,000; and the others below RMB 14,000, with Guizhou the lowest at RMB 12,431. Considering such factors as worker's education levels and productivity, Shaanxi, Chongqing, Sichuan, Guangxi, Inner Mongolia, Gansu and Guizhou have relatively better labor costs (Fig. 8.9).

8.2.1.10 Financial Market

In the 1990s, the MNCs' continuous expansion of the investment generated their external financing needs, that is, to obtain investment funds from the financial market of the country where their parent company and its subsidiaries are located and the international capital market. Therefore, the financial market conditions of the host

Table 8.12 Financial industry development in western China, Unit: RMB 100 million

Province/region/municipality	Added value of finance and insurance industry	Various deposit balances of financial institutions	Balance of savings deposits of urban and rural residents at the end of the year
Sichuan	262.31	9905.30	5902.70
Shaanxi	41.76	6446.48	3533.97
Yunnan	94.02	5140.50	2430.28
Chongqing	93.45	4727.72	2545.85
Guangxi	66.43	4202.84	2561.34
Xinjiang	70.87	3427.48	2518.00
Inner Mongolia	30.57	3298.15	1973.60
Gansu	65.26	2895.86	1586.66
Guizhou	49.87	2777.50	1350.90
Ningxia	17.00	993.74	514.11
Qinghai	17.71	733.05	352.76
Xizang	15.62	456.30	123.88

Note The added value of the financial and insurance industry in the table is taken from the *China Statistical Yearbook* (2005); the deposit balance of financial institutions, and of the urban and rural resident is taken from the 2005 Statistical Bulletin of each province

country is also an important factor in attracting direct investment from multinational companies. Table 8.12 shows that Sichuan, Shaanxi, Chongqing, Yunnan, and Guangxi have the more developed financial industry; followed by Xinjiang, Inner Mongolia, Gansu, and Guizhou and finally Ningxia, Qinghai, and Xizang.

8.2.2 *Principal Component Analysis of the Environment for Foreign Investments*

In order to analyze the differences in the investment climate of various provinces in western China from multiple perspectives, on the basis of the above qualitative analysis, we use principal component analysis (PCA) to further analyze the major differences from a quantitative perspective.

Indicator selection

When conducting a quantitative analysis of the environment for foreign investments in western China, we found economic scale, infrastructure density, population quality, urbanization level, among others, have a significant impact on the total amount of FDI in a preliminary regression analysis of various related variables in 30 provinces (municipalities and autonomous regions) across the country. Therefore, the research group selected the following 12 indicators, shown in Table 8.13.

Table 8.13 Raw PCA data concerning the environment for foreign investments in western China

Province/ region/ municipality	GDP (RMB100 million)	Population density (persons per sq. km)	Level of urbanization (%)	Gross fixed capital formation (RMB100 million)	Proportion of persons with a college degree in the population aged 6 and above (%)	Proportion of the workforce in the tertiary industry (%)
Inner Mongolia	2712.08	20.15	47.20	1809.26	6.63	30.59
Guangxi	3320.10	206.90	33.62	1296.55	5.18	31.34
Chongqing	2665.39	380.73	45.20	1552.99	3.64	32.33
Sichuan	6556.01	178.79	33.00	2587.14	3.62	29.63
Guizhou	1591.90	229.65	26.90	878.85	4.47	30.60
Yunnan	2959.48	112.06	29.50	1352.78	3.84	19.62
Xizang	211.54	2.25	18.93	168.45	0.94	26.88
Shaanxi	2883.51	180.73	37.23	1649.28	7.23	31.53
Gansu	1558.93	58.20	30.02	639.82	5.67	27.71
Qinghai	465.73	7.49	39.25	319.02	4.51	32.31
Ningxia	460.35	88.55	38.00	379.72	7.16	28.69
Xinjiang	2200.15	12.27	37.20	1239.50	9.89	32.60

Note The GDP figures in this table are based on the *China Statistical Yearbook (2005)*; the population density is obtained by dividing the year-end numbers from the *China Statistical Yearbook (2005)* by the area of each province; the level of urbanization is calculated based on the data provided in the 2005 Statistical Bulletin of each province; the gross fixed capital formation, proportion of persons with a college degree in the population aged 6 and above, and proportion of the workforce in the tertiary industry are provided by the *China Statistical Yearbook (2005)*

Province/ region/ municipality	Fiscal revenue (RMB 100 million)	Fiscal expenditure (RMB 100 million)	Total savings of urban and rural residents (RMB 100 million)	Per capita disposable income of urban residents (RMB)	Ratio of built-up urban area to the size of administrative division (%)	Total retail sales (RMB 100 million)
Inner Mongolia	196.76	564.11	1355.51	8122.99	0.00591	891.96
Guangxi	237.77	507.47	1971.67	8689.99	0.03003	973.41
Chongqing	200.62	395.72	1896.56	9220.96	0.06272	955.01
Sichuan	385.78	895.25	4333.82	7709.87	0.02856	2383.95
Guizhou	149.29	418.42	912.83	7322.05	0.01954	517.56
Yunnan	263.36	663.64	1766.50	8870.88	0.01087	884.87

(continued)

Table 8.13 (continued)

Province/ region/ municipality	Fiscal revenue (RMB 100 million)	Fiscal expenditure (RMB 100 million)	Total savings of urban and rural residents (RMB 100 million)	Per capita disposable income of urban residents (RMB)	Ratio of built-up urban area to the size of administrative division (%)	Total retail sales (RMB 100 million)
Xizang	10.02	133.83	91.90	9106.07	0.00059	63.70
Shaanxi	214.96	516.31	2519.94	7492.47	0.02640	966.49
Gansu	104.16	356.94	1217.38	7376.74	0.01101	535.84
Qinghai	27.00	137.34	260.50	7319.67	0.00143	115.60
Ningxia	37.47	123.02	377.70	7217.87	0.03560	137.76
Xinjiang	155.70	421.04	1371.83	7503.42	0.00366	482.07

Note The total savings of urban and rural residents in this table derived from the data of 2003, in China Statistical Yearbook (2005); fiscal revenue, fiscal expenditure, total retail sales and others are from China Statistical Yearbook (2005); the ratio of the built-up urban area to the size of administrative division is derived by dividing the built-up urban area by the area of each province as recorded in China Statistical Yearbook (2005)

8.2.2.1 Nondimensionalization

We use the following formula for the purpose of standardization.

$$x_{ij} = \frac{x_{ij} - \overline{x}_j}{\sigma_j} \text{ When } \sigma_j = 0, \quad \text{let } x_{ij} = 0$$

The results are shown in Table 8.14.

8.2.2.2 Principal Component Analysis (PCA)

We employed SPSS to compute the standardized data. Results are shown in Table 8.15.

In Table 8.15, the eigenvalue of the first principal component is 6.22, the variance contribution rate is 51.84%, and the cumulative variance contribution rate of the first five components is 96.20%, indicating the variation in the aforementioned 12 original variables.

After SPSS computation, we obtained the PCA loading matrix, as shown in Table 8.16.

From Table 8.16, principal component 1 can be interpreted as an economic scale, in which indicators such as GDP, gross fixed capital formation, fiscal revenue, fiscal expenditure, total savings of urban and rural residents, and total retail sales bear a relatively large load. Principal component 2, viewed as population and urban density,

Table 8.14 Standardized PCA data concerning the environment for foreign investments in western China

Province/ region/ municipality	GDP	Population density	Level of urbanization	Gross fixed capital formation	Proportion of persons with a college degree in the population aged 6 and above (%)	Proportion of the workforce in the tertiary industry
Inner Mongolia	0.25	– 0.93	1.67	0.96	0.64	0.32
Guangxi	0.62	0.76	– 0.14	0.21	– 0.02	0.54
Chongqing	0.22	2.32	1.41	0.58	– 0.72	0.82
Sichuan	2.59	0.50	– 0.22	2.10	– 0.73	0.04
Guizhou	– 0.43	0.96	– 1.04	– 0.41	– 0.35	0.32
Yunnan	0.40	– 0.10	– 0.69	0.29	– 0.63	– 2.85
Xizang	– 1.27	– 1.09	– 2.10	– 1.45	– 1.95	– 0.75
Shaanxi	0.36	0.52	0.34	0.72	0.91	0.59
Gansu	– 0.45	– 0.59	– 0.62	– 0.76	0.20	– 0.51
Qinghai	– 1.12	– 1.04	0.61	– 1.23	– 0.33	0.82
Ningxia	– 1.12	– 0.31	0.44	– 1.14	0.88	– 0.23
Xinjiang	– 0.06	– 1.00	0.34	0.12	2.12	0.90
Province	Fiscal revenue	Fiscal expenditure	Total savings of urban and rural residents	Per capita disposable income of urban residents	Ratio of built-up urban area to the size of administrative division	Total retail sales
Inner Mongolia	0.30	0.62	– 0.14	0.17	– 0.79218	0.25
Guangxi	0.69	0.36	0.42	0.94	0.59411	0.39
Chongqing	0.34	– 0.15	0.35	1.67	2.47253	0.36
Sichuan	2.10	2.13	2.55	– 0.39	0.50973	2.75
Guizhou	– 0.15	– 0.04	– 0.54	– 0.92	– 0.00868	– 0.38
Yunnan	0.94	1.08	0.23	1.19	– 0.50707	0.24
Xizang	– 1.48	– 1.34	– 1.28	1.51	– 1.09779	– 1.14
Shaanxi	0.47	0.40	0.91	– 0.69	0.38559	0.38
Gansu	– 0.58	– 0.32	– 0.26	– 0.84	– 0.49911	– 0.35
Qinghai	– 1.32	– 1.32	– 1.12	– 0.92	– 1.04948	– 1.05
Ningxia	– 1.22	– 1.39	– 1.02	– 1.06	0.91396	– 1.01
Xinjiang	– 0.09	– 0.03	– 0.12	– 0.67	– 0.92162	– 0.44

Table 8.15 Computation results of principal components

Principal component	Eigenvalue of principal component	Variance contribution rate	Cumulative variance contribution rate
1	6.22	51.84	51.84
2	2.28	19.00	70.84
3	1.81	15.10	85.95
4	0.70	5.83	91.78
5	0.53	4.42	96.20
6	0.27	2.22	98.42
7	0.14	1.14	99.56
8	0.03	51.84	99.78
9	0.02	0.19	99.97
10	0.00	0.02	99.99
11	0.00	0.01	100.00
12	0.00	0.00	100.00

includes indicators such as population density and the ratio of built-up urban area to the size of administrative division that bear a large load. Principal component 3, interpreted as a demographic component, includes such indicators as the level of urbanization and the proportion of the population with a college degree to the population over the age of 6. Principal component 4, viewed as the income level factor of urban residents, includes the per capita disposable income of urban residents that bears a relatively large load. Principal component 5, viewed as the level of industrial development, includes the proportion of employees in the tertiary industry.

8.2.2.3 Weights for Principal Components

$$W_i = \frac{\lambda_i}{\sum_5^{i=1} \lambda_i}$$

where

W_i is the weight assigned to the ith principal
λ_i is the eigenvalue for the ith principal component.

The computation results are shown in Table 8.17.

8.2.2.4 Comprehensive score of principal components.

The results are shown in Table 8.18.

Table 8.16 PCA loading matrix

No.	Indicator	Principal component 1	Principal component 2	Principal component 3	Principal component 4	Principal component 5
1	GDP	0.992	0.061	− 0.010	0.015	0.040
2	Population density	0.375	0.884	− 0.040	0.145	0.087
3	Level of urbanization	0.166	0.178	0.892	− 0.026	0.264
4	Gross fixed capital formation	0.956	0.069	0.233	0.046	0.071
5	Proportion of persons with a college degree	0.016	− 0.117	0.672	− 0.667	− 0.002
6	Proportion of the workforce in the tertiary industry	− 0.030	0.183	0.307	− 0.235	0.890
7	Fiscal revenue	0.975	0.122	0.048	0.046	− 0.111
8	Fiscal expenditure	0.973	− 0.056	0.008	0.005	− 0.163
9	Total savings of urban and rural residents	0.967	0.151	− 0.038	− 0.068	0.056
10	Per capita disposable income of urban residents	0.091	0.164	− 0.029	0.933	− 0.186
11	Ratio of built-up urban area to the size of administrative division	0.247	0.930	0.163	0.092	0.077
12	Total retail sales	0.976	0.109	-0.071	0.030	0.077

Table 8.17 Weights for principal components

Principal component	Eigenvalue of principal components	Variance contribution rate	Cumulative variance contribution rate	Weight
1	6.22	51.84	51.84	0.54
2	2.28	19.00	70.84	0.20
3	1.81	15.10	85.95	0.16
4	0.70	5.83	91.78	0.06
5	0.53	4.42	96.20	0.05

Table 8.18 Principal component scores concerning the environment for foreign investments in western China

Province/region/municipality	Score of principal component 1	Score of principal component 2	Score of principal component 3	Score of principal component 4	Score of principal component 5	Comprehensive score
Sichuan	2.38	– 0.20	– 1.08	– 0.31	0.65	1.09
Chongqing	0.07	2.21	0.89	1.49	0.56	0.73
Guangxi	0.40	0.46	– 0.04	0.55	0.39	0.35
Shaanxi	0.51	0.39	0.26	– 0.90	0.20	0.34
Inner Mongolia	0.42	– 1.31	1.73	0.71	0.30	0.29
Yunnan	0.53	– 0.35	– 0.06	0.78	– 2.72	0.13
Xinjiang	– 0.05	– 0.99	1.06	– 0.92	0.26	– 0.10
Guizhou	– 0.32	0.74	– 1.26	– 0.95	0.24	– 0.27
Gansu	– 0.40	– 0.23	– 0.54	– 0.87	– 0.50	– 0.42
Ningxia	– 1.22	0.95	0.57	– 1.14	– 0.82	– 0.49
Qinghai	– 1.10	– 0.81	0.10	– 0.04	1.21	– 0.68
Xizang	– 1.22	– 0.86	– 1.62	1.62	0.24	– 0.97

8.2.3 Types of Environment for Foreign Investments

Based on the above quantitative and qualitative analysis, static and dynamic analysis, as well as expert opinions, we divided western Chinese provinces into five types depending on the environment for foreign investments. Those within the same category are naturally similar in investment climate while those falling into different categories exhibit a significant difference.

8.2.3.1 The First Type

The first type includes the Sichuan-Chongqing region (Sichuan, Chongqing), the Guanzhong Plain (Shaanxi) and the Pan-Beibu Gulf region (Guangxi), where the overall economic strength, scale, returns, and development are the best of western China. They feature strong economic development prospects, research and technological innovation; solid and sound infrastructure and policies; large local market capacity and high level of urbanization with many megacities and large cities of extensive influence over the neighboring areas; superior location and environment with convenient inter-regional connection; and better quality of the labor force. Therefore, they are more competitive to attract foreign investment, an ideal destination for high-tech enterprises, market-seeking and efficiency-seeking multinational companies to make direct investment.

8.2.3.2 The Second Type

The second type includes the regions around Dianchi Lake (Yunnan), Baotou-Hohhot (Inner Mongolia), and along the Northern Xinjiang Railway (Xinjiang). Their investment climate has the following features: (1) The provinces where these regions are located are expansive and have long border lines, which is the geographical advantage of FDI for both the host country and the investing companies. This region has advantages but also needs to compete with neighboring countries in attracting direct investment from multinational companies. (2) These regions have unique and abundant resources that call for further development, suitable for resource-seeking MNC's direct investment. (3) These regions feature "uneconomical spatial layout". The population is highly concentrated in the areas around Dianchi Lake, along the northern Xinjiang railway, and around Baotou-Hohhot but scattered in other areas. Except for a few large cities, the secondary cities are not well developed. As a result, the urban economies of scale cannot be effectively brought into play. (4) The economic and market scales are relatively large but the cost of developing the secondary market is relatively high.

8.2.3.3 The Third Type

The third type includes two provinces: Gansu and Guizhou. Although located in the western transportation hub, they have an unfavorable natural and geographical environment with low economic aggregate and development. The income level of local residents is low and their buying power is limited; the overall education attainment of the population is relatively low.

8.2.3.4 The Fourth Type

This type includes Ningxia, where the characteristics of investment climate are as follows: small total economic volume with medium level of economic development and competitiveness in foreign direct investment calculated on a per capita basis and per square kilometer in the western region; no big cities with poor infrastructure; low population density; low income levels and limited purchasing power; small local market size; weak industrial supporting capacity. However, with sound railway and highway transportation, this type has certain location advantages and market potentials.

8.2.3.5 The Fifth Type

This type includes Qinghai and Xizang, where the investment climate features: small economic aggregate, low economic development; few (or no) big cities, poor infrastructure; harsh weather; low population density; lowest education level in the western region; small local market size; inconvenient transportation and higher cost of transporting products or materials; the weakest industrial supporting capacity in the western region.

8.3 Gaps Between the Central, Eastern and Western Regions in Investment Climate

For the regional economic development in China, due to the differences in economic development, locations, nature resources, and cultural environments, as well as the uneven promotion of market-oriented reforms, the investment climates are quite different between the eastern and the western regions. In recent years, improving the investment climate has become a top priority in western China. As a result, the overall investment climate is better, the city's appearance has improved, and the service functions have been significantly enhanced. Although investment competitiveness is remarkably better now, there are still many gaps between the western region and the central and eastern regions in terms of investment climate.

8.3.1 Natural Environment

8.3.1.1 Ecological Environment

A joint report on the "Current Situation of the Ecological Environment in the West" conducted by The State Environmental Protection Administration, the Chinese Academy of Sciences, the State Bureau of Surveying and Mapping, local governments of the 12 provinces, and relevant scientific research departments shows that The ecosystem in the western region is currently evolving from "structural damage" to "functional disorder". The unreasonable development of water resources has resulted in drying up rivers, shrinking oases, and the receding groundwater levels. In addition, glaciers have retreated, snow lines have risen, natural wetlands have shrunk, lakes have become salinized and even dried up; the area sees soil erosion in the western region (excluding Xizang) totaling 104.369 million hectares, accounting for 62.5% of the total of the country; desertification area in the western region totals 162.556 million hectares (statistical data of Inner Mongolia, Gansu, Ningxia, Shaanxi, Xizang and Xinjiang), accounting for more than 90% of the total of the country. The total area of desertified land in the five southwestern provinces is 7.295 million hectares; since they are highly concentrated and leading to serious damages, this is one of the most prominent ecological and environmental problems in Southwest China. Furthermore, due to ecological damage, sandstorms and droughts have significantly increased since the 1990s; the incidence of flooding has increased by nearly 50% in the 1990s compared to the 1980s.

8.3.1.2 Natural Resources

The western region, rich in natural resources, is particularly advantageous in this regard. Its total hydropower reserves account for 82.5% of the nation's total, and discovered water energy resources account for 77% of the country's total; However, only less than 1% is utilized. This region also has considerable mineral resources and reserves. According to the proven reserves, coal in this region accounts for 36% of the country's total, oil accounts for 12%, and natural gas accounts for 53%. Among the 140 kinds of proven mineral resources in the country, more than 120 kinds are found here with the highest reserves of rare earth minerals in the country and even in the world.

8.3.2 Legal and Administrative Systems

8.3.2.1 Legal Systems

So far, China has introduced a series of laws and regulations to protect the legal rights and interests of foreign business, including *Sino-Foreign Joint Venture Enterprise Law*, *Sino-Foreign Cooperative Joint Venture Enterprise Law*, *Foreign-Invested Enterprise Law* and their enacted regulations and regulations. However, this institutional arrangement also has certain flaws: First, the legislative powers of the central and local governments are not clearly defined, and local legislations are very different across the nation. Second, the regional tax incentive policies are different. Since 2001, the state has begun to adjust some policies on tax and income distribution. However, the preferential policies enjoyed by the Western Region Technology Development Zone and Border Technology Cooperation Zone have also been included in the list of revision and cancellation. Cancellation of preferential policies in the western region can only weaken its strength in attracting investment. Third, the "dual-track" legislative model that separates legislation for domestic capital and foreign capital is obviously contrary to the principle of equality in the market economy. Fourth, there is still no special law to follow for the development of the western region (Dou 2006).

8.3.2.2 Government Administration

Institutional obstacles generally exist in the government administration. First, there are many administrative interventions from the government, the project approval process is cumbersome, and the idea and culture of law-based administration have not yet been established. Second, too many functional departments but with no clear division of functions often leads to the buck-passing or finger-pointing situations. Third, the administrators lack experience in managing enterprises according to international conventions. Fourth, the service cannot keep up with the development needs of foreign-funded enterprises. The economy management department obviously prioritize management over coordination and service (Dou 2006).

Governments across the western region have made great efforts in law enforcement and have been fruitful. However, compared with the coastal cities, some officials in this region are more old-fashioned and narrow-minded, only setting their eyes on immediate interests and departmental benefits in the process of fulfilling their duty. By inconveniencing the administrative processes for business, charging random fees, or collecting unjustified fines, they create a negative image of the law enforcement, which has a direct impact on the investment climate.

8.3.3 Economic Environment

8.3.3.1 Economic Structure

Overall, the restructuring of ownership structure and industrial structure progresses slowly. So far, the state-owned business occupies a larger share in the whole economy, while the non-state-owned and non-public-owned economy is underdeveloped. Since the industrial structure is not advanced with lagging labor force restructuring, the entire economy is supported by traditional industries. The industrial upgrade is mainly hampered by the challenges in establishing new leading industries as well as the existing problems stemming from government system, policy and stock structure. The specific situations include the low industrial concentration, decentralized resource allocation, and social resources inaccessible to leading industries, resulting in low-tech emerging industries and less competitive products. The tertiary industry is mainly built on traditional industries such as commerce, catering services, and transportation. The technology-driven services, consulting, and education, which directly serve the primary and secondary industries, are severely underdeveloped; the underdeveloped financial securities market weakens a sustained economic development. These conditions have seriously affected the inflow of foreign capital. Compared to the development of high-tech industries in various regions, the western region has a slight advantage in the aerospace manufacturing industry, and see a small gap in the electronics and communication equipment manufacturing and pharmaceutical manufacturing with the eastern and central regions (Table 8.19).

8.3.3.2 Markets

Market factors mainly include market size and economic development level. The larger the market size and the higher the level of economic development, the greater chance to attract FDI. At present, the western region has smaller market size, and especially lacks a sound market mechanism. In some regions, the credibility of the market economy has not yet been established and the rules of the game of the market

Table 8.19 Key indicators of national economic and social development of the western region in 2004

Indicators	Nation's total	Western region	Share in the nation's total (%)
GDP (RMB 100 million)	136,875.9	27,585.2	16.9
Primary industry	20,768.1	5368.8	25.7
Secondary industry	72,387.2	12,230.0	14.8
#Manufacturing	62,815.1	9527.6	13.5
Tertiary Industry	43,720.6	9986.4	16.7

Source From Table 2.7 of the *China Statistical Yearbook (2005)*

economy have not been fully respected. With a segmented market, it is difficult to attain market scale benefits. In addition, the market environments in the western region are quite different, and the characteristics of the "dual economy" are more significant. (Table 8.20).

(1) Calculated based on the data from Table 17.13 of the *China Statistical Yearbook (2005)*

International researchers often use product prices and GDP per capita to determine the relationship between income and commodity consumption, which is named the price-to-income ratio. It can be calculated by the following formula:

$$\text{Price-to-income ratio} = \text{average unit price of a certain commodity}/\text{GDP per capita}$$

Generally speaking, the price-to-income ratio for product entry is about 3, while the threshold for general consumption of products is 1.5. Hou and Yin (2006) used this data to determine the corresponding relationship between GDP per capita and commodity consumption in different regions of China, as shown in Table 8.21.

Based on this, we analyze the consumption levels of the 12 provinces, as shown in Table 8.22.

Table 8.20 Wholesale and retail markets with a turnover over RMB 100 million in western China in 2004

Year	Number of markets	Number of vendors	Business areas (10,000 m^2)	Turnover (RMB100 million)	Wholesale	Retail
Western region's total	394	281,531	1821.8	1980	1582.5	397.2
Share in the nation's total	11.7	12.6	14.6	7.5	7.5	8.0

Note

1. The western region's total in this table does not include the data for Xizang

Table 8.21 Relations between GDP per capita and consumption

Stages	GDP per capita (RMB)	Consumption level	Note
1	Less than 500	Poverty	Food
2	500—1500	Subsistence level	Food, clothing
3	1500—1700	Practical and durable goods	TV, electric fans, and so on
4	7000—20,000	Durable goods of high quality	Computers, cameras
5	20,000—100,000	Cars	Transportation means
6	100,000—500,000	Cultural and real estate investment	Vacation houses, travels
7	Over 500,000	Wealthy	Social status, charity

Table 8.22 Analysis of consumption stages in western China by province

Province/region/municipality	GDP per capita (RMB)	Value adjusted by price-to-income ratio (RMB)	Stages
Guizhou	4215	6323	3
Gansu	5970	8955	4
Yunnan	6733	10,100	4
Guangxi	7196	10,794	4
Shaanxi	7757	11,636	4
Xizang	7779	11,669	4
Ningxia	7880	11,820	4
Sichuan	8113	12,170	4
Qinghai	8606	12,909	4
Chongqing	9608	14,412	4
Xinjiang	11,199	16,799	4
Inner Mongolia	11,305	16,958	4

Note The per capita GDP in this table derived from Table 3.4, *China Statistical Yearbook (2005)*

In addition, based on the analysis of the 2004 GDP per capita, ten out of the 31 provinces in China have entered the fifth consumption stage, but none of them is in the western region.

8.3.3.3 Infrastructure

Due to the constraints of geographical and historical factors, the construction in the west has been lagging. The complex topography and climatic conditions lead to poor transportation; low railway coverage, low-grade roads, mountainous and remote locations, all make transport difficult and expensive. The urban infrastructure

Table 8.23 Transportation and communication infrastructure of 12 western provinces in 2004

Indicator	Nation's total	Western region	Share in nation's total (%)
Length of railways (km)	74,408	27,062	36.4
Length of roads (km)	1,870,661	757,258	40.5
# highways Rivers (km)	34,288 123,337	8638 30,782	25.2 25.0
Passengers transport (100 million passenger-km)	16,309.1	3381.2	23.3
Freight transport (100 million ton-km)	69,445.0	7899.3	12.7
Post and telecommunications business volume (RMB 100 million)	9712.3	1843.4	19.0

Source Table 2.7 from the *China Statistical Yearbook (2005)*

is backward, without driving effects on the neighboring areas. The IT environment is not well established, making it difficult to keep abreast of some international and domestic situations. The current IT environment cannot meet the needs of investors. These factors directly affect the MNCs production, transportation, communication and product sales, discouraging their consideration of the direct investment. Under-developed infrastructure has greatly increased transaction costs. Although labor costs in the west are relatively low, expensive transaction costs may still make the cost of products higher than that in the east (Table 8.23).

8.3.3.4 Financing Channels

It is mainly reflected in three aspects: first, the challenges are very few direct financing channels and unsound capital market; second, small amount of bank deposits and poor quality of assets limit financial support; third, unsound structure of financial enterprises restricts the source of funds.

8.3.3.5 Costs

(1) Labor cost

The lack of skilled labor and export-oriented and compound talents makes it difficult to meet the talent demands of foreign-funded enterprises. Besides, the cost to recruit these talents in the western region is significantly higher than that in the eastern region. Therefore, the western region actually doesn't have any advantages in this regard.

(2) Land cost

As an important factor of production, land is a crucial investment for the manufacturers. Especially in China, land transfer is mostly a one-time payment for use rights, which has a greater impact on manufacturers' investment decisions. Generally speaking, there is no obvious gap between the western and eastern regions in land use fees.

(3) Tax rate

Based on the report entitled "Improving Investment Environment and Improving Urban Competitiveness: Investment Environment Ranking of China's 23 Cities" published by the Research Bureau of the World Bank in December 2003 (this report is to measure the tax burden from the perspective of the effective tax rate system by using all taxes and charge fee related to sales), Table 8.24 shows the effective tax rates of 18 cities in China.

Table 8.24 shows that the effective tax rates of cities in western China are generally higher than those in eastern and central regions. The effective tax rate in Nanning is 2.49 times that of Shenzhen, Lanzhou is 2.62 times that of Shenzhen, and Guiyang is 2.72 times that of Shenzhen.

(4) Transaction costs

An important feature of the investment climate in western China is high transaction costs. Compared with the eastern region, the western region has more examination and approval items, which takes a longer time and increases the cost or investment risk. The market economy here is not regulated, often resulting in chipping away profits from foreign investment. For example, the prevailing practice of unjustified charges and fees increases the investors' cost. breach of contract is a serious problem and disputes usually don't get resolved in a timely manner; intellectual property rights are not well guarded with frequent infringements, and so on. Restricted by various factors, transaction costs are relatively high in the western region, and the investment risk and business loss is greater than that in the eastern region. These to

Table 8.24 Effective tax rates in 18 Chinese cities

Eastern region		Central region		Western region	
City	Tax rate (%)	City	Tax rate (%)	City	Tax rate (%)
Shenzhen	3.9	Zhengzhou	6.0	Chongqing	6.7
Jiangmen	5.6	Wuhan	6.7	Kunming	7.9
Hangzhou	5.8	Changsha	6.9	Xi'an	8.3
Wenzhou	7.5	Nanchang	7.1	Nanning	9.7
Dalian	8.0	Changchun	7.5	Lanzhou	10.2
Benxi	10.3	Harbin	8.6	Guiyang	10.6

some extent offset the slight advantages of the western region in labor, land costs and resource prices.

8.3.3.6 Degree of Export Orientation

The economy in western China is less export-oriented. In 2004, this region accounted for only 3.18% of the nation's total imports and exports of goods based on locations of business entities; only 3.48% of the nation's total import and export of goods based on domestic destinations and sources; only 0.93% of the total import and export of goods by foreign-invested enterprises of the nation, lower than the above two indicators and indicating that the export-oriented foreign-invested economy in the western region was lower than the national level (Tables 8.25, 8.26 and 8.27).

8.3.4 Human Resources

There is a talent shortage, especially in the fields of advanced technology, management and entrepreneurship, in the western region. Talent development here is facing many problems and difficulties, which in turn restrict the economic, technological and social development. First, the unbalanced structure and distribution of talent presents a challenge. The limited number of high-caliber professionals are mainly concentrated in colleges, research institutes, and large enterprises in the cities. Only a small number of them work at county or lower levels. Senior professionals are much needed, and a brain drain is particularly prominent among senior managers and outstanding entrepreneurs. Second, the level of education of the population is far lower than that in the eastern region. The illiterate and semi-literate population accounts for a large proportion of the total population, with only a few college and university students. In addition, the low "return home rate" of college graduates is another problem. Third, the talent management system still has much room to improve. The problems of talent shortage and waste coexist, as existing talents are not fully utilized. Fourth, there is a certain gap in ideology. The current team of leaders is far from being able to meet the needs of regional development in terms of their qualification or best performance.

8.3.5 Technological Environment

Technologically, the western region lags behind other parts of China, and the business volume of the technology market is relatively low. From 1998 to 2004, business volume of the western region as a share of the nation has been fluctuating around 13%, see Table 8.28. According to the statistical data of China's high-tech industry development ("High-tech Industry Trends" No. 9), in 2004, the high-tech industry

Table 8.25 Western China's imports and exports (based on locations of business entities) and share in nation's total

Region	2000			2003			2004		
	Import and export	Export	Import	Import and export	Export	Import	Import and export	Export	Import
Western region's total (USD 10,000)	1,716,629	992,660	723,969	2,793,013	1,624,287	1,168,726	3,670,162	2,058,619	1,611,543
Share in nation's total (%)	3.62	3.98	3.22	3.28	3.71	2.83	3.18	3.47	2.87

Note Calculated based on data of Table 18.10 from the *China Statistical Yearbook (2005)*

Table 8.26 Western China's imports and exports (based on domestic destination or source of goods) and share in nation's total

Region	2000			2003			2004		
	Import and export	Export	Import	Import and export	Export	Import	Import and export	Export	Import
Western region's total (USD 10,000)	1,861,315	1,031,472	829,843	2,999,637	1,599,413	1,400,225	4,022,353	2,075,133	1,947,221
Share in nation's total (%)	3.92	4.14	3.69	3.52	3.65	3.39	3.48	3.50	3.47

Note Calculated based on data of Table 18.11 from the *China Statistical Yearbook (2005)*

Table 8.27 Total imports and exports of foreign-invested enterprises in western China and share in nation's total

Region	2000			2003			2004		
	Import and export	Export	Import	Import and export	Export	Import	Import and export	Export	Import
Western region's total (USD 10,000)	253,088	123,666	129,422	432,284	181,907	250,377	616,339	238,030	378,308
Share in nation's total (%)	1.07	1.04	1.10	0.92	0.76	1.08	0.93	0.70	1.17

Note Calculated based on data of Table 18.12 from the *China Statistical Yearbook (2005)*

in the western region registered a total output valued at RMB 139.004 billion, the output value of new products at RMB 42.365 billion, the product sales revenue of RMB 133.451 billion and export delivery value of RMB 13.35 billion, accounting for 5.11%, 8.24%, 4.92% and 0.96% of the nation's total respectively (Table 8.29).

Table 8.28 Turnover of technology market in western China and share in nation's total

Region	1998	1999	2000	2001	2002	2003	2004
Western region's total (RMB 10,000)	576,665	839,181	858,677	979,709	1,110,306	1,464,976	1,603,682
Share in nation's total (%)	13.23	16.03	13.20	12.52	12.56	13.51	12.02

Note The data are calculated based on Table 21.48 in the *China Statistical Yearbook (2005)*

Table 8.29 Comparison of key economic indicators of high-tech industries in western China and the whole country

Region	Gross output (RMB 100 million)	New product output (RMB 100 million)	Product sales revenue (RMB 100 million)	Export (RMB 100 million)
Western region	1390.04	423.65	1334.51	133.50
Nation	27,185.55	5138.38	27,145.99	13,929.14

Note The data are calculated based on China Statistical Yearbook (2005)

8.4 Strategies to Improve the Environment for Foreign Investments

Among the many factors that affect the investment climate in the western region, some factors, such as geographic location, economic foundation, and division of labor between it and the eastern region, take time to change. However, most of the factors, especially those related to institutions and laws, can be improved in the near future through efforts. At this stage, the western region should pay equal attention to soft and hard issues regarding investment climate. While strengthening infrastructure construction such as transportation, communication, and water supply, as well as developing human resources, local governments should regulate and improve the soft environment such as institutional and legal protections. In addition, governments at all levels should combine the advantages and characteristics of the region to make a long-term plan to promote economic development.

(1) Update the legal system and improve law enforcement (Sun 2006). First, strengthen the concept of the rule of law and the law-based administration at all levels, establish and develop legal intermediary service agencies, and enhance legal protection on the development of the west. Second, step up in improving the local legal system in every province; include the improvement of the investment climate into legislation. Third, ensure that laws are faithfully implemented, executed and enforced, so as to effectively protect the investors' legitimate rights and interests. Fourth, strengthen the legislative work related to the development of the western region; gather all practical experience, and gradually include the key tasks and effective practices into legislation; implement and enforce laws and regulations on foreign-related economic activities to provide legal protection for the legitimate rights and interests of investors. Establish and improve a sound arbitration to handle economic disputes in a timely manner.
(2) Improve the market environment for foreign investors. Regulate the market to ensure open, fair and fair market competition, combat counterfeit and shoddy products, and protect intellectual property rights. Standardize the credit system, establish and improve corporate and personal credibility checks as soon as possible, and strengthen legal sanctions for contract breaches. Strengthen education, establish concepts and social customs that uphold commitment, honesty, and fair competition, and form professional ethics and credibility that adapt to the market economic system. Cultivate and develop commodity and factor markets, and improve the market system.
(3) Improve services for foreign investment. Governments at all levels in the western region, by complying with laws and regulations, should speed up the transformation of functions to provide quality and efficient administrative services for enterprises, markets and society. The priority endeavor should include simplifying and standardizing administrative procedures, taking investors complaints seriously, and heightening service-oriented awareness.

(4) Create a society of culture and humanities. A nice humanistic society should be warm, honest, harmonious, open, civilized, and ethical. People in the western region should open their minds, abandon the outdated and conservative concepts. When embracing the idea that everyone is an investment climate-by improving every individual the productivity will improve, we can minimize the cost of human society and environment.

(5) Establish an assessment matrix as the foundation to manage and evaluate the soft investment climate. Establish an evaluation matrix for the investment climate in the western region, conduct regular qualitative and quantitative analysis to evaluate various factors of the investment climate, and regularly communicate the current situation and expectations for improvement, aiming to attract more multinational investors interests in this region.

(6) Strengthen the development of human resources and promote coherent flow of talents. Increase investment in basic and vocational education, and improve the overall quality of human resources through training. Actively cultivate the labor market and talent market. Provide employment information services for job seekers, and gradually realize the transparency of recruitment. Remove institutional barriers to talent mobility. Gradually remove the household registration restrictions and departmental restrictions, and implement policies to encourage talents to move to this region. Relax the restrictions on the proportion of intangible assets such as intellectual property as human capital investment, and create a sound legal environment for retaining local talents and attracting talents from the eastern region and from foreign countries. Create a healthy climate of respecting knowledge and talents and an environment in which good managers and entrepreneurs can thrive and multiply.

(7) Create a sound financial environment. Cultivate and actively develop the western capital market; improve the financial service system in the region. Accelerate transforming the shareholding scheme of state-owned commercial banks; improve the rural and urban cooperative financial organizations and non-bank financial institutions including securities companies, finance companies, financing companies, and trust investment companies. Expand the market space for corporate financing. Increase corporate bond financing for major projects and key enterprises in developing the region, and issue more special bonds for the construction of railways, major highways, and power plants. Establishing a market mechanism favorable for enterprises to develop capital in the region.

8.5 Conclusion

The government of the western region should conduct an in-depth analysis on the specific investment requirement for different types of FDI; by building upon the findings and combining with the regional spatial differences, they can improve the environment for foreign investment in a targeted manner.

In areas of the first category, the key to improve the investment climate is to establish a modern financial center. To further develop the west needs to build up the southwest-northwest economic growth pillar centered on Chengdu, Chongqing and Guanzhong with industrial leapfrogging strategy. Chengdu-Chongqing area is rich in resources, and strong in science and technology with a relatively sound industrial system. Therefore, it can promote industrialization through synchronizing the development of traditional industries, resource-based industries, and high-tech industries. The Guanzhong area (central Shaanxi Plain) is rich in history and culture and strong scientific research. Therefore, high-tech industries and tourism can facilitate its industrialization process. The Pan-Beibu Gulf region, located in the southwest sea passage, should fully utilize this important geographical advantage and focus on developing modern service industries, such as logistics, and export processing industries.

In areas of the first category, the key measure is to adopt differentiated strategies to accelerate economic development. The strategy for the three provinces of Xinjiang, Yunnan, and Inner Mongolia should be "promoting development through opening up". Since these three provinces share borders with some surrounding countries, they have geographical advantages in developing border trade. Therefore, opening up can result in a major breakthrough in development, which will promote border trade. By forming a diversified investment system through actively seeking foreign capital, these areas can accelerate the improvement of industrial structure, thereby enhancing the investment climate.

It would be a long process to improve the investment climate in the five provinces or regions of Gansu, Guizhou, Ningxia, Qinghai and Xizang. And the process requires the local governments' support. The central government should provide major funding in infrastructure construction so as to improve the investment climate and lay a good foundation for economic development in these areas.

References

Anand, Jaideep, and Andrew Delios. 1996. How Japanese MNCs have matched goals and strategies in India and China. *The Columbia Journal of World Business* (fall).

Broadman, Harry G., and Xiaolun Sun. 1997. The distribution of foreign direct investment in China. *The World Economy* 20 (3): 339–361.

Bu, Bu. 2001. German companies' investment in China and their promoting systems. *Shanghai Economic Research.*

Chen, Chunlai. 1997. *The Location Determinants of Foreign Direct Investment in Developing Countries.* Working Papers 1997–12, University of Adelaide, Chinese Economies Research Centre (CERC).

Chen, Xiangdong, and Guido Reger. 2006. The Role of technology in the investment of German firms in China. *Technovation* 26: 407–415.

Coughlin, Cletus C., and Eran Segev. 2000. Foreign direct investment in China: A spatial econometric study. *The World Economy* 23: 1–23.

Cassidy, John F., and Bernadette Andreosso-O'Callaghan. 2005. Spatial determinants of Japanese FDI in China. *Japan and the World Economy.*

Guelle, Françoise. 2001. The links between Japanese investment in Asia and de-industrialization in Japan. In *The Changing Economic Environment in Asia*, ed. By Bernadette Andreosso-O'Callaghan, Jean-Pascal Bassino, and Jacques Jaussaud, 52–61, Chap. 3. Palgrave Macmillan Books.

Hatch, Walter, and Kozo Yamamura. 1996. *Asia in Japan's Embrace: Building a Regional Production Alliance*. Cambridge University Press.

Hao, Hongmei. 2002. On China's environment for foreign investments. *Economic Relation and Trade* 2000 (2).

Hou, Jingxin, and Weihong Yin. 2004. *Regional Economic Analysis*. The Commercial Press.

Hou Jingxin, and Yin Weihong. 2006. *Methods for Regional Economic Analysis*. Commercial Press.

HU Hanjun, WANG Jiliang. 2005. Analysis of Influencing Factors of Regional Distribution of Foreign Direct Investment in China. Social Sciences, 5: 27–33.

Ling, Dou. 2006. Institutional factors of foreign investments to Shaanxi. *Journal of Zhengzhou Aviation Industry Management College* 2006 (6)

Lu, Minghong, and Zhen Pan. 2002. Assessment and comparison of investment environment in various regions of China: 1990–2000. *Management World* 11.

McFadden, D. 1974. Conditional Logit Analysis of Qualitative Choice Behavior. In: Frontiers in Econometric, Academic Press, New York, 105–142.

Sun, Jun. 2002. An analysis of determinants of choice of FDI locations in China. *Economics (Quarterly)* 2.

Sun, Haiming, and Xiaolei Zhao. 2003. *Annual Report on China's Regional Economy—Domestic and International Regional Cooperation*. Shanghai University of Finance & Economics Press.

Sun, Yuxian. "Basic Strategies to Improve Foreign Investments to the Western Region". Social Sciences Review. 2006 (11).

Sung, Kang Jin, and Hong Shik Lee. 2006. The determinants of location choice of South Korean FDI in China. *Japan and the World Economy*.

Wang, Xuhui. 2006. Analysis on the location change and influencing factors of foreign direct investment in China. *Journal of International Trade* 4.

Wei, Houkai, Canfei He, and Xin Wang. 2001. Latest theory and research on geographical determinants of foreign investment. *Journal of Shanghai Administration Institute* 4.

Wu, Haiying. 2006. The impact of Japanese firm's investment behavior and trend on western China's competitiveness for FDI. *Ningxia Social Sciences* (5).

Xiao, Zheng, and Victor Geistleger. 2001. Determinants of foreign direct investment and their differences between coastal and western regions of China. *World Economy* 3.

Uncited References

Aghion, Philippe, and Peter Howitt. 2004. *Endogenous Economic Growth Theory*. Beijing: Peking University Press.

Alcacer, Juan. 2000. The role of human capital in foreign direct investment. *Transition*.

Alfaro, Laura. 2003. *Foreign Direct Investment and Growth: Does the Sector Matter?* Harvard Business School, Working Paper 14.

Amirahmadi, Hooshang, and Weiping Wu. 1994. Foreign direct investment developing countries. *The Journal of Developing Areas* 28: 167–190.

Asako, Kazumi, and Soichi Shinohara. 1999. *Introduction to Japanese Economy*.

Balasubramanyan, Vudayagiri, M. Salisu, and David Sapsford. 1996a. Foreign direct investment and growth in EP and IS countries. *Economic Journal* 106: 92–105.

Balasubramanyam, Vudayagiri, M. Salisu, and David Sapsford. 1996b. *Foreign Direct Investment and Growth: New Hypothesis and Evidence*. Working Paper EC7/96, Department of Economics, Lancaster University.

Bende-Nabende, A., and J.R. Slater. 2000. *Long-Run Determinants of Private Capital Formation in Development Countries*. Processed: University of Birmingham Business Enterprise Institute.
Blomstrom, Magnus, and Ari Kokko. 2002. *FDI and Human Capital: A Research Agenda*. OECD Technical Papers no. 195, OECD Development Centre.
Blomstrom, Magnus, and Fredrik Sjoholm. 1999. Technology transfer and spillovers: Does local participation with multinationals matter? *European Economic Review* 43: 915–923.
Blomstrom, Magnus, and Hakan Persson. 1983. Foreign investment and spillover efficiency in an underdeveloped economy: Evidence from the Mexican manufacturing industry. *World Development* 11: 493–501.
Blomstrom, Magnus, Ari Kokko, and Steven Globerman. 2001. *The Determinants of Host Country Spillovers from Foreign Direct Investment: A Review and Synthesis of the Literature*, ed. by Nigel Plain.
Borensztein, E., J. De Gregorio, and J-W. Lee. 1998. How does foreign direct investment affect economic growth? *Journal of International Economics* 45: 115–135.
Cao, Fusheng, and Yuemin Ning. 2000. Experience and lessons from the developed countries in developing underdeveloped areas. *World Regional Studies* 9 (2).
Cao, Fusheng. 1993. Building a new joint development between the eastern and western China. *Journal of Social Sciences* 3.
Castellacci, Fulvio. 2001. *A Technology-gap Approach to Cumulative Growth: Toward an Integrated Model Empirical Evidence for Spain, 1960–1997*. DRUID Working Papers, forthcoming.
Chen, Fuming, and Mingjie Rui. 2006. A study on regional investment environment improvement based on three-dimensional space. *Economic System Reform* 1.
Chen, Langnan, and Jinghuang Chen. 2002. Empirical study on the impact of foreign direct investment on China's economic growth. *World Economy* 6.
Chen, Youliang. 2003. Some thoughts on the global expansion of western multinational corporations. *World Economy and Politics* 5.
Chenery, Hollis B., and Alan M. Strout. 1996. Foreign assistance and economic development. *The American Economics Review* 56 (4): Part 1, 679–733.
Cheng, Huifang, and Xiang Ruan. 2004. Analysis with gravity model on the location choice of foreign direct investment in China. *World Economy* 1.
Cheng, Huifang, Xinlu Pan, Qunyang Du, and Yi Zhao. 2003. Comparison of foreign investment environment and countermeasures in Zhejiang and Shanghai. *Zhejiang Social Sciences* 2.
Cheng, Huifang. 2002. International direct investments and open endogenous economic growth. *Economic Research* 10.
Chinese Embassy in Spain. 2002. *EU's Policies for Underdeveloped Regions and What China can Learn from Them.*
Choe, Jong Il. 2003. Do foreign direct investment and gross domestic investment promote economic growth? *Review of Development Economics* 7.
Cimoli, M. 1988. Technological gaps and institutional asymmetries in a North-South model with a continuum of goods. *Metroeconomica* 39: 245–274.
Cimoli, M., and L. Soete. 1992. A generalized technological gap trade model. *Economie Appliqué* 45 (3): 33–54.
Cohen, Wesley M., and Daniel A. Levinthal. 1990. Absorptive capacity: A new perspective on learning and innovation. *Administrative Science Quarterly*, 35: 128–152.
Cui, Daoling, and Zhicheng Ren. *Journal of International Trade*, no.3 (2006).
Cui, Xinjian. 2001. Microcosmic theory of FDI: OL model. *Management World* 3.
Dai, Qian, and Zhaoxia Bie. 2006. FDI, human capital and economic growth. *Economic Research* 4.
De Mello, Luiz R. Jr. 1996. Foreign direct investment in developing countries and growth: A selective survey. *The Journal of Development Studies* 34 (1).
De Mello, Luiz R. Jr. 1999. Foreign direct investment led growth: Evidence from time series and panel data. *Oxford Economic Papers* 51.

Dees, Stèphane. 1998. Foreign direct investment in China: Determinants and effects. *Economics of Planning* 31: 175–194.
Deng, Dacai. 2000. The unbalanced eastern-western institutional arrangements and the institutional reform in western China. *Shanghai Economic Research* 1.
Department of Foreign Investment Administration, Ministry of Commerce, People's Republic of China. 2006. *Report on Foreign Investment in China, 2005.*
Desai, Mihir A., C. Fritz Foley, and James R. Hines, Jr. 2005. *Foreign Direct Investment and Domestic Economic Activity.* NBER Working Paper 11717.
Dornbusch, Rudiger, Stanley Fischer, and Richard Startz. 1998. *Macroeconomics*, 7th ed. McGraw Hill and Dongbei University of Finance & Economic Press.
Dosi, Giovanni et al. 1992. *Technical Change and Economic Theory.* Science Press.
Du, Jiang. 2002. An empirical analysis of foreign direct investment and China's economic development. *World Economy* 8.
Dunning, J.H. 1998a. Location and multinational enterprise: A neglected factor? *Journal of International Business Studies* 29 (1): 45–66.
Dunning, J.H. 1995. Reappraising the eclectic paradigm in the age of alliance capitalism. *Journal of International Business Studies,* 26: 461–491.
Dunning, J.H. 1998. The changing geography of foreign direct investment: Explanations and implications. In *Globalization, Foreign Direct Investment and Technology Transfer: Impacts on and Prospects for Developing Countries*, ed. by Nagesh Kumar. London: Routledge.
Dunning, J.H. 1973. The determinants of international production. *Oxford Economic Papers* 25 (3): 289–336.
Dunning, J.H. 1980. Toward an eclectic theory of international production. *Journal of International Business Studies* 11: 9–13.
Dunning, J.H. 1977. Trade, location of economic activity and the MNE: A search for an eclectic approach. In *The International Allocation of Economic Activity*, ed. by Bertil Ohlin, Per-Ove Hesselborn and Per Magnus Wijkman. London: Macmillan.
Dunning, J.H. 1986. *Japanese Participation in British Industry.* London: Croom Helm.
Dunning, J.H. 1993. *Multinational Enterprises and the Global Economy.* New York: Addison-Wesley Publishing Ltd.
Dunning, J.H., Zu Kweon Kim, and Chul-In Lee. 2007. Restructuring the regional distribution of FDI: The case of Japanese and US FDI. *Japan and the World Economy* 19: 26–47.
Economic Research Institute of the State Planning Commission. 1996. Research on China's regional economic development strategy. *Management World* 4.
EEAG. 2002. *Report on the European Economy.* Munich.
European Commission. 2000. *Structural Actions 2000–2006.* Belgium.
Fagerberg, Jan. 1987. A technology gap approach to why growth rates differ. *Research Policy* 16: 87–99.
Glass, Amy, and Kamal Saggi. 1998. International technology transfer and the technology gap. *Journal of Development Economics* 55: 369–398.
Helpman, E. 1984. A simple theory of international trade with multinational corporations. *Journal of Political Economy* 92: 451–471.
Hu, Anshun, and Yongtao Niu. 2003. On improving the investment environment in western China. *Qinghai Finance* 9.
Hu, Feng. 2001. The background, content and effects of Thailand's adjustment on foreign investment policy. *Journal of Guizhou University of Finance and Economics* 5.
Hu, Zuliu. 2004. Three major issues concerning China's introduction of foreign capital. *International Economic Review* 2.
Jiang, Guojie. 2002. Analysis on the characteristics and location factors of foreign direct investment. *Journal of International Trade* 7: 12–16.
Jiang, Jinfan. 2004. The functions of foreign direct investment in China's economic growth. *World Economy* 1.

Jiang, Xiaojuan, and Ling Du. 2001. The latest theoretical research on transnational investment. *World Economy* 6.
Jones, Charles. 1995. R&D-based models of economic growth. *Journal of Political Economy* 103: 759–784.
Kanemori, Hisao, and Yasushi Konishi. 1990. *A Reader of Japanese Economics*. Toyo Keizai.
Kasahara, Shigehisa. 2004. The flying geese paradigm: A critical study of its application to East Asian regional development. *UNCTAD Report* 169.
Krugman, Paul. 1979. Increasing returns, monopolistic competition, and inter-national trade. *Journal of International Economics* 9: 469–479.
Krugman. 2001. *New Theory of International Trade*. China Social Sciences Press.
Kukawka, Pierre. 2001. *L' Europe par les régions*. Presses Universitaires de Grenoble.
Kwan, Chi Hung. 2002. Flying-geese pattern of economic development: An empirical analysis based on US import statistics. *NRI Papers* 52.
Lai, Mingyong et al. 2002. China's competitiveness in attracting foreign direct investment. *Nankai Economic Research* 3.
Lai, Mingyong, Qun Bao, and Xiaoxiao Yang. 2002a. A study on China's competitiveness of foreign direct investment. *Nankai Economic Research* 3.
Lai, Mingyong, Qun Bao, and Xiaoxiao Yang. 2002b. Competitiveness of foreign direct investment: Theory and empirical research in China. *Shanghai Economic Research* 6.
Cheng, Leonard K., and Yum K. Kwan. 2000b. What are the determinants of the location of foreign direct investment? The Chinese experience. *Journal of International Economics* 51 (2): 379–400.
Li, Yining. 2000. New *Ideas for Regional Development—The Impact of China's Unbalanced Development and Countermeasures for Modernization*. Beijing: The Economic Daily Press.
Li, Chunli. 2002. Understanding and suggestions for improving the investment environment in western China. *China Price* 11.
Li, Juheng. 2002. Location selection of FDI and China's regional economic development. *China Soft Science Magazine* 6.
Li, Ping. 1999. *An Empirical Study on the Theory of Technology Diffusion*. Shanxi Economics Publishing House.
Li, Tieli. 2005. *On Boundary Effects and Cross-Border Sub-Regional Economic Cooperation*. China Financial Press.
Li, Xiaoying, and Xiaming Liu. 2005. Foreign direct investment and economic growth: An increasingly endogenous relationship. *World Development* 33 (3).
Li, Xin'an. 2006. An empirical analysis on the correlation between China's FDI clustering effect and regional economic growth. *Finance and Trade Research* 4.
Li, Yuju, and Peng Zhang. 2003. Transportation cost: An explanatory variable from export to foreign direct investment. *Management Science* 4.
Li, Zhongmin. 1999. *Human Capital: A Theoretical Framework and Its Application to Explain Some Problems in China*. Economic Science Press.
Liang, Qi. 2003. Investment and industrial agglomeration of multinational corporations. *World Economy* 9.
Liang, Yun. 2001. What does chongqing have to attract foreign investment: Analysis of Chongqing's improvement of environment for foreign investments. *Economic and Trade* 8.
Liu, Qing, and Shuming Ren. 2005. A study on the transformation of MNC industrial transfer. *Economics and Management* 10.
Liu, Wei et al. 1999. Ranking and evaluation of city investment environment in Jiangsu province. *Economic Geography* 2.
Liu, Xiuling. 2003. *Foreign Direct Investment and Technology Transfer*. Economic Science Press.
Losch, August. 1995. *The Spatial Organization of the Economy*. Chinese translation. The Commercial Press.
Lu, Chunhua, and Hua Sun. 2003. On improving the investment environment in western China. *Guangxi Economics and Trade* 9.
Lu, Dadao et al. 1997. *Report on China's Regional Development*. The Commercial Press.

Lu, Di. 2003. Foreign investment and China's economic development—Evidence from industrial and regional analysis. *Economic Research* 10.
Lu, Minghong. 1999. Institutional factors and the distribution of international direct investment: An empirical study. *Economic Research* 7.
Lu, Minghong. 2000. *Geographical Determinants of International Direct Investment*. Nanjing: Nanjing University Press.
Lucas, R.B. 1993. On the determinants of direct foreign investment: evidence from East and Southeast Asia. *World Development* 21: 391–406.
Lucas, Robert E., Jr. 1990. Why doesn't capital flow from rich to poor countries? *American Economic Review* 80: 92–96.
Luo, Changyuan. 2006. FDI, domestic investments and economic growth—Evidence from China's interprovincial panel data 1987–2001. *World Economics* 4.
Lyu, Feng. 2006. On the importance of foreign investments to the development in western China. *Market Modernization Magazine* 5.
Mang, Li. 2003. Industrial clusters: A new approach to attract FDI. *Journal of Tianjin University of Commerce* 9.
Mao, Yunshi, and Jing Yuan. 2005. Multinational corporations' strategies for direct investment in China: Trends and characteristics. *Management World* 9.
Mao, Yunshi. 2005. *Multinational Corporations' Strategies for Direct Investment in China*. China Financial and Economic Publishing House.
Monash University of Australia, Asian Development Bank, National Development and Reform Commission of China. 2003. *The Utilization of Foreign Capital in the Western Region*.
Ni, Haiqing, and Yangui Zhang. 2006. An empirical study on the relationship between human resources and FDI in China. *Journal of Central University of Finance and Economics* 12.
North, Douglass, and Robert Thomas. 1989. *The Rise of the Western World*. Huaxia Publishing House.
North, Douglass. 1978. *Institutions, Institutional Change and Economic Performance*. Shanghai Joint Publishing.
North, Douglass. 1991. *Structure and Change in Economic History*. Shanghai Joint Publishing.
Pei, Nanfei, and Karin van der Esch. 2004. The impact of FDI on developing countries. *China and World Economy* 12 (6): 109–117.
Qiu, Huifang. 2001. Spatial distance—Analysis of industry differences in transnationalization index of multinational corporations. *International Trade* 12.
Romer, P.M. 1990. Endogenous technology change. *Journal of political Economy* 98 (5).
Ruttan, Vernon. 1978. *Toward a Theory of Induced Institutional Innovation*. Shanghai Joint Publishing.
Sanchez-Robles, Blanca, and Marta Bengoa. 2002. *Foreign Direct Investment, Economic Freedom and Growth: New Evidence from Latin-America*. Universidad de Cantabria, Economics Working Paper 4/03.
Shen, Kunrong, and Qiang Geng. 2001. Foreign direct investment, technology spillover and endogenous economic growth—Econometric test and empirical analysis of Chinese data. *China Social Sciences* 5.
Shen, Lisheng, and Yunfa Zhu. 1999. *Human Capital and Economic Growth*. Social Sciences Academic Press.
Smarzynska, Beata K. 2002. *Spillovers from Foreign Direct Investment through Backward Linkages: Does Technology Gap Matter?* World Bank Working Paper.
Study Group to Europe on Regional Foreign Investment Policies. 2001. EU regional policies. *Research Report of the Development Research Center of the State Council* 42.
Sun, Qian. 2002. Determinants of foreign direct investment across China. *Journal of International Money and Finance* 21: 275–295.
Qu, Tao, Milford B. Green. 1997. *Chinese Foreign Direct Investment: A Subnational Perspective on Location*. Routledge Press.
The National Land Agency of Japan. 1999. *National Land Statistics*.

Tian, Guiming. 2002. *Multinational Corporations' Overseas Direct Investment and Host Country Incentive Policy Competition*. Beijing: Economic Press.
Tian, Yipeng. 2006. Japan's 'countermeasures for low-density' and regional coordinated development in the second half of the 20th century. *Journal of Contemporary Asia-Pacific Studies* 10.
Toyo, Keizai. 2001. *Overview of Regional Economy*.
UNCTAD. 1996. *Incentives and Foreign Direct Investment*. Geneva: United Nations.
UNCTAD. 1998. *World Investment Report 1998*. New York: United Nations.
UNCTAD. 2002. *World Investment Report 2002: Transnational Corporations and Export Competitiveness*.
Van der Beek, Gregor, and Larry D. Neal. 2004. The dilemma of enlargement for the European union's regional policy. *European Public Law: EU eJournal*.
Vernon, R. 1996. International investment and international trade in the product cycle. *Quarterly Journal of Economics* 80: 190–207.
Veugelers, Reinhilde. 1991. Locational determinants and ranking of host countries. *Kyklos* 44: 363–382.
Wang, Bin. 2001. *Introduction to International Regional Industrial Structure Analysis*. Shanghai People's Publishing House.
Wang, Chengqi, Jianhua Zhang, and Hui An. 2002. Foreign direct investment, regional differences and economic growth in China. *World Economy* 4.
Wang, Dingding. 1992. Theories of institutional innovation. *Economic Research* 5.
Wang, Fuxin, and Ruizhi Jiang. 1998. Analysis of the correlation between China's utilization of foreign investments and economic development. *The Journal of Quantitative & Technical Economics* 5.
Wang, Jian, and Xu Kangning. 2005. FDI location, industrial agglomeration and heterogeneity—A case study of Jiangsu. *Economic Sciences* 4.
Wang, Lei. 2004. A literature review on industrial clustering from the perspective of multinational corporations. *Nankai Economic Research* 5.
Wang, Weidong, and Guoqin Xue. 2003. Evaluation of regional investment environment. *Journal of Shaoxing Humanity* 6.
Wang, Yanli, and Chuanzhe Liu. 2006. Human capital and FDI technology spillover—evidence from China. *Statistics and Decision* 17.
Wang, Yiming. 1997. An international comparison of regional economy and regional policy in the period of rapid growth. *Review of Economic Research*.
Wang, Zengtao. 2002. The analytical framework and significance of the geographical selection of foreign direct investment. *International Finance Research* 3.
Wang, Zhile. 2003a. *New Development Trends of MNC Branches in China*. Xinhua Publishing House.
Wang, Zhile. 2003b. *Report of Multinational Corporations Investments in China, 2002–2003*. Economic Press.
Wang, Zhipeng, and Zinai Li. 2004a. Foreign direct investment, spillover effects and endogenous economic growth. *World Economic Papers* 3.
Wang, Zhipeng, and Zinai Li. 2004b. Foreign direct investment, spillover effects and endogenous economic growth. *World Economics* 3.
Weber, Alfred. 1997. *Theory of the Location of Industries*. Chinese translation: The Commercial Press.
Wei, Houkai, Canfei He, and Xin Wang. 2002. *The Decisions and Public Policies on Location of FDI in China*. The Commercial Press.
Wu, Feng. 2001. Foreign direct investment and agglomeration effect. *Economic Perspectives* 6.
Wu, Haihua. 2004. *Foreign Investment and Economic Development*. Economic Science Press.
Wu, Jinming, Pan Zhang, and Zengqi Zhao. 2005. Industrial chain, industrial supporting radius and enterprise viability. *China Industrial Economics* 2.

Wu, Linhai et al. 2002. *On Technology Transfer of Multinational Corporations to China.* Economy and Management Publishing House.
Wu, Shimin. 1996. Investment issues in the development of western China. *Qiushi* 14.
Wu, Xuehua, and Huixin Yang. 2004. An empirical study on China's manufacturing industry agglomeration. *China Industrial Economics* 10.
Xu, Bin, and Jianmao Wang. 2000. Trade, FDI, and international technology diffusion. *Journal of Economic Integration* 12.
Xu, Luodan, and Weihong Tan. 2004. A literature review of foreign direct investment. *World Economy* 3.
Xue, Qiuzhi, and Shenggang Ren. 2005. New theory on multinational corporations: From the perspective of location and clustering. *Journal of Fudan University (Social Science Edition)* 1.
Yang, Haiyan. 2005. FDI and China's economic growth: An empirical study from 1998 to 2003. *Eastern China Economic Management* 8.
Yang, Jianlong. 2000. *Game Theories on Foreign Investment and Strategies.* Economic Science Press.
Yang, Xianming, and Runmin Fu. 2002. Thoughts on foreign direct investment and industrial upgrading in China. *Journal of Yunnan University (Philosophy and Social Sciences Edition)* 1 (1).
Yang, Xianming. 2000. *Stages of Development and Foreign Direct Investment.* The Commercial Press.
Yang, Xinfang, Lijun Ren, and Hongqin Li. 2006. An empirical study on the 'squeezing' effect of foreign direct investment on domestic capital: The impact of FDI on China's economic growth from the perspective of capital formation. *Journal of International Trade* 9.
Yao, Shujie, Genfu Feng, and Kailei Wei. 2006. A study on the relationship between foreign direct investment and economic growth. *Economic Research* 12.
Yin, Huafang, Zhen Pan, and Minghong Lu. 2006. A study on measurement and validation on China's foreign direct investment industrial policy: 1979–2003. *Management World* 7.
Yu, Yongding. 2004. The impact of FDI on China's economy. *International Economic Review* 2.
Zhang, Kevin Honglin. 2005. Why does so much FDI from Hong Kong and Taiwan go to mainland China? *China Economic Review* 16: 293–307.
Zhang, Keyun. 2001. *Regional Economic Policy: Theory and Practice of EU Countries.* China Light Industry Press.
Zhang, Tianding. 2004. An empirical study on the impact of FDI on China's economic growth. *World Economic Research* 10.
Zhang, Tianding. 2004. Foreign direct investment, transmission mechanism and China's economic growth. *The Journal of Quantitative & Technical Economics* 10.
Zhang, Xiaotong. 2000. *Econometric Analysis.* Economic Science Press.
Zhao, Fang. 2003. On the relationship between technology and institutions and the impacts on economic growth. *Contemporary Economic Research* 1.
Zhao, Fuhou. 2006. Comparison of foreign direct investment on the economic growth of China's three major regions. *Modern Finance and Economics* 7.
Zhao, Jianglin. 2004. Development of foreign investment and human resource: A summary of China's experience. *Economic Research* 2.
Zhao, Wei. 2006. Human capital and technology spillover: An empirical study based on import transmission. *China Soft Science Magazine* 4.
Zheng, Jianghuai, and Chunliang Gao. 2005. Capital transfer, optimal industrial support and policy change of international manufacturing industry. *China Industrial Economics* 2.
Zhong, Changbiao. 2000. Theory and validation of the relationship between foreign investments and regional economic growth. *The Journal of Quantitative & Technical Economics* 1.
Zhong, Ruoyu, and Yiming Yuan. 2004. Research on industrial supporting capabilities of Shenzhen. *Journal of Shenzhen University (Humanities and Social Sciences Edition)* 5.
Zhou, Chunying, and Bo Wang. 2006. On long-term balancing and dynamic between foreign direct investment and China's economic growth. *World Economic and Political Forum* 3.

Zhu, Ting. 1996. Characteristics and problems of foreign investment policy liberalization in the 1990s. *Journal of Lanzhou Business School*.

Zhu, Ying. 2000. Globalisation, foreign direct investment and their impact on labour relations and regulation: The case of China. *The International Journal of Comparative Labour Law and Industrial Relations* 16 (1): 5–24.

Zhu, Xinmin, and David Shaw. 2001. *Management of Industrial Declining Areas in Europe and America*. Southwestern University of Finance and Economics Press.

Zhu, Shaojie. 2006. Analysis of foreign investment strategy based on FDI industrial agglomeration. *Reform and Strategy* 7.

MIX
Papier aus verantwortungsvollen Quellen
Paper from responsible sources
FSC® C105338

If you have any concerns about our products,
you can contact us on
ProductSafety@springernature.com

In case Publisher is established outside the EU,
the EU authorized representative is:
Springer Nature Customer Service Center GmbH
Europaplatz 3, 69115 Heidelberg, Germany

Printed by Libri Plureos GmbH
in Hamburg, Germany